T0354805

The Foundation Book of Primes

- 2nd Edition

Body of Work
By

F. Dot

authorHOUSE®

AuthorHouse™
1663 Liberty Drive
Bloomington, IN 47403
www.authorhouse.com
Phone: 1 (800) 839-8640

Published by AuthorHouse 06/22/2015

ISBN: 978-1-5049-1919-7 (sc)
ISBN: 978-1-5049-1918-0 (e)

Library of Congress Control Number: 2015910089

Print information available on the last page.

Dedication

This book is dedicated to my family and friends who helped me during a period of almost complete destitution. Without their help, no book that I authored would every have been published. The elite tried to condemn me and extinguish my livelihood for not subscribing to their beliefs based on privileges and lordships of the few. For these elite who found it preferable to condemn and exclude, the same fate awaits you! However, I will be disappointing them. My focus will be on the birth and growth of a sentient movement that will bring environments for those who seek to develop their abilities towards universal awareness and atonement. I am deeply grateful to wise thinking sentient predecessors who, unbeknownst to them, have helped me with this book's prime foundation.

Dedication – 2ⁿᵈ Edition

This book is dedicated to all sentients everywhere in the Nexus Expanse and Beyond. The path towards higher levels of awareness continues with this second edition. The path is yours to take. Expand on this edition towards All-That-Is.

Table of Contents – Second Edition

PART – I

Second Edition Inclusion

Introduction

More Content Being Released

The writings by this scribe are needed in these times of transitional and post-transitional experiences. Hence, some topics may have much more content being released than others depending on the point along the transitional timeline and depending on sentient readiness. Those topics tend to stream more when the need is greater.

Putting A Spin On Historical Facts

There is a tendency to skew historical references to put a "spin" on "historical facts" by removing "unpleasant" feudal-states' terrorist and destructive events. This scribe's goal is to present more factual cause and effect stories to be told that have been buried or hidden by the elites for the purpose of keeping them from being told. This scribe has presented sufficient information so that the reader can research further should she wish to. The recommendation is to dig deeper so that the reader can experience the disturbing facts for oneself.

Escape Velocity

The intent of this scribe is to show how one can gain "escape velocity" in order to achieve sentient awareness than from the state of being anchored to ground. This may take a concerted effort to escape.

F. Dot

Broadening The Reception And Bandwidth

It is of her-storical importance that this scribe is broadening the reception and bandwidth of higher levels of awareness and insights. This scribe's writings are expanding to be in sync with the Nexus Pentarchy Prime Expanse.

PART – II

Supporting Materials and Reflections of Prime Importance Second Edition Inclusion

PART - II

Recent Historical References (RHR)
on Former Belief Systems
- The State of Affairs

Paranoid

There are those who claim that members can cross borders freely. As it can be shown in Recent Historical References, this is simply not true. One must have privileges which are primarily given to a small number of members as compared to the societal pool by being granted exclusive "travel papers". Without these travel papers, crossing is made extremely hazardous to one's existence. Shoot to kill becomes the standing orders for illegal crossings by non-violet members. Paranoia in having secure borders sets in. It is a quandary why there is fear of other members who are no threat to them. They just want to cross. The fearful are truly paranoid. They may need to seek out mental health services. Are you paranoid?

There Is A Choice

In Recent Historical References, one can find numerous references to rationed health care privileges. However for the few privilege elite, there is unlimited access. Does this seem right to you? It is a quandary to think that societal members have accepted this warped healthy premise view as fair and equitable. The elitists have it so they are not worried. The end result is that the masses have severely diminished health and will have to survive on their own. In this hostile environment, it may be best to move and live in Nature's environments to improve one's health. There is a choice.

Spontaneous Rejections

During the Transitional Period Towards a Nexus Pentarchy Prime Framework, subjects of feudal-states who were selected and have abided by feudal laws did amass considerable properties of value as measured by feudal-state constructs' level of statuses. The hoarding and the extraction from the natural environments went on unabated even when the natural treasures were being depleted to exhaustion. The natural environments that were dying or dead were of little consequence as supported by feudal laws just as long as the privileged elites were comfortable in their micro surroundings. As time passed, the pool of elites became smaller and smaller while the masses being excluded became larger and larger and were the ones denied access to basic needs for sustenance. The results produced massive and violent assaults on the masses to contain them. The masses reached the level of awareness of the existence of barren wastelands and waste waterways being perpetrated by the hoarders. Survival of the environments was finally made acutely realized when the casualties yielded the effects of accelerated death and destruction directed towards the excluded. It was through spontaneous rejections through demonstration and resistance protests that the tide towards calamity was abruptly reversed. The expiration of all feudal systems was the only remedy to take in reversing the non-sustainable practices of hoarding and depletion of Nature's resources. A caretaker framework by caretaking sentients was crafted. Executioners of natural surroundings would no longer have elitist statuses. Confinement of members who promoted grave harmful activities through their participation ensured viable environments for all inhabitants. Sentient environments proliferated due to their astute caretaking activities. By striving towards sentient understanding through these activities, it will raise your level of awareness as it pertains to you and your surroundings and, by extension, to your at-one-ment with All-That-Is (ATI).

Cherished Judicial Venues

In Recent Historical References, "illegal aliens" as defined and proclaimed by the "greatest nation state of its time" were chased and hunted with the aim of extinguishing their presence from the perimeters of this "great country" with the objective of achieving a 100% success rate. Their laws required that this completion rate be attained. The aliens were not anointed "subject classification" to be able to participate in its societal domain. They were viewed as not worthy of inclusion and were denied all access to cherished judicial venues. One must have legal standing to participate. By stripping away all judicial standings, sentients were damned.

Hollow Substance

In Recent Historical References, refugees fleeing due to grave survival causal events and then tried to enter nation-state perimeters were driven back towards their respective nation-states that they were subjects to. They were denied entry into the particular nation-state due to being non-subjects of this nation-state in their attempt to find refuge from grave harm. The deterrent goal of this particular nation-state is for non-subjects to not make the journey in the first place. The fates of the forced repatriation of these non-subjects often resulted in their torture and corporeal termination within their respective feudal perimeters as proclaimed by repatriated feudal terrorists. There are many more examples of similar non-sentient practices by "great nation states" of their time. These "great" societies' legal discrimination enforcement practices brought the hollow substance of these great societies to light and the absence of what truly constitutes a "great society". Being hollow is just a shell that can easily be cracked. Consider being a sentient and the remedy will become clear to you. Do you want to take a crack at it?

Muted With A Shrug

In Recent Historical References, "international bodies of water" where identified for any ship registered with any nation-state to have unobstructed travel access through them. Oftentimes, these bodies of water were used as dumping grounds by the nation-states and inter-nation-corporations. None were held to caretaking responsibilities of these bodies of water. If there were caretaking rules for the care of these bodies of water, they were often ignored all together. The same lack of caretaking responsibilities happened to "international air space". It is only when the land, air, and waterways were within feudal nation-state borders that caretaking responsibilities were considered due to their border demarcations that afford them with "defensible perimeters" whereby overwhelming use of force was used in the defense of them. The sounding of the pollution alarms were muted with a shrug. These bodies of water were not in their nation-states' "back yards" to worry about them. Eventually, the alarms got louder and were heard only after the pollution washed onto their shores. The pollution was then in their back yards. How could this be? It is baffling to us today to understand how they could not know the answer to this question. Maybe it is because of their limitation in only seeing what is in their back yards. What a convenient blind spot.

Poetic Justice Illustrated

In Recent Historical References, non-harmful marijuana plants were destroyed by man-made fires because of artificial laws that state that it is illegal to grow them. These and similar feudal "war on" campaigns to snuff out Nature's Life Forces were done using precision executions. The high success rates may have been too successful in the application and used to also snuff out enemy feudal lords and their subjects. In time, Nature will make adjustments to the assaults made on her by producing balancing conditions to extinguish anti-life forces. When massive assaults are perpetrated on life forces that have not shown any ill-will towards the perpetrators, then counter-conditions will be done to correct these destructive acts in demonstrating who is the true superior caretaker. Nature took care of us all in the beginning. Man is the only specie that chose to purposefully make extinct an unacceptable number of species. As Nature would remind inhabitants from time to time, those actions committed onto the least of thee, do it onto Her. This is poetic justice illustrated.

Onus Of Subject-hood

In Recent Historical References, nation-state governing agencies would often push the onus of subject-hood -- otherwise known as citizenship – onto subjects of feudal lords. This puts members in double jeopardy whereby if they cannot show "proper legal papers" from a list of acceptable ones, they are considered non-citizens and unworthy of the rights and privileges anointed to citizens. Oftentimes, they would be denied sustenance, health promoting care, and legal protection be availed to them when caught without identity papers. In "great" nation-states, they were even shackled and confined in "secured confinements" as if they were hardened criminals. In actuality, the nation-state's responses by their enforcers are the true crimes being committed, which were sanctioned by the state. The enforcers are part of the "law enforcement" agencies, which were granted the ability to perform terrorist activities with impunity. In a Nexus Pentarchy Prime Framework, these activities are not sanctioned and are not given impunity. In this Sentient Framework, Sufficient Force Doctrine is the mantra, which specifically excludes all terrorist promoting activities. No one is a subject to a feudal lord. No one can be discarded at the privilege of a feudal lord. Feudal lords need not apply. There is no place for them in a Sentient Expanse.

Superior Societies

In Recent Historical References, the "rule of law" as practiced by the greatest nation-states of their time is the legal cover used to oppose frameworks that are contrary to their "ideal" version of a "just" framework. Forced into submission by any means necessary was the option of choice used to squash other frameworks. Heavy non-citizen casualties resulted when superior weaponries were deployed even when no grave harmful acts or the propensity for the same were exhibited by non-citizens. The opposing views were to be silenced by these kill-containment campaigns. These campaigns were sanctioned by those same "superior societies" who adhere to the oppressive rule of law. These frameworks are violent by their very architecture nature. Campaigns of terror were also used to suppress non-adherence members and to expel all non-members even when these non-members were already present before being invaded. "First strike eradication" was the option of choice for these terrorist constructs. Looking for an alternative? Consider joining a sentient sustaining framework. Start with the word.

Now That You Know

During the Transitional Period Towards a Nexus Pentarchy Prime Framework, it is odd to comprehend that the "greatest" nation-state the world has ever known at the time was perceived to be the "greatest" defender of life, liberty, and the pursuit of freedom. Yet, it fell precipitously short in achieving this noble goal. Its grasp was unattainable by its very construct. The sad truth is the the onus fell to the individual members to fight and claw their way up in ensuring that the defender pillar of the greatest nation-state remained erect. Some sentients were within the perimeters of this once great nation-state who could do no other than be a sentient in ensuring sentient pursuits were championed and not this pillar of inadequacy. The lesson here is that member sentients had to take charge and not some artificial construct. Others needed to follow their lead and rise to the state of sentient-hood in order for a framework to be architect and erected for all sentients to be free to traverse anywhere in the known dominion and beyond. No pillar walls called "borders" are ever needed. It came to be realized that the sole purpose for these walls was to keep subjects in or non-subjects out. Now that you know, are you in or out?

Combative Stance

In Recent Historical References, the legal militarization of terror was widely practiced by feudal nation-states as a response to civil disobedience behaviors and demonstrations against "law and order". The combative stance was around the question, whose laws and whose perspective constitute order? A legal framework to promote terror anywhere demonstrates their feudal attempts to artificially construct a legal framework for them to execute summary enforcement orders. Chipping away at feudal elites' power was totally unacceptable as determined by the elites. The elites view their power as their inherited right. As viewed by them, it is their right to hoard power. The masses are to be damned. For sentients, there is nothing just about their non-sentient-based actions. We require that sentients be in charge. A replacement Sentient Framework is what is needed. In this framework, there are no terror responses, just wise outcomes.

Ethos Of Doing Business

In Recent Historical References, the hoarding of riches through virgin environment extractions and pillaging until depleted was the feudal construct ethos of doing business. The environments' damaging affects and, indirectly, the inhabitants whose survival depended on them were of no consequences. The ethos of doing business was the primary focus. Nothing else mattered. This ethos was supported by feudal systems known as governments that were chartered with business-focused practices that were heavily influenced by the beneficial business-centric entities' continual campaigns to dissuade sentient caretaking practices from being implemented. The business entities' responses can then state that their actions and practices were in keeping with existing regulatory rules and regulations and hence, their actions are "justifiable". Can we ever say that these assault practices are ever justifiable? If the answer is not in the affirmative, then you are a sentient aware of the true riches that need to be nurtured.

Good Grass

In Recent Historical References, eliminate the opposition as the way to silence any and all "terrorists" of feudal systems was the common rallying call made when their thrones were in jeopardy. It is like weeding the lawn so that only "good grass" would be allowed to grow, which can be used as an analogy for this rallying call. However, as was learned, constant weeding is needed to allow for "good grass" to flourish. Weeds just keep coming back up. Similarly, those officials in governmental constructs were fearful of anti-government activities. The fear was to lose believers of these artificial constructs. In response, fear must be instilled throughout using extermination campaigns for anyone who dares to stand against them. Often, eradication actions tended to be done along nationality or religious lines for those who "obviously" represent differences from the "status quo". When their visual abilities can see only along nationality and/or religious lines, then germination will take root for extermination to take place. Given this singular identifying view, then eradication is nothing more than genocide by any other name. There is no good grass growing here.

Of Lordly Importance

Has there ever been a defensible perimeter in Recent Historical References that endured the test of time? Feudal attempts at defensible perimeters were erected. However In time, all have been made obsolete. So why spend a great deal of time, effort, and resources in defending them? Based on the historical references, perimeters were created by feudal lords in their feudal attempts to keep non-subjects out and, more importantly, to keep subjects in. Subjects were important to feudal lords as wealth generators to be used for any lofty projects they consider of lordly importance. Subjects are property for purposes of taxation and to extract anything else that was deemed to have value. The sentient answer is neither. A sentient is not a property to any feudal lord to be used or discarded at the privilege of a feudal lord.

Went Elsewhere

Feudal systems, by definition, are constructs with exclusivity granted to the privileged few. No one else can enjoy the same privileges the constructs have to offer. Others must subscribe to their inherited worth to help sustain their privileged power. By not being inclusive to all, their expiration is predetermined once their "privileged worth" has evaporated. This was done when the other non-privileged would no longer subscribe to these exclusionary artifacts and then went elsewhere.

Feeble Attempts

In Recent Historical References regarding times when military did feudal lords' bidding, it was considered "an honorable act" to be a member of the military and perform her duties. If military soldiers were taken prisoner and then later released from captivity, they return as "heroes". For the opposing military who lost the battle or war, the victors did not considered their soldiers' actions as those of terrorists. This is because the victors would be shunning with the thought that they could have been on the losing side and did not want to be labeled as terrorists themselves. All soldiers want to think that they were doing noble deeds. Both sides would follow established rules of engagement so that soldiers are respected. They participated in a noble profession is the main notion. These rules did not appear to apply to non-military civilians with ideas and plans that were carried out for the termination of feudal-states. These non-military civilians were labeled "terrorists" by feudal states. This "label permit" allowed for the torture of individual civilians up to and including being put through violent deaths. Weapons of mass destruction deployments were considered acceptable responses when those termination acts are viewed to keep victorious feudal states in power. How odd that states were afraid of civilians that normally do not have access to weapons of mass destruction. If they did, it was found to have been planted so that evidences can be used to prove that their "reign of terror" campaigns are absolutely necessary. So, as individuals, you are making "powerful" states be very terrified. If you have only stones to use, then take along a sling and witness the powerful response you trigger. In historical terms, the actions taken by feudal constructs were feeble attempts to silence you.

Blending In

In Recent Historical References with each increasing generational focus, chemical and genetically altered foods were introduced with the result being the sterilization of the environments from the original state of natural habitats. This posture ensures that feudal lords can control everything and keep subjects dependent on them for sustenance. Feudal subjects would be forced to stay within artificially maintained environments and constructs. To be one with nature would then be severed and, by extension, disconnected from being one with All-That-Is. Sentient pursuits will then be thwarted from blossoming. The unforeseen consequence of the singular focus in the sterilization of the environments by the propagators is to be stuck-in-time. Are you one of them because you do not know how you got here in the present? Consider returning to your origins in your blending in with the natural surroundings. Be a caretaker. It will yield a breath of fresh air.

It Does Not Bode Well

In Recent Historical References, "undesirables" were slaughtered with the aim at their extinction. In this way so the argument goes, only believers remain. Why was this practice allowed to go unchecked by terrorist states? It was propagated by the stated objective to wipe out the opposition to its logical end. Historical references repeatedly show this to be an habitual conduct of feudal nation-states. The behavior was institutionalized by the repetition of the same stated objective with the result being extinction events happening time and time again. With this belief conditioning, then believers are themselves practicing terrorist acts by their very conditioned nature in not doing anything about them. However, this view is not universal when one looks at Nature's other inhabitants' acts of environmental cohesiveness when conditions are bountiful. There are no predators exhibiting behaviors that would have the singular purpose of making extinct any groups of other predators or their prey. For believers, one may need to observe Nature to learn a way out of the vicious cycle of extinction behaviors. They are not based on natural instincts. It also does not bode well to be a terrorist. It ought to be instinctive to at least try. Be one with nature and your instincts will return.

Gamesmanship

Weapons of mass destruction (WMD) are to be made obsolete. This option will no longer be allowed to exist with the singular purpose of annihilating "the enemy" before the enemy strikes with its own weapons of mass destruction. In Recent Historical References, this gamesmanship was affectionately called "the arms race". What they were racing towards was total annihilation on both sides. With the elimination of these weapons, should grave harmful actors choose a destructive path, then their acts will have a muted outcome and be messy and difficult for them to complete due to there being no WBD to gain access to. This ought to dissuade them from from following through with grave harmful acts. The actors will get a push-back from a sea of societal members who have chosen the non-grave harmful acts path and are not at a disadvantage due to the removal of all WMD everywhere. Sufficient Force Doctrine would then apply. Hence, a sea-wall will stop all advances and wash away those who contemplate their own self-destruction.

Nation-State Of Birth

In Recent Historical References regarding corporations, an entity was defined by most nation-states whereby global entities of this type were able to be at many locations around the world at the same time. This is very out of place because nation-states were restricted to their perimeters to a large extinct. Those who wanted to expand their "spheres of influence" required the use of or the threat of military protracted forces. The outcome was for other nation-states to "get in the game" in order to have parity in their sphere of influences too. In almost every case, the military industrial complex fed on itself with the propagation of the same for other nation-states to acquire the same military industrial complex. Flexing their muscles was often carried out. This is nothing more than terrorist outreach by any other name. What other type of entity can propagate the expansion of military might everywhere? The answer is entities called corporations. They had unique "entity traits" of global objectives and goals with no expiration dates. They are in a position to offer military industrial grade products and services to anyone for a price. Their interests are to promote the military industrial complex. They are huge. The end result to all of this effort is the fine art of ratcheting up the threat of terrorism in order to protect corporations' livelihood. No right-sizing here, only global domination. In summary, a corporation is a conceptual definition born in one nation-state. It grew and became cancerous. Now, its tentacles are found in other nation-states. To remove this cancerous growth, the definition has to be undone in its nation-state of birth.

Perimeters

In Recent Historical References, "great nation-states" deemed it necessary to "secure their borders" by erecting "border fences" along their perimeters with the purpose of keeping non-citizens out. Or, was it to keep citizens in? It can go either way sitting on the fence. The impacts to Nature's environments and all those who are natural inhabitants to them were of little consequences when the preservation of feudal constructs was of supreme importance. The premise is that all inhabitants are "subjects" to feudal lords and have more value than "non-subjects", which are kept out of their perimeters. The global view beyond perimeters was mostly non-existent. Later with the borders secured, hoarding was propagated by driving the expansion of their perimeters. Exclusionary practices were defined in legal terms to ensure undesirables were expelled from their perimeters so as to not degrade the property holdings of the respective feudal states. Today, it is quizzical in a Sentient Framework why entities from historical times had low self esteem and accepted the notion that a few elites can hold more valuables than the masses combined. We are sentients. No perimeters are needed to keep us in or out. Quizzical indeed!

Nature's Diversity

When artificial constructs like feudal laws condemn species of Nature through executions and eradication using legal reviews and court orders as the basis for such actions, then Nature will in turn eradicate the artificial constructs by reducing them to rubble. Many great societies of Recent Historical References have been left barren whereby later archaeologists can only guess as to the cause or to not even having a clue as to these great societies' demise. It is Nature's diversity that makes the biosphere habitable and not those of toxic practices. The specie who likewise constructed barriers to Nature's Diversity's well being by promoting "thrash and burn" practices will find itself burned to a crisp when they are likewise returned to Nature as ash.

A Lease Arrangement

It is on the whims of property owners in whether environmental good stewardship practices will be performed or not. In a Sentient Dominion Expanse, duty caretakers are in charge and not property owners. No member owns property. It is a lease arrangement. As can be shown using Recent Historical References, property owners stripped and then hoarded what they considered to be wealth holdings from value-rich resources with the end result of leaving properties in toxic waste conditions with the environments unable to readily sustain Nature's habitats let alone thrive anytime soon. In contrast, there is no sentient premise that artificially defined properties can be owned by anyone other than Nature. Sentients know better who the true stewards are and it is not the owner.

Favorably Rich Environmental Conditions

For millennia as shown in Recent Historical References, favorably rich environmental conditions would sprout "great civilizations". These same "great civilizations" would eventually lay barren reflecting the once favorably rich environmental conditions being depleted of the riches, which then would become barren first as the predictor of the great civilizations' demise. Reflecting differently, historical references also show that those atoned societies became great environmental stewards taking only sufficient environmental resources while at the same time promoting sustainability in maintaining the environments in their original pristine conditions. Their astute stewardship did achieved higher levels of awareness and societal longevity. They were truly great sentient societies. These societies continue their stewardship even when invading external war armadas came to "claim" the pristine environments for themselves only to pillage these environments to exhaustion and ultimately resulted in barrenness. Unbeknownst to these armadas, they would in the not too distant future be laid buried never to expand further on their invasions. The armadas' members would then find themselves being reborn to a dramatically constricted favorably rich environmental conditions to help aid them in a greater atonement (at-one-ment) quest towards a spiritual self awareness state. By having less favorable surroundings, these returning members would not be so distracted. The journey can begin now if you wish. The limitations are based on one's earnest desire or lack thereof towards a self awareness state. Should one find herself asking the question, "How did I get here?", then she may have a long ways to go.

Far Away Lands

In too many incidences found in Recent Historical References, a number of "supreme nation-states" watched while genocide was taking place elsewhere in faraway lands. They did not want to get involved. After all in their elitist "reasoning", the distant populations experiencing genocide inflicted on them are non-citizens of supreme nation-states. In short, they have no worth or value for protection afforded to their citizens exclusively. The upstanding citizens could only watch in horror due to their extensive pliant and placid behavior shaping by their nation-states. Little did they know that genocide could happen to them due in large part by their obedience-shaping practices by feudal-states. Disposal option is one of the options on the table for consideration by feudal lords. However, this could only happen in faraway lands, correct?

Rewarded With A Treat

In Recent Historical References, feudal systems are framed in elite terms to the detriment of their subjects. Subjects are grouped en masse. Hence, mob rules apply for the masses. How is it, figuratively speaking, that the tail is wagging the dog? Is it because the dog – or is it the tail? – can easily be rewarded with a treat? Indeed, treats were showered on the elites to keep them loyal. You will not find this in a Nexus Pentarchy Prime Framework. It is framed for all sentients at all levels of awareness to be included in Nexus Dominion discussions and activities. Prime degrees of separation from the Foundation Prime to the Nexus Prime are small. There are no mob rules to contend with. Wise sentient remedies rule.

So Called Threats

The "greatest nation-state" of its time as is described in Recent Historical References had a commanding military reach that stretched the entire world. The reach was not so much to protect "friendly" nation-states as it was often alluded to. The umbrella mission and goal was to protect this great nation-state from all threats. The protection of its nation-state came above all others. This is not the case in a Sentient Framework. Any reach stretching the entire Nexus Dominion Expanse and Beyond is afforded the same level of protection for all sentients. No need to determine who is friend or foe. Any so called threats are considered to be at the Nexus Pentarchy Prime Dominion and Nexus Pentarchy Prime Rapid Response Auspices are in readiness mode to take any and all appropriate actions and activities regarding grave harmful acts. The Auspices are guided by Nexus Sentient Prime Directives and associated remedies.

High Bar Standard

In Recent Historical References, examples can be found in the legality of death promoters. One alarming example is that of the promotion and sale of addicted tobacco products. These products were given legal protections whilst their "healthy use mystique" was clouded in secrecy. Even after the "scientific research communities" proved the fatal end results for users, the producers continued to enjoy legal protection from deep restrictions or banishment. This took a very long time to prove due to the influence by the tobacco products producers who sponsored much of the early scientific researches that produced dampened and "incomplete findings requiring more research". At the same time tobacco products were provided legal cover, non-lethal competitor products were given no legal protection for use by placing them on the "gravest" of harmful drug banishment list that had the affect of totally banning their use by any entity. No blind judiciary rulings are found here in rendering which drug is more harmful. This placement of non-harmful drugs on a list had the effect of the escalation in the financing of the greatest of all wars on drugs to keep them away from consumers. This resulted in "legal enforcement" activities that ultimately were nothing more than death squads to counteract the producers and distributors of the alternative products, which have the result of producing countering death squads that were shaped over time to match the legally shielded enforcers' escalating military-equivalent campaigns against them. One might conclude that the illegal death squads were the product of the legally sanctioned ones. The byproduct on this war effort included the incarceration and, at times, death sentences to a very large number of individual users and collateral bystanders. In summary, one can find many examples of legal operators-of-death prevalent in Recent Historical References. The very high profits by producers and distributors were to be protected at all costs. The "gravest" of harmful drug banishment list maintained by nation-state death-squads were to be adhered to by using any means necessary in their non-use by any entity, which included access to all necessary treasury assets as needed. In summary, an artificially set "high bar standard" produced death squads on all sides of this standard with disastrous results.

What Is Really Going On

We do not need to rely exclusively on "the facts" in making sentient decisions and wise outcomes. In numerous Recent Historical References, "the conclusive facts" were stretched and twisted to the point of actually making them very incomplete of all of the related "hard facts" in order to advance non-sentient selfish decisions and outcomes. These decisions were not based on well informed information and the complete set of facts. The decisions made were a cover for far more sinister objectives. To avoid horrors from even starting, require that sentients be in charged. They would have far more insights as to what is really going on and take appropriate actions.

Above The Law

In Recent Historical References, apartheid was institutionalized in the fabric of many nation-states. The dominate aggressor race to include its cultures, religions, beliefs, pedigree heritages, to name a few, promoted practices through artificial laws and institutions that stripped personhood and participation to those who were indigenous originals to the land or are viewed as inferior to the "superior" aggressor race. These practices encouraged turning a blind eye to genocide of "indigenous and inferior races". The intent was to make these indigenous and inferior races extinct so that no one will "challenge" their superiority ever again. More often, much smaller populations of inferior races remained so that their diminutive size could not effectively challenge the superior race ever again. The dominance practices continued with the privileged and made institutionalized based on the rule of law. The practices gave cover to hide behind the "established legal statutes" to oppress the non-privileged who had none. In summary, the rule of law can justify any terrorist act with the force of law and with impunity. Genocide should never be above the law. The law will have to be dismantled.

Diplomatic Immunity

In Recent Historical References, important interactions between nation-states were done through "diplomacy". Each nation-state could have small defensible perimeter "embassies" erected in other nation-states in order to perform sanctioned embassy activities as if it was within that specific nation-state of the embassy in adhering to its rules of conduct. This afforded the staff of these embassies the privilege of "diplomatic immunity" from any violations of the host's nation-state rules of conduct and its laws up to and including grave harmful acts from prosecutions. When observed or impending feudal conflicts that could lead to wars were present, then the embassy staff members were ordered to leave the host nation-state that they were in. It is with great comfort that in a Nexus Pentarchy Prime Dominion Expanse, there is no diplomatic immunity. Therefore, those who commit grave harmful acts can be remedied to zero.

In the Dominion Expanse, there is no need for embassies because there are no nation-states to have a reason in having them built. Hence, feudal wars have been effectively reduced to zero, as it should.

To Be Marginalized

As long as there are feudal constructs, there will always be terrorist states. Having subjects defined as properties of the state will always mean enslavement for us all. When sentients are prohibited from entering or leaving border perimeters, it means that we share in the notion that we are marginalized by the state to what it means to be a sentient. In Recent Historical References, atrocities and oppression directed towards subjects were enforced due to "lawful" rulings. Only feudal elites were considered as performing lawful duties. The masses were to be damned and marginalized. Do you want terrorists to continue to be in charge or do you no longer want to be marginalized by insisting that sentients be in charge? There is no reason to be damned any longer. The choice is clear.

Submitted Claims

In Recent Historical References, there are many references to the horrors of genocide by feudal systems that planned and implemented campaigns to eradicate those native originals occupying lands that were being invaded by the great feudal militias of their time. These originals were not subjects (properties) of feudal states, which meant they had little value so as to be discarded from the premises simply for being in the way of feudal lords' "submitted claims" to the same. These originals did not subscribe or bowed to feudal lords and needed to be removed completely through genocidal practices. With their numbers greatly reduced or completely wiped out, the non-believers of feudal systems would never be able to rise up ever again and be a threat to their feudal expansions and dominance. The genocides were codified in feudal laws even when this term was never used. The judiciary outcomes produced the same enforcement results.

Those in royal robes were present during the executions, but did nothing to stop them. There judiciary orders were lawfully carried out. Looking at related references, can anyone claim that the law does no harm? Do not be fooled. It does.

Rights Of Sovereignty

In Recent Historical References, feudal constructs did not want to interfere in each other's internal matters due to respecting each other's treasured feudal "rights of sovereignty" even when genocidal acts were being committed by another sovereign feudal construct. Historical records do show that the then non-genocidal practicing constructs have also practiced genocide to the point of extinction earlier in their histories. The thinking at the time is to eliminate the threat to their belief systems even when those who aligned with and are loyal subjects to their belief systems committed atrocities against "savages" and "terrorists" by armed invasions. Victory included the acquisition of instant wealth for their troubles. The labels of those who were threats to the conquerors were used to justify campaigns base on "the rule of law". Hence, laws enacted were made to justify their own "rules of engagement" resulting in inconsequential atrocities as viewed by them. From these references, one can only conclude that the true premise for "the right to sovereignty" was actually to export state-sponsored terrorism everywhere. A nation-state can only interface with another nation-state. Removing the "fringes" of societies ensure that these interfaces remain intact. Nation-state building was the rallying call to duty. From the elites' perspective, it is a noble life-long endeavor to promote "the rights to sovereignty". Given this, here are some questions to ponder. Do you want to do a noble deed? Is it by contributing to the export of terrorism everywhere is how one can demonstrate one's noble deeds? Is this the defining trait to have true nobility? Consider removing terrorist endeavors from the list of noble things to do. In order to accomplish this, it requires the expiration of all feudal constructs. Only in this way can "cruel and inhumane" events can be extinguished. Sovereignty is then no longer a right.

Kicked In On Reflex

In Recent Historical References, a supreme feudal state known the world over promoted and propped up other feudal states so long as their policies aligned with itself. Should feudal states choose to align themselves with another instead even when reaching out to neighboring feudal states, exclusionary practices and penalties kicked in on reflex. A Manifest Destiny Doctrine was even crafted earlier in its historical timeline to validate the acquisition of territories for itself through military means if necessary. Now, isn't that a kick?

Claim-Rights Expedition Practices

An earlier greatest nation-state of its time as described in Recent Historical References promoted and perfected the nearly complete set of genocidal extinction practices on the original native inhabitants during the reign of terror clearing of non-citizens campaigns in its takeover of environments to be their legally acquired feudal claims for the same. This precedence was practiced in future rising of newly-formed great nation-states using numerous prior to their times historical precedence setting nation-states that came before to support their newly acquired claims. The precedent setting great nation-states in essence promoted terrorism around the world. The feudal terrorist claim-rights expedition practices continued long past the time when all the final perimeters encompassing all known lands were drawn. Takeover campaigns did continue. The terrorists had history on their side. We can all learn a lot from history.

The Ultimate Pursuit

When acceptance of sentient pursuits in feudal systems is initially recognized in a precedence event and then is later nullified, then this is due to the realization that all feudal-judiciary constructs would have the affect of a house of cards come tumbling down. The campaign to terrorize is instead accepted in order for them to "contain" feud subjects and to "ward off" non-feudal subjects in order for "order" to be restored. The main elitist's thrust for order is so that the coupling of the feudal-system and the judiciary remains intact, which seems to be the normal historical response as supported by Recent Historical References. Their true intent is to ensure power is reserved to a few non-sentients. Not much judicial thought was given to weigh abuse of power on its merits, just more of the same judicial misconduct rulings. The first judicial misconduct set the precedence for the later ones in producing the final ultimate feudal desirable outcomes. In summary, nothing much of interest happened due to these ultimate pursuits, just a bunch of elites being stuck-in-time.

Personhood Anointment

In Recent Historical References, even compatible "great nation-states" did not want to merge to be even greater. That would mean a concentration of power to an even smaller number of elites. The oddity that is described in these references is that a man-made construct called a "corporation" having "personhood" status was able to "merge" its personhood with other "like-minded corporations" and be the only "entity" that can span across two or more "great nation-states". The dilemma with this is the answer to the next question. Can a great nation-state be really that great, or is it a corporation with stealth invasion capabilities the "greatest" of the two artificial constructs? The more astounding puzzle is the next question. How can a man-made artificially constructed great nation-state give birth to a creation called a corporation that is not made by man, but did ultimately gave precedence to its personhood existence that can enjoy all the privileges granted to all other persons? This creation can then reach out to the judiciary for enforcement rulings that can execute any means necessary to ensure a corporation the right to survival protection. Yet, it is severely handicap. A corporation cannot use senses that can see, hear, speak, taste, and touch like a vast majority of persons can. What we are observing is an example of judiciary precedent setting misconduct in the extreme. No sentient can survive in a judiciary's perimeter reach. A sentient is a lower class personhood type to that of a corporation. A sentient does not have stealth invasion capabilities. To overcome this extreme misconduct, it may take extreme measures to nullify its affects. Can you think of any like removing personhood anointment to corporations? We need a fair playing field. A person can only be in one feudal nation-state sphere of influence game at one time. Of course the prefer measure is to expire all feudal nation-states and their judiciaries. Sentients everywhere would not call this extreme measure. It is the sentient thing to do. We require that sentients be in charge so that extreme measures are not needed.

Too Steep In Cost

In Recent Historical References, laws and regulations were passed and implemented that had the effect of requiring the making of goods and the performance of services significantly more expensive. Yet, when it came to the care and maintenance of Nature's cornucopia, the expense was considered too steep in cost to do. Poisoning and complete extractions were considered cost effective, reasonable, and acceptable. The prevailing practices did not need any adjustments. The reasoning is that Nature is too vast to be of concern during those times was the assumption that was given. This acceptance view of Nature's abundance promoted the raping of Nature with future grave consequences. The needs of "number one" were of paramount to any "distant" projection concerns. The assumption was that there was plenty of time to deal with any issues in a far distant time. Yet, the cries of Nature were deafening. For the vast majority, no one heard them. Insisting that you do not hear anything and that it is not of your concern does not abstain you from experiencing in kind the same anguish that Nature experienced. When that happens, you then ask yourself this question. How did I get here? I guess that you will have to experience it for yourself. Caution, you might even cry out.

Valuable Commodities

In Recent Historical References, the "rule of law" had as its baseline a set of feudal laws that applied to primarily corporeal and artificial "subjects" of feudal states with provisions that were expensive in its implementation.

The provisions required the sacrifice of monetary treasuries through the generation of wealth by feudal subjects and through the tapping of Nature's environments by the extraction practices of resources deemed to be of valuable commodities, which all contributed to the upkeep of these feudal constructs. A set of limited-in-scope laws were passed that addressed what to do with non-subject inhabitants. For non-subjects, the question as to the value of these labeled types for legal identification is that their concern by feudal elites hardly registered. The expense allocation for their upkeep contributed to the additional sacrifice of monetary wealth that eventually became transfer payments to providers. Prison farms and enclosures were constructed to house and keep "convicts" are examples of non-subject inhabitants' provisions based on the significant increasing numbers of those who were confined. These convicts had also the distinction of being condemned to last their entire lives and to be excluded from elite and privilege circles of society during this time. This lifetime condemnation was of no consequence. Through provisions, value was added to each convict due to the cost of taking care of every one of them. This added-value was realized to business and feudal apparatuses that benefited from this arrangement in providing the necessary goods and services deemed appropriate. By convicts being incarcerated over extended periods of time, then constant and regular revenues were realized by this cottage industry. Hence, non-subjects became valuable commodities. In addition to what is described above, a set of limited-in-scope laws that addressed the "health" of natural environments were likewise passed. The references show that Nature's environments took a very heavy hit for feudal constructs' upkeep. The prevailing view at the time was that the natural resources on the whole were of little or no value and therefore, ignored by the wealthy elites. Only a small percentage of the resources were deemed of sufficient value to be extracted to depletion, which also impacted the adjoining natural surroundings to no longer be vibrant of Nature's Living Wonders. The historical saying, "What you sow, so shall you reap!" To paraphrase for what is really going on for the topic being discussed, "What you do not sow, so shall there be nothing to reap!" To be barren is the result that often occurs and not the projected elite's paradise of wealth accumulation. The limited cost set aside to maintain the current landscape is determined to be sufficient by feudal elites. Subjects will be so compliant as to follow them over the cliff. This would be acceptable since there is nothing of value below to disturb the surroundings. One can wait for feudal constructs to fall off the cliff to construct a Sentient Framework, but why would you? Feudal constructs benefit only a few elites. Awake to your sentient-hood and see that blind compliance robs you of who you really are and the contributions you can make to everyone around you and to Nature's Living Wonders. This is the environment that will help you grow as a sentient. No need to be a subject any longer.

The Lucky Ones

For the few remaining minority races left in the world, are they the lucky ones? Luck had nothing to do with it when Recent Historical References highlighted the exposed terrorism practices that were routinely practiced by "great" nation-states of their time. Their failed exclusionary policies left great numbers of great and rightfully proud societies to perish by their mighty military invasion campaigns. It was, at times, only when extinction of a race was eminently made aware to the self-reflective victors did a reversal view occurred. Only with this awareness did it lead to the exclusionary policies order be suspended by the overseers of the lucky ones remaining as viewed by the victors. Extinction would have tagged the great nation-states in historical terms with committing genocide. Regrettably, this was their singular motivation for a very long time. Do not be fooled. Genocide did take place for some races, but not to completion for others. The remedy for genocide has been shown to be the extinction (expiration) of feudal terrorist-states by any other name.

Decimate

The word 'decimate' came from the Roman era as described in Recent Historical References. It was created to describe a line of solders in formation whereby the commander in that event ordered the execution of every tenth solder in the line. These executions were done to motivate all the other soldiers who were left standing to exhibit complete loyalty at all times and to follow all military readiness and combat orders by their commander-in-chief. This was done to ensure that the "superiority" of the Roman Empire of its day was maintained. This "technique" was not applied during the European's "conquest" of the Americas. Decimate was not applied to the "indigenous" Native Americans whose numbers were quite significant when the Americas were first "discovered". For a number of centuries after the "discovery" of the Americas, the mortifying historical references showed that for a large number of tribes that were present at the time of discovery, much less than one in ten were left to carry on. In fact, a disturbing number of tribes were obliterated from the face of the Earth while the remaining tribes came close to extinction themselves. The campaigns in decimating the Native Inhabitants resulted in redefining the campaign usage of the term to more accurately be genocidal campaigns. In this way, the "non-civilized heathens" by dramatically reducing their numbers could not effectively rise up and be a challenging adversary to be able to have a chance in fighting the "civilized European societies" ever again. In this atrocious way, it will ensure the survival of "great" terrorist nation-states. These historical genocidal practices did "inspire" other nation-states to also remove "indigenous" and "undesirable" inhabitants from their "civilized" societies. It has historical basis since it has been done before, so the argument goes. However, is this how we identify a mighty empire by its genocidal leanings?

Observations and Perspectives
on Historical References
- The State of Affairs

Officiate

Feudal elites are not discriminating in their "official" duties in office holder selections. They would instead officiate the discrimination against those who do not subscribe to their feudal beliefs framework that condemns and hoards.

Darker Days

Feudal lords will say, "we are moving beyond our dark days that we recently experienced!" This was uttered to promote faith for its construct. However, what history shows over and over again is that darker days are yet to come. These dark days can only stop when feudal systems expire once and for all.

Life Condemnation Castes

One "felony" conviction does not cast a corporeal entity to be caste for life. Only in feudal constructs do feudal lords condemn a corporeal entity for life. In these constructs, life is temporary and it is feudal constructs that endure. In order to promote sentient pursuits, all feudal constructs are to be expired. In this way, life condemnation castes will cease to be practiced, as they should.

Be Smug About It

To snuff out one's livelihood and be smug about it is a trait of a terrorist. These systems make property of us all to be disposed of "at will" by feudal lords. The solution is the expiration of all feudal systems. No sentient is disposable. We require that sentients be in charge to ensure that this does not happen.

Spiritual Acumen

The affects of judicial decisions still contribute to the results of non-judicial outcomes by elitists and feudal lords. They ensure that the masses are to be damned through the practices of exclusion. An exclusionary construct is, by extension, a terrorist state and cannot long endure. Power by the few cannot stand firm when there is a finite access to enforcement elites (latchkeys) whereby their membership ranks diminishes over time due to the practices of exclusion having the affect in reducing the candidate pools. The fights to advance within the ranks by the membership pools also contribute to barren and sterile results. Those with spiritual acumen will not be a party to such terrorist constructs. The practice of exclusions will drive the "faithful" away when shown the light for inclusion. The choice of being in the dark or of being in the light will become clearer for all who seek from whence we came. All who seek will find illuminating paths to take. It starts with the uttering of the word, which has always been a part of each and every one of us. The word was there in the beginning. Some of us just lost our way back.

Towards Favorable Societal Experiences

There is this notion by the feudal elites that they can create the desired outcome exclusively without any input from the masses. These elites have executed psychological shaping in its intensity to keep the masses subservient for all basic needs or denials. The masses conclude that individually, a single member cannot possibly stand up to the elite monoliths. As separate individuals, the masses are no match against the elitists' hoarding of power and wealth. They have the power only because the masses see no hope for a different structure. When the masses understand and see the glimmer of hope of a Nexus Pentarchy Prime Framework and the contribution of every member's influence towards favorable societal experiences, then collectively, the individual is not alone and can be a part of a greater dominion without the need for elitist power dominance. All is no longer hopeless. It begins with the selection of your chosen Pentarchy Prime Foundations. Make your selection wisely.

Disruptive Terrorist Focus

Collectively as can be found in numerous Recent Historical References, we historically killed ourselves in great numbers and were not readily able to get our heads around this continual death spiral. Yet, "great" nation-states of their time were much more concern with a few "disruptive terrorists" who may do harm by coming to their shores than the much greater numbers killed within other nation-states' perimeters during the great wars that they fought in. If these few "terrorists" do arrive on its shores, then confine them in maximum security confinement centers would have been the sentient approach to take. Instead, what may be the true reason for this posturing by feudal nation-state elites is to keep its subjects more fearful of external harmful elements than to be concern about remedying the true terroristic elements being promoted within the same great nation-state perimeters and external. Upon reflection, this pasturing was the primary intent all along backed by the officiating elites of its time. In summary, nation-states cannot be made to be less terroristic in nature. All must expire so that all grave harmful acts can be heightened and be the primary focus, as they should. It is the Nexus Dominion Collective that has universality remedies in the forefront for the benefit of all. In this way, protection is not afforded just to the few elites. Rather, it is afforded to all sentients everywhere as part of one of the Nexus Pentarchy Prime Tenets. Consider making it your focus.

Superior Constructs

In Recent Historical References, societal norms of "superior nation-states" promoted the destruction of useful artifacts and the indiscriminate harvesting and clearing of natural preserves and resources. The extinction of species and depletion of resources were the outcomes of these superior constructs. When the natural resources were completely depleted, then the search for to-be-found resources was carried out to discover and acquire them through the use of overwhelming force and destructive military campaigns. Genocidal activities through forced expulsion or eradication were also practiced whenever discovery of new Nature's riches are found for extraction. The demise end result could not be prevented for these great military-based societies holding to the notion of "property rights" that prevailed instead of adopting the Doctrine of Wise Usage (DWU) used in the Nexus Pentarchy Prime Framework. We are today humble to those early Nexus Pentarchy Prime Founders for their foretelling acumen in preventing total extinction to include even our own species from similarly reaching extinction outcomes.

Choose Life

In Recent Historical References, nation-states that promoted subject executions would most likely, by extension, promote fetal executions. If a nation-state were to end all executions, will fetal executions likewise end? There is not an adequate sampling of historical references to conclude one way or another. Subject executions became fashionable way before all other executions became fashionable. For sentients, all executions are fatal. By collectively choosing life over death, this choice will promote the end to all annihilation and mass destruction. Choose life.

To Be Mobile And Pursue Their Dreams

In Recent Historical References, there is the notion that the "rule of law" makes it possible for people to be mobile and pursue their dreams. This is simply not correct. People themselves made it possible for people to be mobile and travel throughout the Expanse by skirting the law. Laws were passed to keep feudal systems, and, by extension, feudal land-based lords in keeping feudal subjects in the fold of feudal ownership. This is how feudal systems collapse due to their ineffective use of terrorist tactics and activities. Eventually, feudal subjects no longer would put up with oppression. In more recent times, an extraordinary effective and flexible spanning framework was spawn to allow sentient issues and concerns of prime importance to be remedied by the right-sizing of the optimal Degree Prime Dominion determined by the Rule of 5 (Ro5) to review and craft remedies on issue and concern review requests. In this way, all sentients are participants in their self-pursuits and spiritual development by their selection of leader caretakers throughout the ascension line of prime degrees.

Demonstrative Form Of Terrorism

In Recent Historical References, the finality of a member's fate for a non-grave harmful act event requiring confinement or condemnation ruling registration for the duration of the member's life expectancy by medieval judiciary constructs and enforced by nation-state agents is a demonstrative form of terrorism inflicted on members. A member is condemned for life by these cruel medieval torture chambers without hope for stigma removal and still be expected to be a contributing member of society through drastically reduced limited means. Only if members have actually performed or have the propensity of grave harmful acts shall they be confined in all cases. When a historically termed "victim" is healed psychologically and/or physically, then confinement and "probation" ends, which would most likely be the earliest, or when the predefined maximum confinement/probation end decree rules apply. As sentients, we are not in the condemning business. Providing adequate conditions for a return to sentient health is the type of practices that ought to be promoted.

Legal Exclusions

The practices of legal exclusions of sentients that do not have the propensity of grave harmful acts promote terroristic behaviors and practices by any other name. Those who believe and promote them have the propensity for grave harmful acts and very often will advance and project such belief systems on non-feudal subjects through military assault campaigns in carrying out exclusionary orders. They will pursue the development of ever newer and more destructive weapons of mass destruction in accomplishing this manifesto. Escalation feeds on itself. Do you still want to believe? Ask yourself this question instead. What would a sentient do? If you cannot answer this last question, then you do have a long ways to go.

Cleanly Executed

In Recent Historical References, one will find the executors of terrorist campaigns to be at the highest echelons of society who oftentimes are not those on the "front lines". In their realm of existence, the executions are "clean". Do not be fooled. There is nothing "clean" about grave harmful acts on a grand scale. Total annihilation "cleanly executed" is the order that is being carried out.

Class Correction

Elites are part of the inclusion class. The vast numbers of societal members are part of the exclusion class. There will be a class correction to this abstract oppression-imbalance decree at which time, weapons of mass destruction will be made moot. The few elite will no longer be protected from the masses by exclusionary-based weapons and overwhelming enforcement campaigns. Be a part of a Sentient Framework and help make weapons of mass destruction obsolete.

More Of The Same

Government ought to not be confined to a political-based arena. Duty caretakers with capabilities ought to be the norm. Otherwise, ill behavioral practices on societies are ever present due to political interference. By extension, law-based constructs do not contribute to incubators of caretaking norms. Rather, exclusionary practices became the norms with the resulting condemnation and execution rulings directed towards sentients and sentient environments. So, is your thinking still more of the same? Consider a sentient alternative.

Sea Of Troubles

In Recent Historical References, feudal land-based systems left vast environmental sea areas on the planet outside of legal "jurisprudence and protection". They served as dumping areas for wastes and toxins while also stripping these vast sea areas of their "valuable" resources. This is a classic example of non-land-claim exception of "self governing" fragility domains that were non-sustainable and resulted in tragic consequences being inflicted on these vast areas to include all the inhabitants who also reside there. In addition, outside nation-states would conduct military exercises that put extreme stresses on these ecosystems and be dumping grounds for arsenal wastes. These are the historical legacies by the "great feudal states" of their time. Do we really want to return to the same extreme sea of troubles? Sentients would drown in them.

Partner Up

Other "partnered" feudal states are accomplices to the greatest feudal state of its time when these other partners did not protest non-sentient behaviors toward even their own sentients. They are in the same league as the greatest of them all. Hence, sentients are not seen, not heard, not touched, not tasted by their presence, and definitely not spoken about. These voids will not endure. Sentients everywhere, partner up so that we can be seen, heard, touched, tasted with our presence, and definitely spoken about. There is no need to hide. We are sentients. The Expanse is ours.

Shared By All

Feudal constructs promote environmental contagions due to "jurisdiction" voids whereby they are void of even a semblance of feudal construct's jurisdictional protections. The intent is to strip valuables from them to depletion and fill the extraction sites with toxic wastes; and then leave. As sentients are quite aware of, these assaults and toxins have a way of dispersing to once "protected" feudal domains. In the end, the suffering is shared by all. Hence, there are really no voids. The get filled by the same carriers that created the voids in the first place.

The Grim Reaper

Overwhelming force is the doctrine used by the "greatest nation-state" to squash the "enemies of the state", so labeled, without reservation no matter how many non-combatants have been snared, albeit unceremoniously terminated, in the process. Since these non-combatants are "non-citizens", hence non-subjects, their importance and value are moot as viewed by this greatest nation-state. This perspective reduces all to rubble. No "great" nation-state could possibly be viewed as great when destruction results in fallow lands and in waters by its wake. Whenever a nation-state advances are present or in the vicinity, the grim reaper is close behind. Instead of promoting terrorist constructs, promote a framework that is truly a caretaker of sentient values. This framework makes war obsolete due to expiration of feudal states and nullification of their border perimeters. Terrorist advances are no longer appealing.

Feudal Attempt

The elitists are losing their believers through attrition. They are desperate to replenish their ranks. Choose to not replenish their moats and castles. It would be a feudal attempt.

Considered A Nation-State Matter

In Recent Historical References, "international laws" permitted death squads to flourish in feudal-based societies. The resulting findings show that these laws did not protect sentients because it was considered a nation-state matter protected by international laws. The resulting remedy that was crafted is the expiration of all feudal-based constructs so that Pentarchy Prime duty caretakers can perform their stewardship activities to ensure a protective environment.

Pay Homage

The "greatest nation-state" that ever existed as recorded in Recent Historical References did terrorized its subjects by having a perceived "greatest army" of highly paid, legally sanctioned, judiciary and enforcement soldiers whose numbers are greater than the combined armies of legal judiciary and enforcement soldiers of most of the less-than-greatest nation-states that were also present at the time. With their construct, "power" over its environments to include the masses of its subjects was considered supreme and superior to all other constructs. This construct suffocated astute and noble duty caretaker that performed activities to benefit and to nurture the viability of all of Nature's inhabitants. Even the privileged elitists who found themselves with diminishing wealth kept their beliefs anchored in their absolute allegiances to supremacy judiciary construct. This construct was later proven and demonstrated to be found to be inferior to the optimally and noble stewardship of effective caretaking activities without assaulting the living and breathing life forces of surrounding environments. Time demonstrated that this stance lead to its own suffocation and demise.

With fewer resources to hoard over the course of time by its long-term premeditated annihilation of state-decreed adversarial enemy campaigns in maintaining their appetites to hoard and retain their "innate rights" to wealth and power, abandonment of these nation-states occurred to area perimeters of ever-constricting and congested bastions of resource-rich environments. With their diminished wealth, a replacement framework promoting life-replenishment and life-sustaining caretaking practices was erected. Our vibrant sustainable environments are directly attributed to the founders of our sentient promoting framework we enjoy today. These founders are truly our greatest saviors. Let us pay homage,

First-Helping Policies

The race to acquire basic needs resources is being propagated by elitists and hoarders of these resources so as to enjoy the privileges that the masses cannot afford. The truth of the matter is that the resources are being squandered and being driven to diminishing reserves and towards extinction. These short-term yields are not indicators of an advanced society, but rather, one that uses force to deny segments of societal members their rightful access to them. The constructs that support this existence is reinforced by perpetual wars and conflicts in order to perpetuate their "great" statuses from all others. Do not be fooled. The first-helping policies exhibited by "great constructs" are to ensure impoverish existence for the masses. Wasteful practices are the norms in these "great societies". Be not shy. Insist on sharing the resources for the benefit of all. Take only what you need, which is a very effective and sustainable practice.

Nothing Exceptional

You will have to give up your feudal attempts for control of your borders and your preemptive strikes beyond them in your feudal attempts to secure them. Feudal posturing have always lead to wars, which results in destruction of once pristine environments and vibrant habitats. There is nothing exceptional worth noting regarding borders except that they are eye sores.

Valiant Responses

The domestication and docile shaping of feudal subjects produce numbed behaviors whereby responsive caretaking activities are muted in favor of the stodgy framework for the "rule of law". Good Samaritan responses are penalized while hoarding, wealth, and power are admired. In Recent Historical References, one can find numerous examples whereby calamities, which could have been dwarfed, were allowed to propagate into catastrophes long before valiant and desperate responses were allowed. They were allowed for reasons of the preservation of hoarding, wealth, and power by the same bad-actor elitists.

Fluent Righteous And Favorable Outcomes

Why would anyone believe in a construct that cannot respond, to a high degree, effectively and in a timely fashion, regarding grave or urgent matters? The answer may lie in the notion that one is a subject of a feudal master's behavior shaping efforts for all subjects to be loyal believers in the acceptance of the false notion that the feudal system is always just and correct in its actions. In Recent Historical References, one can find many references that this notion is bankrupt in producing fluent righteous and favorable outcomes. The greatest flaw is that subjects are expendable to that of feudal systems.

Allegiance To Fiefs

With feudal nation-states, iron curtains that were once removed are hung again in providing judicial cover to once again blanket their subjects from sentient pursuits. These events are used as reminders for those who do not believe in feudal fiefdoms. Terrorist practices by nation-states are their only means to force allegiance to fiefs.

A Constitution To Give Credence

As provided in numerous Recent Historical References, a nation-state constitution is the basis for an artificial construct with the presumption that it will endure for the ages. The fallacy by many during those times is that the articles of incorporation have it right. Even if not 100% right, the premise is that it cannot get any more perfect. This belief in a false premise condemns us all. Terrorist practices are assured because of this false premise. In all cases, "great nation-states" have crumbled due to rigid adherence to them for their existence. They snapped. Attempts will be repeated again and again until nation-state elitist officials get it right, which turned out to never happen. The allegiance, then, is for the right to terror and to obliterate all enemies of the nation-state who also adamantly feel that they likewise have it right and will defend that right. This ought to not be the objective. A constitution ought to declare the highest goals to be implemented and be updated or replaced with higher goals to be implemented as greater understanding and insights are forthcoming. It will come to past that promoting a Sentient Framework will endure for the ages. It will not need a constitution to give credence to its framework since it is not a a nation-state that would need one. Sentients are in charge.

Its Time Did Run Out

All those with access to "state secrets" were selected due to their abiding obedience to their state-sponsored religion. Terrorism practices continue uninterrupted without end due to the annihilation of any dissent by non-believers. If a privileged actor dares to go against the oath of its religion, she is unceremoniously discharged for not remaining true to the cause. There would also be efforts and campaigns to place non-believers (non-elitists) in harms' way. These are nothing more than terrorist tactics by any other name. In Recent Historical references, incarceration of non-believers in great numbers was the legal option of choice for the "greatest nation-state" of its time. It is comforting to know that its time did run out. It found itself running out of funds and places to put the chosen non-believers for daring to utter the word. Imagine, the elitists feared the word the most!

For sentients everywhere, there is no crime in uttering the word. The word heightens our awareness on being sentients. Believers would not understand what it means to be one. They are blind to their cause only.

Helplessness

In Recent Historical References, the only legally constructed "entity" that was allowed to execute sentients; the only legally constructed "entity" that held sentients as property; the only legally constructed "entity" that exclude sentients in dominion activities; the only legally constructed "entity" that hoards resources by having first pickings over the viability of sentients' health; the only legally constructed "entity" that did all of these and others; do you know what entity this was? It was a feudal nation-state having a judiciary to carry out its standing orders. Do not be fooled. It is an artificial state. For sentients everywhere, be secure in your view that this entity can never be a sentient. No wise outcome can come from it, only perpetual sufferings and tragedies to ensure the the "rule of law" is supreme based on erroneous standing orders. Why would anyone give unwavering supremacy to it? The answer may be due to one does not consider herself a sentient and instead would surrender to the notion that she is a subject of feudal lords. There is hope for her in the understanding that not everyone shares her view and has chosen not to be stuck-in-time and have moved way beyond a stationary point. As a sentient, you can shine a light for her to see a different way out of her helplessness.

Sentient Pursuits

A life of privilege in feudal nation-states requires overwhelming "enforcement" of exclusionary laws. No caretaking framework is present in these artificial constructs. Hoarding in numerous forms became the ruling objective for privileged superiority. Feudal systems are based on this framework. Deny resources to undesirables were practiced in these feudal states in their last feudal attempt to dwarf any uprising for what became to be known as The Awakening of Sentient Pursuits. For the non-privileged, it was eventually realized that a caretaking framework is all-inclusive and would replace all other feudal nation-states combined. Feudal lords need not apply. All sentients in the Nexus Expanse are welcomed. Feudal borders were no longer needed and were removed. Removal proved to be great for the environment as well.

Co-existing In Balance And Harmony With Nature

Assault on Nature's environments and their inhabitants continues when feudal constructs are present. If you want to promote a peaceful co-existence with Nature, then all feudal systems are to be expired. Insists that sentients be in charge. Sentients will then insist on a caretaking framework that, by its very architectural nature, can co-exist in balance and harmony with Nature. Hoarding is not an indicator of superiority, caretaking is.

Barren And Toxic Remains

In Recent Historical References, societal subjects did have new vehicles and dwellings in comfortable surroundings. However, this was made possible through death and destruction left in their wake due to the extraction zones located in once naturally pleasant surroundings. These zones were extracted to exhaustion resulting in barren and toxic remains. The decision was to ensure that extraction costs remain low, which meant that to restore the zones to once naturally pleasant surroundings was determined to have unacceptable costs. This determination accepted the notion that there were at the time a very large number of zones with naturally pleasant surroundings remaining in continuing to do the same to these zones. In their minds, it would be a long time before complete extraction of all the zones would occur and therefore, there was no need to worry about this now. Over time, extraction practices became very efficient having lower and lower time durations for the extractions. The race for hoarding valuable resources through extractions ensued leaving behind ever more barren and toxic zones. Historical references do show that this longevity extraction campaign pushed us to the precipice of extinction. This is their legacy. Will it be shown to be ours as well? Let us learn from their wakes that which they left behind. There is very little time left.

Weakened Through Starvation

A feudal state is defined as an elitist construct that hoards and rations environmental resources to the detriment of other viable inhabitants. To sentients, this is of particular grave concern when denial of fair access to these resources by non-elite inhabitants is practiced. By weakening the non-elite inhabitants through starvation, this ultimately resulted in their extinction. Here is another example of an extremist terrorist practice. You will find no sentient who would abide by this practice. Hopefully, you will likewise not abide by it too.

Inherently Greater Collective Power

Death and destructive activities by lethal force is indicative of terrorist states. In this way, feudal subjects can be unceremoniously and summarily terminated when "the greater good" is argued and then determined. Translation, any resistance group for the rule of law and, indirectly, nation-states are to be squashed by using "any means necessary" to ensure the greater good. Right-sizing of group dominions spanning members of the identified group or groups have no legal framework in feudal nation-state constructs. Oftentimes, peaceful assemblies are viewed with suspicion and fear as a "front" to overthrowing nation-states. To prove that the fear is justified, state-sponsored infiltrators will join the peaceful assemblies and eventually acting out terrorist acts for all to see. In that way, brutal "crackdowns" of these "violent demonstrators" would then be "legally justified". The true reason for the fear by the feudal elites is their fear of losing their unchecked power. Continuing to believe in powerful elites negates the masses' inherently greater collective power. The power is not reserved for the few. Consider choosing to share power throughout the dominions.

Resumption Of War

War is an inevitable consequence when there are exclusionary terms and practices regarding who is a feudal societal entity with all the rights and privileges thereof granted. War is not inevitable when all sentients are included in a dominion. If you hear someone asking this question, "Are you a societal member or citizen?"; or this question, "Are you in or out?"; or this question, "Are you with us or against us?"; then war is on the horizon for everyone. Either way you answer the question that is being asked during the heighten alerts during the multi-feudal societies' "Many Millennia War", the resumption of war is on the horizon.

Disobedience

A prison is a creation of a feudal construct. Confinement in a prison reinforces the concept of perimeters that feudal lords will fight to the death to maintain. The intent is to confine the spiritual essence as a way to enforce feudal lords' right to property. This also includes the confinement of subjects of feudal lords. Abuse, torture, and death await those who are. Loyalty and obedience are expected from all subjects of feudal lords. Do not be fooled. Spiritual essence can never be confined in such prisons. It is also natural to find an escape out of prisons. So, if you are disobedient and find yourself boxed in, then work on your spiritual essence. This awareness needs to be attained in order for one to be set free and escape from a torturous death.

We Will Move On

There is no need to prop them up any longer. All anti-sentient feudal systems need to expire. This will occur as sentients everywhere apply remedies to expire existing "laws on the books" in greater numbers, which will have the effect of making feudal constructs obsolete. This also will be true for "cross-border corporate entities" by default. We require that sentients be in charge. Psst! Elitists will continue to think that they are the only ones here. Their kingdoms will turn to rubble when sentients leave their perimeters and enter sentient-based dominions. After a lengthy period of time, elitist will realize that others were here and would ponder as to where have they all go. Let us continue to let them think that they are still the only ones here. We will move on.

Violators

Regarding an "overthrow" threat of an artificial "nation-state", how odd this must sound. Feudal lords' premise on actions to take for overthrow "violators" is to wreck havoc on the masses in order to "eliminate" the smaller number of those who have oppose them. Overwhelming force is their credo. These assaults are based on their fear that they would lose control of the situation and by extension, there rights to positions of power. In reality, their rights-to-power was never theirs to begin with. The eliminations of those who opposed them are never the expected results that the feudal lords have stated would happen when the plan was first executed. Sentients everywhere will learn of elites' vulnerabilities and use them to take actions to expire all artificial constructs. For lasting results, we require that sentients be in charge. Care to partake?

Identity Burden Of Proof

In Recent Historical References regarding feudal states and their judiciaries, the onus is on the citizen (subject) to prove herself that she is who she declares her identify to be. For sentients, the onus for the identity burden of proof ought to be on the feudal states and their judiciaries to prove citizen identities since they have extensive records on most everything on society's makeup, as it should be. Insist that this be so. As is evident, they have access to substantially more resources than what a citizen would have. Citizens can hasten the certification process by coming forward with identity papers. In all cases, the wait ought not to be long for passage. Temporary identity papers can be issued until confirmation identify papers are given. With temporary identity papers, passage is on a visitation basis only, as it should. By confining or severely restricting those without proper papers is a barbarous practice.

Democratic Nation-States

There is nothing democratic about "democratic nation-states" (DNS). The reason is that when members from one democratic nation-state traverse another DNS, the members are excluded from the democratic process and yet are still compelled to comply with all practices of the traversed nation-state. Hence, non-members have no influence in the democratic process due to exclusionary practices. There is nothing universal here. To truly be considered democratic, then the governing nation-state spanning both DNS is needed so that all can participate in the democratic process. This is repeated when more than two DNS are spanned. In Recent Historical References, a governing body called the "United Nations" was charted to address matters spanning numerous nation-states. However, this was doomed to failure from the start due to the disparate democratic and non-democratic nation-states juggling to be the greater influencing party to the concerns of the day. A "security council" was even created that consists of permanent and a select number of non-permanent members with the permanent members having veto power regarding any issue resolution being voted on. Oftentimes due to the veto power of the few, there are reference examples of genocidal events that were executed by member states which festered unabated for very long periods of time to the horrors of non-permanent members. Clearly, this was not a democratic process with participatory rights given to all. A significant number were even executed for the singular purpose of keeping them from participating in nation-states' matters. Their views were to be silenced. In summary, non-members have no influence in other DNS. To truly be considered democratic, then a governing body such as a more inclusive version of The United Nations will be crafted by member DNS of the greater dominion and not be dominated by a few members of the dominate council. From this more inclusive United Nation version, more inclusion work still needs to be done. The ultimate issue to address is to include all subjects of DNS in the democratic process. Historically, subjects are owned by their respective feudal nation-states with no influence capabilities on the collective states except possibly the state that "owns" them by way of "property rights" due to being subjects of a particular nation-state. As a subject for the vast majority of them, one is reduced to being a slave having wealth value for feudal elites. The challenge is to include subjects of all feudal states to have inter-DNS influence capabilities so that a totally inclusive version of the United Nations will then be viewed as truly democratic. This idea was a non-starter by the few feudal elites.

Free Enterprise

In Recent Historical References, the "free enterprise" framework – otherwise known as commerce -- promoted hoarding of resource extracted riches with very little regard to the consequences of discarding waste byproducts anywhere and everywhere with no thought given to reclamation. The societal trash was dispersed everywhere or placed in land-based mountain heaps or discharged into waterways. The unending cycles of newly discovered natural resource riches extractions were promoted unabated, thereby stripping native inhabitants of sustainable natural surroundings for their own survival, which ultimately lead to the extinction of a large number of species. The "superior human masters" knew not what the consequences would be by their callous indifference. Instead, the choice made was not to give it even a cursory thought. The riches are vast so their impacts would be small, so the argument that given. Do not be fooled. Little did these masters know that their fates await them due to their discharges of their stewardship in these matters. In time, all things are balanced out even when it means that a waste-land and waste-water type surroundings will be provided to them for their dramatically reduced spiritual environments in which to develop in. The once declared masters will not know how they got to where they are upon arrival. That insight is best left hidden so that their focuses can be on a narrower path in the basic pursuits of survival using the same very constricted available resources that they help create. Their journeys are extended significantly in their quest to return to the prior point where they left off. Pondering the choices made, why would anyone want to start all over again on a spiritual quest?

Unnoticeable

A quizzical notion existed in Recent Historical References as to why a large percentage of the population behave in a manner as to not have even a remote care for others. Their interests were primarily focus on hoarding material "wealth" to the detriment of others. This behavior was propagated by the very feudal constructs that existed at the time. These constructs induced those behaviors by wrongly promoting the spoils to the victors. This was the state of mind at the time. Fortunately for us, the references show that there were those who would be caretakers of those less fortunate. These caretakers did not buy into the hype. It is obvious today that when a system is based on hoarding and not on caretaking for all, then the result is to neglect those not as fortunate and hence, be unnoticeable of their plight. The way forward from this imbalance is for a caretaking framework.

No Apologies

To the "greatest" nation-state to have ever existed in its glorious moment in time, are you proud that other nation-states have followed your lead? Your leadership that is being referenced is the execution of, by the military and police deployments, genocidal mission campaigns on indigenous inhabitants who were present before the righteous acquisition takeover crusades. If you are the greatest nation-state, then you should not apologize for the crusades by those who follow you because that is what all great feudal states do. They provide protection to a select number of subjects and pummel all non-subjects. To speak to the contrary to your actions reflects poorly on your superiority in the overwhelming use of an armed military that leaves death and destruction everywhere in its wake. Isn't this the way to measure a great nation-state? Non-sentients are in charge. Again, please do not make any apologies. Why start now? It does not bode well for you. Your luster will diminish. On the flip side for all those sentients who are being pummeled, take heart. Know that the Many Millennia Reign of Terror War will abruptly end in the not too distant future. Keep the faith. Your time is near.

A Crime To be A Sentient

Feudal systems make it a crime to be a sentient yearning to be free to travel anywhere in the known world. Only a select few are permitted to roam in cross-systems' perimeters with proper papers. The vast majority are much more restricted. This is a disturbing premise that is upheld with the use of any and all forces deemed necessary. There is much misguided fear in these systems that can decide to terminate any sentient at will to protect their perimeters. This scribe's will is not with them. Are yours?

Healthcare

Healthcare delayed is healthcare denied. Serious patient illnesses cannot wait for political discussions or discourse as were practiced in Recent Historical References by nation-states. There are no politically-based denials in the Nexus Pentarchy Prime Framework. Dominion remedies are based on expedient caretaking attainment goals. Insist on adequate care and in a timely fashion.

To Collect Their Rightful Share

Feudal constructs are based on the holdings of property. Subjects are also comprised in these holdings. Wars are carried out against other feudal actors who want to hoard the same holdings for themselves. The objective is to collect their rightful share of the hoarders' holdings. Feudal actors who feel threatened will use "any and all means necessary" to eliminate the threats. Oftentimes, "rules of war" are supposedly agreed upon whereby non-holdings subjects are "fair game" for elimination. In a Sentient Framework, there is no "rules of war", the use of "any means necessary", nor the "fair game" practices of eliminating non-holdings subjects. In a Sentient Framework, holdings of subjects have no meaning and the Nexus Pentarchy Prime Sufficient Force Doctrine guides the Sentient Expanse in reducing all grave harmful acts to zero. The state of grave harmful acts to zero is a very good place to be in.

Obtrusive Fences

In Recent Historical References, constructions of border fences were erected. The singular purpose for them was to keep subjects in or non-subjects out or, more commonly, both. However, the fences did more than that. The ignorance on the unintended consequences had the affect of performing an assault on Nature and the Life Forces that were nurtured by her. The unintended consequences of this expansive reach marked the promotion and hoarding of Nature's abundant riches. Or, could this have been the strategic objective all along? Imagine how unimaginatively foolish this constant tug of war regarding border perimeters has been. This tug of war lasted for a very long time and became known as The Many Millennia War. Do you think that we can do without these obtrusive fences? They really serve no sentient purpose.

Attuned Humans

In Recent Historical References, one of the weapons of mass destruction used in deep waters was the sonic boom bombs that destroy living creatures from the inside out. Internal organs and underwater hearing of such creatures as whales, dolphins, and other non-human sentients would explode leaving them unable to navigate the waters and painfully, would slowly die. Many would be beached along the shore unable to return to the waters. In almost all these cases, their deaths follow soon after. The sonic boom bombs have frequencies that have a multiplying stronger sonic boom effect in water than in air due to the density of water. Those same sonic boom bombs would be muted above water. These sonic boom bombs were detonated far from shore in deeper waters where no humans or a very small number of them would know about what were actually going on. This turned out to be not the case. There were those who could hear their cries and see their excruciating painful death. Others likewise could also if they were just attuned and be receptive to them. Only when there are overwhelming numbers of attuned humans that feel the excruciating pain can the tragedies be exposed for all to hear and to also demand that there be a complete halt to all of these bombings. Consider not being silent any longer when human-causing tragedies do occur. Be receptive to halting the source for all this grief.

Laid To Rest

The feudal construct is the vanguard, defender, and champion to the feudal premise of property rights. It includes the right to own citizens and the right to value there citizens more than the value of non-citizens. The judiciary is a built-in orator to ensure that these rights are not violated. Hence, the judiciary is anti-sentient by its very conflict-of-interest makeup. For aware sentients, sentients will declare emphatically that they are not properties to any feudal lord or to any artificial construct. One by one as this awareness is ascended on the citizenry; the expiration of feudal constructs will take hold until all has been laid to rest. We then become caretakers to each other, as it should.

Experiencing Both Sides

In Recent Historical References, high levels of state-sponsored incarcerations and executions are indicators of terrorist states. There are two sides to incarcerations, those who are looking in and those who are looking out. Don't think that anyone will be left in or out. At different times, one will have experienced both sides until one is no longer stuck-in-time due to choosing a different course of action than that of a terrorist. When one looks at her condemning or condemned predicament and transform it in terms of being a caretaker challenge, then this most likely can be your way out. Take it.

Good Stewardship

There was this dominant notion that the rights to property will ensure good stewardship, which has been disproven to be the case as provided in numerous Recent Historical References. It is absurd to say that all property owners are by definition – or by "the force of law" – the best stewards of property holdings, which includes claims to natural surroundings. What has been shown is that the "undesirables" of Nature's species collective by these owners were to be exterminated and that Nature's riches were to be extracted to exhaustion. When depleted, the next parcel of property was exhumed. It is a quandary how it was determined that this viewpoint defined good stewardship. Even the force of law did not help matters much to sway good stewardship.

Perpetual Battle

Denial of basic sustenance was practiced by "great nation-states" of their time on "enemies of the state". Those who aided these hunted enemies were also included in this classification. This practice even went against "humane" treatments articulated in charters by "world bodies" whereby the same great nation-states were signatories to them. This practice of condemnation fed on itself as to be reflective. After a while, these same signatories could not see their own humane reflections by what they projected. What they saw instead where their nemeses being reflected by their own reflections. Sadly, they became stuck-in-time in a perpetual battle that never seemed to cease and unaware of their own reflections.

Cloaking Of The Law

In Recent Historical References, the "cloaking of the law" by nation-states was practiced and institutionalized in shielding their activities from dissertation. For the elites, this afforded them the ability to cloak all destructive behaviors and practices prohibited to the masses. The more appropriate translation for this is, "the law of secrecy and judiciary misconduct". Hence, there is no transparency for efforts to be taken to dismantle non-sentient institutionalize constructs due to their cloaks. In this way, feudal institutionalize terrorism can continue unabated. There was also no escape for subjects of feudal lords given this cloaking capability. For sentients everywhere, getting rid of the cloak is not the objective. Retiring all feudal nation-states is the objective. No one ought to be able to promote and project terrorism in any form. Do not be fooled. There are countless references that demonstrate that a non-terrorist state can ever be achieved. Therefore, do not waste your time and effort. Take the sentient path. Let transparency shine.

To Be A Ward Of The State

There is a phrase found in Recent Historical References that was used in feudal constructs. It is "to be a ward of the state". There is very large number of references that show that the state is ill suited to be a caretaker of anyone. The phrase that is much appropriate to this concept is "to be a property of the state". In this way, the state is well suited to handle any property up to and including the discarding of the same. There is no caretaking exhibited here, only the disposal of property when it is no longer of value. So, are you a "property"? A sentient does not see herself in this way. For her, the choice is clear. Try not to get trapped in being a ward of the state by thinking about it for too long.

Incarceration Was The Tool Of Choice

In the name of security, subjects were incarcerated oftentimes for lengthier stays for law infractions committed than those who committed grave harmful acts. Sentencing activities was just something that judiciary soldiers did by viewing and treating everyone in the same judicial cesspools no matter how minor or major the "crime". These behaviors are indicators of terrorist states that fear being exposed as terrorists themselves by ethical sentients and so they will do "whatever it takes" to shield them from being exposed all in the guise on "the war on terror". Feudal subjects in great numbers who did not commit any grave harmful acts and who were also snared in the states' nets were of no concern. Their dragnets gave very little thought to non-terrorists compared to the singular focus on doing whatever it takes to fight the war on terror in perpetuity, if necessary. They would have first access to any amount of feudal treasuries and resources to sentients bewilderment. To keep this war going, parallel efforts were focused on ensuring that non-believers are silenced as well. Incarceration was the tool of choice. Fortunately, sentients can never be silenced. The word will be uttered. For all those feudal believers, you have the right to be very afraid, be very afraid. The Many Millennia War is coming to an end now that the word is in motion.

Composition

In Recent Historical References, a citizen – otherwise known as a feudal subject -- of a nation-state – otherwise known as a feudal construct – is classified as being a property of a particular state being examined. A non-citizen is not classified as being a property of the same state being examined. If you believe in nation-state constructs, then you believe that privileges and rights are reserved only to citizens as long as you are still classified as one. Hence, you are viewed to be of "value" to the state as long as you remain classified or can be made to be unclassified as a citizen when it suits the nation-state. It is a simple legal maneuver to not be classified as one. Hence, you are only valuable to the state as long as you are a citizen. For those who are not citizens, then the view of that particular state is one of a terrorist state. It is in this manner that terrorism was propagated throughout the known world. To end terrorism, all nation-state constructs have to expire. In a Sentient Framework, a sentient cannot be declared a non-sentient even while beyond the corporeal Expanse. The framework is structured such that its composition contains no terroristic elements. Terrorism is considered the same as grave harmful acts and will be remedied quickly by the Nexus Pentarchy Prime Rapid Response Auspices to bring all grave harmful acts to zero.

Sanctimonious Owners

Land grabs of Nature's pristine environments resulted in the parceling of lands so that every piece of land is owned by a land owner. These land owners would remove or eradicate all undesirable species from their "legally acquired" parcels. – As an aside, it is disconcerting that before the the "rule of law" and subsequent "land grabs", the original native inhabitants did not have any "legal claim" on the land. It is no wonder that the native inhabitants were forcibly removed from the owner's land, if you subscribe to such feudal concepts. – The species that did survive the eradication are domesticated ones to be used as the owner's sees fit to do. Nomadic species quickly became extinct due to the erecting of perimeter fences or markings. Should nomadic species cross into their perimeters, a high percentage of these species were hunted for sport. How sanctimonious are the owners who think that they have tamed and domesticated the "wild frontiers". This sanctimony didn't last for long. Nature may appear to have been domesticated. In reality, it became dormant. When a tipping point is crossed, then the landowners will find themselves washed away or displaced. On the other hand, Nature does respond favorably to sufficient use and extraction behaviors. Duty caretakers of Nature are always beneficiaries of Nature's Cornucopia by performing proper caretaking. In short, be sure to groom Nature. By doing this, you bring out the beauty in her.

No Disconcerting Affects Are Noticed

Invisible is how elites see the masses. Their elitists' self-serving decisions cannot possibly affect anyone, so the elitists conclude. No disconcerting affects are noticed by them. Do the masses notice anything disconcerting? Elitists see no visible affects being observed by the masses. They have the final word on this.

Just Another Caged Zoo Attraction

Feudal systems are anti-sentient. If a subject is not a property of a feudal system with appropriate travel papers, then she is caged like any zoo animal until returned to the owning feudal lord for disposal. These force repatriations are enforced by judicial decree. In summary, keep your travel papers very close or be just another caged zoo attraction.

Not In My Great Neighborhood

How arrogant it is for feudal lords to erect border perimeter fences with the sole purpose to keep non-subjects out. This scene is obscene. Who do they think they are? This is a barbarous behavior of a non-civilized culture. In addition and just as disturbing, Nature's migratory inhabitants are kept from entering or leaving by these fences. The erection of the fence is a terrorist act in the extreme. "Not in my great neighborhood" translates to not being neighborly by any means. The wall represents a toxic relationship. Not to worry. The toxins have a way of leaking back in. This wall was a feudal attempt at constructing a moat around its castle. Nature always manages to find a way to topple even the biggest of grandstands. In time, normalcy will once again return.

Take What Is Sufficient

The greatest nation-state will not relax its hold on world supremacy. After all, it is a hoarder of resources and of property holdings. No sincere Nature's sustainable cornucopia caretaking is practiced here. This "supremacy view" over all other interest views is propped up by the labors of others with some having sustainable interest views. The resources and property holdings are then extracted and collected to depletion. When one steps back and observe what is truly going on, the greatest nation-state would not be so great if everyone else hoarded. When this happens, the greatest nation-state would go to war to "take" what are "rightfully" its holdings. After awhile, nothing is left and the supremacy crumbles due to exhausting its own holding reserves. Consider not waiting for this depletion to happen. Conserve today. There is just so much to go around. Keep your share hidden. Insist that the greatest hoarder take what is sufficient for its needs.

Authorship Copyrights

Nation-states who proclaim to be protectors of authorship copyrights have legal cover to use the author's body of works without the award of monetary royalties to the authors. In this way, these feudal states can use the works by these authors with impunity in performance of their duties. Legal cover always has a way of sanctioning abuses. This is but one example of misconduct that permits egregious behaviors by elites.

Still On The Fence

The "greatest nation-state" of its time did object to the Nexus Pentarchy Prime Framework. As the Nexus spanned more and more into less than greatest nation-states' perimeters, these nation-states did expire so that the Nexus Expanse can lay the foundation for environments that will be suitable for sentient pursuits. The "greatest nation-state" would be one of the the last few to remain. By then, sentients in great numbers would leave its perimeters. Its greatness would be a dwarf of its former glory until the staunchest of the believers are the only ones remaining and unable to protect their perimeters. A Sentient Framework is by far the preferred framework of choice. No one needs to go to war to establish and maintain its "great" distinction. There is no need to neither "keep non-subjects out" nor "keep subjects in". No territorial perimeters are neither drawn nor artificial border walls constructed. If you can answer the question, "Are you in or out?", then you are still on the fence. – It is a choice to not even have a fence in place at all. – However and you most likely may not be aware of this, you have a long ways to go to get out of being stuck-in-time. You need to consider that you do not have all the time in the world. This world has an expiration date. If you past this date, then you will have to start all over again on a different world, which may not be as favorable to work out notions and develop spiritually. Your journey will be longer and cover a greater distance to complete. Can you see the finish line from where you are? Most likely, you do not.

Violent Tendencies

Of course there are school curricula to advance the study of feudal systems. However, when the outcome is "The Many Millennia War" that promotes death, destruction, and inhabitable environments, how can any of them be a "superior" system or even come close? Also, these systems are especially architect for those of privilege. In addition, you will most likely be excluded from membership based on statistical numbers. One needs to be "invited" into the privileged inner circles. An alternative course of action is the expiration of all barbarous-prone feudal constructs and to replace them with a Sentient Framework that promotes sustainability of the environments and sentient pursuits. Look beyond your immediate surroundings and see the violent wake produced by your beliefs and undying faith in support for the continuation of the same historical outcome norms given above to occur now and perpetually into the future. Eventually, all who look out will be looking in. There are no sparing believers from experiencing the wakes for even the current "protected elites". The waves that produce the wake go above and then go below a harmonious surface. The harmonious surface is the sentient calm. Time is on the sentients' side for the violent waves to subside. It remains violent for others due to their undying belief that the waves will eventually subside. With violent tendencies, the waves will just get stronger.

Recent Historical References (RHR) on Former Belief Systems - Judicial Misconduct

In Reverence

Acting in response to the "rule of law" was prevalent in Recent Historical References. How about acting in response to the "rule of life"? The incubator of life can be realized when allowed to continue. Prior to the incubation, there is only potential. When laws are used to determine realization, then life-force realization is not considered due to not being considered property for value extraction. For sentients, life realization is inspirational and viewed in reverence.

Stigmatized

In Recent Historical References regarding judicial misconduct, a subject may get a sentence that reflects a "serious unlawful act" that did not have anything remotely determined to have committed a grave harmful act. The judicial ruling had the result of being stigmatized as being condemned for life whereby the condemned would be excluded from freely participating in important societal discussions and opportunities. Pursuit avenues where made severely restricted for the condemned. This societal view is "all in the name of justice". Be not fooled. It is not in the name of justice. It is more sinister. Those who condemned will experience the same. One can choose not to condemn.

Sentients Just Don't Fit In

By judicial precedence as recorded in Recent Historical References, a feudal-based non-corporeal entity -- otherwise known as a corporation – was granted the recognition to be considered a "person" in order to have legal standing to enter into a contract with other entities, both corporeal and non-corporeal. This corporation person, – maybe since it was determined to have a heart – was legally permitted to practice exclusionary rights in not hiring corporeal entities that were considered not to be a perfect fit to include all judiciary determined misfits. This precedence to be called a person had an unintended consequence. The artificial entity called a corporation having legal standing as a person had a huge impact on the livelihoods of non-artificial entities by being what could be viewed by non-artificial entities as an employment cartel. This is in line and in keeping with being subjects of a feudal nation-state. Sentients would be puzzled. The judiciaries have shown to favor corporations than sentients. Sentients are not recognized as persons. Only subjects are recognized as persons. Sentients just don't fit in.

The Judiciary Scale

In Recent Historical References, those with financial means have access to "premium justice". Those with greatly reduced or no financial means will have access to rudimentary justice. In feudal systems, the promoted view was that there is balance using the judiciary scale. All would have access to this. Their reality was that those with ample means have a far greater chance to tip the scales in their favor. References do show that no balancing scale was used in this framework. The elites preferred it this way. To remedy this during the Transitional Period Towards a Nexus Pentarchy Prime Framework, if feudal-based judiciaries should have a monopoly in the prosecution arena, then feudal-based judiciaries will have a monopoly in the defense arena. No other representation is permitted in judiciary chambers. In this way, a balanced judiciary scale is assured to a much greater degree than before and it would be more transparent since it can be seen more handily.

F. Dot

In The Best Interest Of The Child

In Recent Historical References when it came to pre-adult sentients, those with "wealth" have overriding "interest" in their non-adult sentient properties as awarded by the state, so say the judiciary with its "guiding principle" used by the measure "in the best interest of the child" in making judicial rulings. In its rulings, a child custody support payments reflect the "wealth" of the child as determined by the wealth holdings of the non-custodial parent. In this construct, wealth was transferred through the confiscation of property holdings of convertible values and the labor earnings of the losing party in a dispute. This is another example of subjects judged as having property values. Of course, elites are viewed with much more highly regard based on their enormous worth value than the masses that are viewed with much less regard based on their minuscule worth value. In a Nexus Pentarchy Prime Framework, no sentient is a property having a wealth value to be bartered. The maintenance upkeep cost, using the same illustration, for every child will be the same. This is to be the sentient view for "in the best interest of the child" whereby the maintenance value is universal. We require that duly certified pre-adult duty caretakers be in charge, in this example, in the caretaking of pre-adult sentients.

Menacing Model

There is no wisdom that is a part of the foundation for the rule of law. It is a conceptual model of a feudal construct in a feudal attempt in keeping its subjects to be in adherence to feudal control. In this conceptual model, subjects are viewed as property. As with all properties, they lose their value and are reduced to dust over time. This same model also applied to the surrounding environments. Valuable properties are extracted from the environments. In time, the environments become barren due to this menacing model. How much value are you worth? If you are a dutiful subject, then your worth reduces value over time. There is just so much that can be extracted.

Mythical Persons

In Recent Historical References, a corporation has been judiciously defined as a "person". However, no one has actually seen this person. This person must be a mythical figure. By extension, the judiciary must also be a mythical person to be able to declare who is a person. Given this view, non-mythical and mythical persons are lumped into the same collection type included in judicial rulings that are made. Logic dictates that a non-mythical person cannot possibly stand up to a Goliath mythical person. She would be squashed very easily. In summary, judiciaries are blind in recognizing a sentient. They have never seen one. For them, it must be a mythical person. For sentients, we require that sentients be in charge. We can see things quite clearly. There are no mythical persons, only the artificially made up ones. Let's be real.

Executioners Of The Law

In Recent Historical References, judiciary administrators are not caretakers of the law. This is a misnomer. Rather, they are executioners of the law. They can issue orders to execute life in its entirety with the backing of the force of law on their side. There are many references in which these administrators feel helpless to do anything about it. Indeed! They are subjects to feudal lords and would loose their positions and livelihood for violating their oath to include extinguishing another corporeal subject. Let us release them from their burdens. Insist that sentients be in charge. In order to accomplish this, it would require removing execution – more commonly known as murder – from their vernacular.

Basis For Terrorist Practices

As can be found in many Recent Historical References, the legitimacy or legal framework for executions is the basis for terrorist practices by feudal systems, both from within and from without feudal perimeters. Those who harbor this legitimacy are themselves terrorists and who, through passiveness shaping, promote this legal terrorism doctrine reach to be everywhere without challenge. The institutionalization of terror made it extremely difficult to remove it. There is no room for a Sentient Doctrine of Sufficient Force in such a legal framework. All decisions must pass absolute or "finality" muster. Anything less is considered "reasonable doubt" so that a final ruling in the affirmative cannot be made. The case is dismissed. In actuality, determination for a less finality ruling oftentimes proves to be the right decision and the wisest.

Lessons Learned

In Recent Historical References, it takes a millennium to advance an incremental judicial guiding principle ideal. What a very poor and sub-standard conceptually-based judiciary construct! Why keep it? There is probably a far better framework that can replace this antiquated construct. No need to return to a barbarous time. Lessons learned ought to yield far superior conceptual models. No need to deliberate for a millennium. Need to catch up.

Judiciary On A Pedestal

There are many examples found in Recent Historical References when one could not depend on the judiciary to help one from serious harm even when one's life depended on it. The matter of one's death is just another case file. One should seriously step back and consider to not to hold up the judiciary on a pedestal. Its existence and the actions it takes are dependent on the "rule of law" for arriving at court rulings to be carried out and not based on one's more urgent welfare and protection needs. Fine-tuning of laws to close these gaps is a fallacy when adequate "laws on the books" are not present. The judiciary is primarily an administrative system of laws and nothing more. Administrators of the judiciary are feudal lords by any other name. Nothing of esteem stature can be produced here. Nothing of eminence can be found here. In summary, there is nothing binding you here. Consider looking elsewhere.

Observations and Perspectives
on Historical References
- Judicial Misconduct

Is At High Risk

"The Rule of Law" is overrated. This construct is extremely costly for the low level returns in benefits that it provides. As part of built-in delay mechanisms, every one of us is at high risk of grave harmful acts! Are you alarmed about this?

Tactical Delaying Constructs

There are those who believe that the construct for the rule of law determines all legal outcomes and that this construct is very stable. The actual results are that the end-determinations are based on a built-in delayed series of decisions by imperfect and flawed actors strung together to achieve "final" resolutions. If there are flawed intermediate decisions made, the final resolution is flawed as well. Should a different series of decisions have been made, a different resolution would have resulted for this same petition. The premise that stable judiciary determined outcomes are realized is also flawed because "new" historical arguments can be revealed to overturn or reverse previous "precedents" made. The tragedy is that extended durations of hardships and suffering to include the extinguishing of corporeal existences would have occurred in order for the more "best and wisest precedents" to be made. In summary, the best and wisest precedents are to occur at some distant future moments-in-time after deliberations by the judiciary. Clinging to such non-sentient responsive judiciary will delay the adoption of Sentient Framework. The earliest the expiration of these tactical-delaying constructs, the sooner that feudal subjects will be subjects no more. Consider promoting a sentient way of life in everything that you do.

Law And Disorder

The demand for the rule of law requires war-like campaign activities against peoples who wish to be left alone so as to promote their peaceful way of life. Overt poking and prodding activities are used to trigger non-peaceful responses to justify the war-like campaign strategies that are carried out in returning to the supposed premise of "law and order". These practices should more accurately be termed "law and disorder".

Insanity Plea

Whoever in the administrator judiciary that spawned the insanity plea precedence "ruling", which permitted no grave sentencing confinement, did not have society's safety interests in mind. All members who commit or have the propensity for grave harmful acts are to be confined away from the general population. Remedies are to be crafted when environmental toxins and hazards are discovered to be found that would alter any other member experiences in the same or similar fate. Law is not a deterrent in these matters. Holes in the law allow members who commit grave harmful acts to be untouchable. In the Nexus Pentarchy Prime Framework, no member with these behaviors is untouchable. There are no holes to fall through. There is no location in the Nexus Expanse that a member can escape to. The Nexus Pentarchy Prime Rapid Response Teams go into action without any delays. They are trained and reviewed for continual fitness at intersperse times during their duty caretaking activities. The primary aim is to continuously strive to bring all exhibited grave harmful events to zero.

In The Way

Legality gets in the way of effective duty caretaking stewardship activities.

Judicial Weight

There are numerous Recent Historical References of legal constructs collapsing under its own judicial weight. They simply could not hold up to a higher bellwether.

Caretaker Arbiters

We are letting judicial constructs with the propensity to condemn be the default caretaker arbiters. This notion of judiciaries as caretakers is an oxymoron. This will not do. Arbiters make horrible caretakers.

Balancing Act

As a citizen of a particular nation-state, you may have a legal right to raise a particular issue for review and judgment to include appeals that can be escalated up through the autocratic judiciary. However, the sentient question that ought to be answer is this. Is the outcome normally a wise one? When one answers this with sentient insights, then the only conclusion that can be made is that the judiciary that is based on artificial laws is a violent construct directed towards its subjects complete with executions in its rulings. The judiciary is truly blind of its unintended consequences. The masses that are affected do not have this same excuse. No balancing act here.

Responsible Way

Judicial review due to its latent hesitant-precedence institution cannot respond in a responsible way when urgent matters are present. It contributes very little to reducing grave harmful acts to zero or provide relief efforts when natural and artificial events of major catastrophic nature would occur. This framework is such as to contribute to greatly diminished optimal responses in bringing the environments back to a standing of wholeness so as to lessen the impact of pain and suffering by the inhabitants. Accept nothing less. Insist that sentients be in charge of truly caretaking activities. There is no latent hesitancy in the sentient activities that are performed. There is no need to get a ruling. Sentients are known to act in a responsible way.

Legal Judicial Limbo

Legal judicial limbo promotes "crimes against humanity" due to needless delays in finality rulings. It is by design that makes this so. Even after centuries of "refinements" in judiciary rulings, the terrorist issue avoidance practices remains ongoing. Is there a sentient looking into this? Better yet, expire this framework and replace it with a sentient one.

Come To Past

The assault of laws that mane, injure, execute, and the like, often do reach the level of "crimes against humanity" as it is historically termed. However, the practices are exempt due to being based on the "rule of law". Also, how can an artificial construct be held accountable for such crimes? Applying incrimination laws towards sentients are not of a criminal nature, if you subscribe to this notion. They are sanctioned by the artificial constructs. The lawful obedience by feudal subjects make these events "acts of war" on sentients everywhere as seen through the eyes of sentients. To bring all acts of war to zero requires the expiration of this and every other artificial construct. We require that sentients be in charge. And so, it has come to past.

Labeled An "Alien"

The artificial construct that defines an "illegal alien" is alien in itself. What sentient entity would make such a definition? No sentient would, only obedient subjects of feudal nation-states. In these feudal systems, there is no legal status in being sentient. Those with privileged statuses would insist that all believe in this notion. Their cover is under the robe of justice. Dare to not believe in such a miscarriage of justice and misconduct. There is no justice for any entity when even one is labeled an "alien". From a different and more enlightening view, no sentient is considered an alien in a Nexus Pentarchy Prime Framework. All sentients are inclusive in this framework. Would you like to be a part of a continuum whereby every sentient can travel anywhere in the known Expanse and Beyond? If so, then disrobe your subject identify label in order to see your true sentient self. What do you have to be afraid of? Aliens?

Returning Back To A Condition Of Health And Vibrancy

The "rule of law" is getting in the way of caretaking duties of the natural surroundings and, by extension, the health and welfare of sentients everywhere. With military apparatuses to ensure feudal perimeters, this becomes very acute for natural spreading and migration of Nature's life forces on either side of the perimeters. Also, wars have been waged to claim more of the natural resources by extending the feudal perimeters. In these border wars, Nature has no legal standing for consideration in the damages that are done by them. Find a way to remove all perimeters and you will find yourself returning back to a condition of health and vibrancy.

Personhood Trauma

Access to "safe" abortion services were demanded by those who view fetal growths as cancerous tissue growths inside pregnant entities. Since these tissue growths were ruled as non-legally defined feudal entities, they cannot possibly be experiencing any personhood trauma. With this view, no legal protections were given to these non-entities, only excruciating pain and suffering experienced towards the end.

The Well Being Of Children

Judicial administrators are not caretakers. They are executioners of the law. Why allow children to be cared for in such a torture chamber? Children are much more fragile than adults and their needs cannot be delayed or ruled on by judicial conduct. Their development years are very short. Caretakers are needed to care for all children. Remove the judicial jurisdictional ownership from its torture chambers and give the ownership to caretakers. Certified duty caretakers can respond much more effectively and with keen interest for the well being of the children.

Sensitive To Prevention Foresight

Passing laws to make something that is grotesque or gruesome illegal so that "something like this will never happen again!" are just hollow words. Until a "law" is passed, similar behaviors and events are still considered to be "legal" and permissible. In the same way, a law can be undone. There is nothing special about laws. They just describe whatever is fashionable at a particular point in time for enforcements. They are fashionably artificial. Countless Recent Historical References can be found that show that unnecessary pain and suffering need to occur for "something to be done" so that "something like this will never happen again!". Artifact crumble and dead remains can be uncovered to prove that the pain and suffering always preceded laws. There are no prevention points of view with this belief system. They are fabrications of feudal attempts to rule with the force of law in keeping subjects in the fold. By one being in the fold, one succumbs to the feudal darkness of terror abyss. Why subscribe to such arcane and cumbersome construct? Why subject yourself to terror? Escape! Consider having sentients be in charge. Sentients wait for no artificial nor non-caretaker artifact to come alive for something to be done. Sentients are sensitive to prevention foresight. Wise remedies are routinely made by those who are aware. Come out of the darkness or pull yourself from the abyss. Join with other sentients. There is no need for you to go through pain and suffering.

Corporations Have Tentacles

It is easy to target individuals. It is not so easy to target "Corporations". Corporations have tentacles across many nation-states that to separate and target them would require enormous perceived strength to overcome them. The perceived strength does not change the fact that they are only artificial constructs. There is no actual personhood in corporations even though they were given this status. They do not bleed. They do not have a heart. They are just figments with no spiritual insights. To put them on pedestals reduces sentients to sub-personhood inferiority status. We require that sentients be in charge. This includes sentients in charge of any consortium registered due to the determination that it would provide effectiveness and economies of scale for the charter that is part of the registration. Sentients makes up a consortium and they are in charge in determining the outcomes.

Bully State

In Recent Historical References, the legal reach of the "greatest nation-state" was thrust onto other nation-states for their compliance. What nation-state would dare to challenge this nation-state? However, when the reciprocal is attempted, it is forbidden by this same "greatest nation-state" that believes its legal framework superior and is to be universally applied everywhere else. In actuality, this bully is guilty of jurisdictional misconducts. It takes a brave state to stand up to a bully. In time, others will gang up to subdue the bully. By combining your efforts, the collective will become greater than any one bully state. There is safety in numbers.

Resist The Addiction

Those of the judiciary robes and other adversarial court jesters believe they are protected by the rule of law when a court order is executed to include the terrorizing and termination of those caught in its judicial web. They consider themselves to be quite superior when in their court purview perch.

The execution may appear to be clean, but violence is needed to carry out the order. Do not be fooled. The jesters' fates await them as well. The court tables will be switched from that of looking out to that of looking in. The question that often comes up in similar scenarios like this one is, how did I get here? She got here by getting stuck-in-time in a vicious cycle initiated by her court protective actions. Choose to get out of a violent relationship. Do not look back or you may be drawn back in to the familiar court dramas. Resist the addiction and come clean. Violence is not the way forward. There is no just way to terrorize and terminate.

The Web Of Justice

"Justice" is served only when the "accused" is first caught in its web. Those who are outside its web can continue to do, by some, heinous crimes like maim, kill, terrorize, and other grave harmful acts. Long periods of time may pass before the perpetrators are "brought to justice". This weakness of the judiciary to include law enforcement actors in bringing them to justice has been shown to be extremely inefficient. Justice, supposedly, will always come through so the choir keeps preaching to us to keep the faith. However, the success rate for catching members who commit grave harmful acts it is not even close to 100%. In the mean time, the same atrocities will still go on unabated. The odds are in favor of those who commit grave harmful acts or the propensity of committing grave harmful acts in not getting caught or given light "sentences" when caught. This gross misconduct is perpetuated as long as subjects continue to be viewed as owned by feudal nation-states whereby "jurisdictions" are drawn for judiciary activities. Instead, consider to pursue a sentient vision. Once this awareness state is achieved, a sentient will always conclude the folly of being faithful to feudal states and their judiciaries. The object then becomes to expire them all and the earliest so that an even higher sentient attainment set of remedy activities can be pursued with achievement levels much closer to 100%. The Nexus Pentarchy Prime Framework has the Rapid Response Auspices that are chartered at the Nexus Degree to remedy all those who commit grave harmful acts or have the propensity of committing grave harmful acts. These activities are described elsewhere in writings by this scribe. When feudal states are no more, then more effective Nexus remedy steps can occur without judicial obstructions. There is no equivalent state in the Nexus Rapid Response Auspices that is similar to the state of being stuck-in-time in a judiciary abyss. The state of being a sentient emanates in all directions within the Expanse and Beyond. The results are impressive.

A Rudimentary Facsimile

By adhering to an artificial construct called a judicial framework whereby all your choices you are permitted to make in your daily experiences are based on judicial premises and not what is needed and necessary in a given situation, then you will experience spiritual starvation that may even lessen your spiritual attainment achieved previously. This may lessen to a significant degree the muffling of inspirational insights of any kind. Artificial constructs have no spiritual atonement nor, by its very deficiencies, can ever achieve even a rudimentary facsimile. There is no "wisdom" in judicial precedents. Its framework has and always will be based on "properties" owned by legal entities. Legal entities include judicial references such as companies, corporations, governmental organizations, and of course, feudal subjects to be granted expansive or contracted pursuits up to and including extinguishing of corporeal existence. In summary, there is neither viability nor wisdom in the judiciary. There is only misconduct. Demand that sentients be in charge in making the wise and necessary caretaking decisions that are needed on behave of all members of the dominion. Choose your leader caretakers wisely.

At The Core

At the core of legal argument is terrorism. That is what nation-state constructs have built into it. Legal terrorism can only be eradicated when all feudal nation-states expire. There is no other way to ensure that terrorist practices are not at the core of any ruling by falling through legal cracks ever again.

F. Dot

Open-Ended

To allow for open-ended legal prosecutions to be initiated in response to grave harmful acts encourages non-action pursuits when it suites the prosecution. Their thinking is that they have all the time in the world to look into prosecutorial cases. This delay-response privilege does not promote a "just" system of "legal protection". On the contrary, spurts of terrorist events can even go unchecked with this open-ended proviso. To avoid these abject inefficiencies, a replacement framework is needed. Start by removing this particular privilege. Implement metrics to keep track.

Measuring Gauge

Arcane judicial beliefs in an artificial judiciary that deliberates with "prudence" and "precedence" promote, by its very arcane peculiarity, very long periods of suffering occurring before rendering "judgments" and also very long periods of suffering occurring after rendering those "judgments". With these beliefs, grave harmful events could be unfolding with no actions being taken by the judiciary until long after the horrors and the unfolding reign of terror events have subsided. Only when "evidence" is collected, "weighed", and "evaluated" by prosecutors and then only when the "evidential findings" are persuasive enough for "charges" to be filed with the judiciary can the long and arduous trial be scheduled and convened. In cases when evidence has been destroyed or hidden, then no action is taken or can related findings be admissible for judicial adversarial proceedings. This jester court behavior continued for many millennia. Subjects who performed grave harmful acts used the cover of the judiciary to "game the system". This flawed system was propagated to other feudal borders with varying degrees of judicial successes for violent perpetrators. The relatively high non-success rates made a mockery of the credo "justice is served". Nothing just is found here. In the Nexus Pentarchy Prime Framework, no border states are carved out. In this framework, the feudal judiciary's own measuring gauge for the premise of "with a reasonable doubt" usage would leave dominion's safety in an unacceptable vulnerable dilemma. Perpetrators of grave harmful acts, which are of extreme concern from all other matters, are handled at the Nexus Pentarchy Prime Umbrella. These matters are of prime importance and ample resources are allocated to ensure rapid remedies are performed. Should members be misidentified as perpetrators, then their recorded entries will be voided and their release from confinement is at the earliest possible. The measuring gauge used is that there is "a high degree of certainty that the member is not involved in grave harmful acts" and not the porous gauge historically used, "with a reasonable doubt". The Nexus Premier Remedy Standard is to diminish all grave harmful acts to zero. In order to accomplish this, start with your beliefs. Assist with the Transitional Period Towards a Nexus Pentarchy Prime Framework so that grave matters are taken seriously and addressed in the most expeditious manner possible without delay.

The Way Out

There are many examples found in Recent Historical References regarding the assault on the Life Forces of Nature to command her to bow to the will of feudal lords enshrined in the rule of law and reinforced by the judiciary. The mere act of an assault supported the intent to make these Life Forces to be non-life forms. The extinguishing of a Life Force ought to be abhorrent to all. As is shown in numerous historical references, barbarous conquerors and feudal lords have always pursued the course of death and destruction even when the original intent was something very different, but escalated to absolute death and destruction. The addiction of defensible perimeters would lead to the same results. Nature's Life Forces allowed our lives to exist and have experiences. The answer is clear to those who understand the way out of this abhorrent abyss. Insist that sentients be in charge. They already have an aerial view on the way forward and around the abyss. Nature Life Forces will be allowed to flourish and to fill in the abyss so that no one else will slide back in.

Very Touching

The rule of law and the judiciary are considered elements of a "civilized" society. One is supposed to "feel safe" in this society. This is very touching.

In actuality, epic campaigns to stem "unlawful" behaviors or events are waged with the use of overwhelming and oftentimes deadly force, which leave great swaps of death and destruction to ensure obedient subjects will kowtow to this reasoning through fear and terror. These campaigns are instigated even when the behaviors or events do not inflict grave harmful acts to other obedient members of society. The reign of terror campaigns are well document in Recent Historical References. One can research this for herself.

Law-Enact Actors

Life goes on, unless the law exterminates. The law does not exist or make a sound until the governing law-enact actors make it so, at which time the law administrators can rule on its merits. The law has the support of enforcers. To ensure societal obedience, weapons of mass destruction are always on the table. Let's sit down and discuss whether this law is what we ought to be doing. Let's not exterminate every again.

Go To Higher Ground

The rule of law and the judiciary will not help sentients when major Earth changes occur. For those ardent believers, the Earth will swallow them up. It is recommended that all go to higher ground, or more precisely, to higher realms of awareness. In order to accomplish this, remove the rule of law so that everyone can go to a safer place. Your pursuit for universal truth can be found there.

Value-Added Arrangement

Judicial rulings are all based on "property". Those with greater property values are treated with favored statuses. All subjects are properties with sufficient or minimal values for more favorable judicial rulings. Judicial rulings for non-subjects will have inferior rulings due to being viewed as properties with legal standing and by extension, to have no value. These

non-subjects are incarcerated in great numbers resulting in a high-growth prison cottage industry, which adds
"value" to non-subjects in their core business of warehousing them. Roundups are very profitable in this type of cottage industry. It does not matter that no harmful acts have been committed by non-subjects to be committed. Judiciary treatment is inferior or non-existent. It is out of their hands. It matters only that value has been added to commodities through incarceration. A select group of wealthy elites have profit handsomely from this value-added arrangement.

Spectators At A Coliseum

In Recent Historical References, a very high percentage of believers subscribed to very inefficient constructs regarding the administering of feudal laws. They were obedient and didn't seem to mind the long wait for "justice to be served". Today, it is very puzzling that believers had blind obedience to constructs with built-in lengthy delays to justice. This is most disconcerting when delays are routine for those who commit grave harmful acts as well. There were no rapid responses to these acts, only legal maneuverings and posturing by opposing judicial adversarial actors. In addition, these feudal constructs would put higher importance on their own subjects than non-subjects, who were viewed with more disdain than one of their own. The societal norms of their time created a culture of being like spectators at a coliseum, cheering and booing to the unfolding atrocities and court proceedings. With the advances made in real-time communications, this same culture norms found atrocities happening in distant feudal perimeters to be more entertaining and safer to watch. Are you far away so that it is safe to watch?

Interim and Post-Deliberation Judiciary Measures

In the "grand scheme of things", feudal constructs have not been present for that long. During that time, hoarding became the order of the day. This lead to rations and denials of basic needs to non-feudal lords or the non-elites of these constructs. Calamity events did occur, which could have been avoided, but was deemed to messy to partake. Judicial misconducts prevented the real-time course corrections that were desperately needed from being carried out at the time of these events. The "rule of law" superseded any and all duty caretaking measures from being applied. All time-consuming "deliberations" that were necessary to arrive at finality rulings deterred those life-saving or cataclysmic prevention measures from being done in a timely fashion. Interim and post-deliberation judiciary measures were applied to ensure that artificial decrees were abide by with absolute precision before, during, and after the rulings are made. The end results were absolute as well. Nature receded and denied all from access to basic needs. For believers of feudal systems, the judiciary did follow all the correct precepts. Using this reasoning, we should be in much greater shape. Has this been your experience?

Tied And Shackled

Feudal judiciary constructs are horrible on prevention and worse yet on remedies. Artificial constructs reduce feudal subjects to property holdings that are viewed as having a long shelf-life. This must be the reason for their very lethargic calamity issue response behaviors for very grave matters that ought to have determined urgent responses instead. Given this irresponsible behavior, the premise is to hold properties until final rulings are provided even when death occurs during the interim. There is no justice when death prevention plays no role in the deliberation process. Their hands and ankles are tied and shackled.

Absolutely Certain

Adherence for the "rule of law" or lawful irregularities regardless if when an outcome results in death, terrorism, destruction, extinction, or the depletion of Nature's riches ought to not be the legacy that we would want to leave to future sojourns. The rule of law is, by design, absolute in its rendering of rulings. Oftentimes through incremental decrees, total elimination is the absolute ruling that will be executed. Are you absolutely certain about the legacy that you want to leave for others to deal with? You may find yourself having to pick up where you left off at a later time.

Performance Is Dismal

A high incarceration rate is a significant indicator of a failed judiciary and supporting law enforcement apparatuses. Clinging to a burning belief that "justice" is superior to all others is a complete tragedy. Nothing can be further from the truth. Justice is not being served. Finality is a misnomer. Judicial decisions are faulty by nature. The end result is that the judiciary is the champion executor of terrorism. Forced adherence to judiciary institutionalize practices are used with the intent to ensure that the few elites retain ultimate power. In this construct, the masses are to be damned. If you answer this question in the affirmative, "Are you one of the damned?", then consider being sentient-aware about the true unjust nature of the judiciary. Its performance for delivering justice is dismal. Therefore, consider discarding it. As more sentients become aware, the elitist's "stature" crumbles. When this happens, the true framework of a just society can be fully realized.

Sentients Are Not Blind

A Starter List of Judiciary Types:

Pre-tragedy Judiciary: A tragedy occurring prior to waiting for a judiciary final ruling.

Pre-drama Judiciary: A wrenching drama occurring prior to waiting for a judiciary final ruling.

Post-tragedy Judiciary: A tragedy occurring due to a judiciary final ruling.

Post-drama Judiciary: A wrenching drama occurring due to a judiciary final ruling.

Non-prevention Judiciary: A judiciary providing no grave harmful acts prevention.

Non-protection Judiciary: A judiciary providing no protection from grave harmful acts.

Non-rapid-response Judiciary: A judiciary that behaves helplessly when grave harmful act events are occurring.

The list of above judiciary types is only a sample of the horrific deficiencies of any feudal-judiciary construct. If the judiciary is supreme in rendering the final ruling, then it fails miserably. The rulings are always prone to being revisited. It is startling that very large numbers of believers were as obedient like flocks of sheep as to enter the chambers of the judiciary with the abiding belief that actions will be taken regarding the prevention, protection, and rapid response to grave harmful acts. To the horrors of the flocks of sheep, what resulted instead was the playing out of grave harmful dramas and tragedies. The conclusion that one could come to is that the judiciary is indeed blind to the matters of great importance in contributing to viable favorable environments for sentient pursuits. Sentients are not blind to this revelation. Are you?

Pre-Judicial Duty

The "rule of law" is an artificial construct. The judiciary administers the law. It is arbitrary and flawed when the judiciaries in robes are "pre-judicial" in their rulings. Also, these rulings are not universally applied due to all of the jesters that make up the judiciaries. Grave harm is done when rulings are not timely, which makes these apparatuses extremely inefficient and consume valuable time especially when lives are at stake. The apparatuses are void of caretaking-centric views of members within their jurisdictions. Members of these jurisdictions are treated as subjects of feudal lords. Members that are not subjects fare far worse. They have no standing in jurisdictional membership pools. Terrorism is the pre-judicial duty and order of the day. Their fates are reduced to chattel slaves. Members of jurisdictions do not fair much better.

Start A Conversation

There is nothing sentient about a corporation or business entity if it is not self-aware. By extension, all artificial corporation or business constructs are not self-aware. Can a sentient even have a conversation with one? In Recent Historical References, the judiciary set a precedence to answer this question in the affirmative. From that point on, this precedence is now enforceable everywhere in various jurisdictions. The judiciary is culpable to the unbridled abuse in power excesses by these corporations and businesses that cannot be reasoned with. For legally protected entities that are not self-aware, how did they manage to have a persuasive conversation with the judiciary to continually acquire more power that spanned many jurisdictions? Wouldn't you be interested in wanting to know? Sentients will take a different path. We require sentients be in charge. Should there be a time in the future when these artificial entities called corporations or businesses become sentient-aware, then we will re-visit this topic by starting a conversation with them to gain their insights. This scribe predicts that this will not happen any time soon. Work instead on promoting a Sentient Dominion framework.

The Transitional Period Towards a Nexus Pentarchy Prime Framework - Transitional Prime Directives

Internet Usage And Cafes

During the Transitional Period Towards a Nexus Pentarchy Prime Framework, Internet usage is allowed to show Summary of Nexus Pentarchy Prime Tenets and Societal Five-Percent-Spanning Recommendations posted online. If more information is needed, then see your leader caretakers. Archival of Prime Directives are not accessible via the Internet. Archival Access Centers like Auspices Library Cafes can be access by Foundation Prime Members for information that is specific to individual members or are affected by their respective ascension degree-primes' Prime Directive Remedies.

Elimination Of The Multiplicities Of Laws

Promote the elimination of the multiplicities of laws that are replicated in overlapping spanning jurisdictions during the Transitional Period Towards a Nexus Pentarchy Prime Framework. When there is a greater spanning set of jurisdictional laws covers 5% or greater of societal members that are identified as Nexus Pentarchy Prime Dominion sentients, then the duplicate set of laws from lesser spanning jurisdictions will be targeted for expiration. This is based on the Nexus Ro5, but modified to be applicable to the interactions with non-Nexus Pentarchy Prime Dominion constructs.

Entry Proviso

During the Transitional Period Towards a Nexus Pentarchy Prime Framework, beware of entry access by feudal institutions. The privileged elites desire to select the best of the best with the entry proviso that those who are selected must leave their meager communities from where they came from. The elites' objective is to reinforce the notion that the masses are to be damned. The claim that anyone can make it to success is muted when only a few are selected for privilege access. The appearance of a large number of "rising stars" still only represent a single digit, less than 5% of the total population of societal members. Given this entry proviso, an alternative framework is underway. Members who are promoted by the favorable environments of the Nexus Pentarchy Prime Framework can continue to participate in the favorable environments from whence they came from. However, those who are lured away by the elites to renounce their bonds with the Nexus communities will have remedies whereby steep "restitution and penalties" will be applied should they return. These Prime Directives are open-ended and expire 25 years after the complete implementation of the Nexus Pentarchy Prime Framework.

Warehousing

In the Nexus Pentarchy Prime Dominion, secure and restricted warehousing of non-grave harmful behavior inmates is not allowed when no resistance by inmates is indicated or present.

For All Intents And Purposes

When a member's activities demonstrate that they, for all intents and purposes, produce or create conditions that results in grave harmful acts by those who profit from them, then the member will be viewed as being a contributing participant to grave harmful acts or the propensity thereof. All duty caretaking privileges that were utilized will be withdrawn and specified in Prime Directive Remedies. As given in a Nexus Prime Tenet, providing for basic needs is not included in the review process leading to findings and the crafting of the remedies.

Officiated To Have Expired

Champions for the "Rule of Law" will need to comply with Pentarchy Prime Directives when non-sentient laws are officiated to have expired. Terrorism in all its forms will have remedies to ensure that its previously "established" environments are no more.

Cartel Attempts

Expire all feudal elitist cartels. Craft prime directives for yourselves. Wisely select leader caretakers to craft prime directives that eventually will span the Nexus Expanse. In every step along the way, the elitist cartels cannot germinate. Cartel attempts are not recognized.

Privacy Matters

During the Transitional Period Towards the Nexus Pentarchy Prime Framework, kiosks are to be made available and be used by Nexus Pentarchy Prime members when there is still interfacing with non-Nexus frameworks. In this way, tracking of members to the individual's base location will not be known due to the shared kiosk hotspots scattered throughout. When non-Nexus "officials" are present due to "official directed orders", members are to dispersed and the kiosks communication changes disabled until Nexus Pentarchy Leader Caretakers spanning the kiosks or their designates identified ahead of time give the all-clear resumption announcement. Kiosk operators will only have knowledge that member entry instruments are valid for member entry. The respective Pentarchy Prime Degree Auspice Transitional Repositories and their operators at secure centers located at different undisclosed locations will validate and monitor kiosk activities. When tampering is discovered, disable and/or removal of hardware is immediately performed. Non-Nexus officials who "execute orders" will be identified for removal remedies up to and including election of more-than-tolerant-of-sentients candidates to replace the current elected offenders. The remedies provided here need to be expand on for the highest possible Auspices anonymity protection from terrorist officials and their enforcement actors. Privacy is a matter of prime importance during this challenging transitional period.

Ascension Appeal Time Frame

During the Transitional Period Towards a Nexus Pentarchy Prime Framework regarding the life cycle of judicial review, the cap for the judicial apex is to be the predetermined maximum at the time from initial review request, which is 25 years. If not completed in this time frame, then the last ascension judicial rulings made is to be final word. The judiciary had plenty of time to decide. Sentients require a responsive judicial due diligence during the transitional period. There is to be no open-ended jurisprudence. For judicial review levels that are less than at the apex degree, the time limit will be based on a decreasing graduated time scale when no further ascension appeal is permitted. Similarly in the Nexus Pentarchy Prime Framework, the maximum time frame and associated decreasing graduated scale are to be used in Review Request Auspices caretaking activities. The maximum of 25 years is given for select provisions described elsewhere in writings by this scribe.

No Need To Be In The Shadows

During the Transitional Period Towards a Nexus Pentarchy Prime Framework, insist that a "person entity" known as corporation be require to secure a passport when crossing nation-state boundaries in order to enjoy the same rights and privileges as non-corporation entities. Since these entities have been granted full feudal-recognized subject-hood, then it is time for all corporations to be given equal protection with their own issued passports. There is no need for them to be in the shadows every again.

Advice To Be Disseminated

During the Transitional Period Towards a Nexus Pentarchy Prime Framework, multiple financial and commercial entities will be established as a strategy for Pentarchy Prime Dominion interfacing with legacy constructs. One "think tank" organization or consortium will be established in each major caretaking category that is charted to provide advice to all the others in that particular major caretaking category. No direct consulting will be performed. Advice is to be disseminated to participating members. This is being done so that financial and commercial entities can distance themselves from receiving scrutiny by feudal lord regulators and inspectors. In this way, the "public" advisories for all Nexus Pentarchy Prime members will act on their own behalf so as to not to be pulled into being charged for collusion by these think tanks The intent is to have no large entities membership groups be singled out for additional scrutiny. The advisory organization will be funded by membership fees and donations from members of the spanning Pentarchy Prime Umbrellas. See other guidelines found elsewhere on this subject.

Non-Compliant Official

During the Transitional Period Towards a Nexus Pentarchy Prime Framework, a significant number of Prime Directives will be crafted having specified remedies crafted. During this interim period, these prime directives will be prioritized separating those that address grave harmful acts having the highest priorities to be worked on. "Elected officials" spanning the identified Prime Degree will be informed of duty caretaking requirements requiring their full compliance based on the Transitional Rule of Five for non-Pentarchy Prime Legacy Constructs. Refusal of compliance will require the need for extended remedies that will be so declared to find a suitable replacement for the non-compliant official.

Write-In Candidates

During the Transitional Period Towards a Nexus Pentarchy Prime Framework, voting for elected officials may require write-in candidates to communicate the non-compliance by the remaining candidates. Whoever "wins" will not have the majority and will be in a weakened state whereby her "victory" will be short-lived. In time, all will be in compliant with prime directives having remedies crafted for clarity and follow-up.

A Time For Rejoicing Is Upon Us

During the Transitional Period Towards a Nexus Pentarchy Prime Framework, sentients of the Nexus Pentarchy Prime will qualify the candidates who will be promoted for official placements even when there is a high probably that some will not be elected or appointed. Over time, the non-qualified "elected" officials will win plurality percentages far lower than 50%, which will significant weakened their "political capital" to advance their unchecked causes. This will be a significant indicator towards rapid ascension of qualified candidates to official placements. This moment-in-time event indicates that the collapse of nation-states is imminent in the not too distant future. By extension, the completion of the Nexus Pentarchy Prime Framework is near. A time for rejoicing is upon us.

Cross-Border-Artificial-Societal Entities

Let it be enough with the disparate collection of feudal cross-border-artificial-societal entities. If there are "corporate entities" that can cross perimeters, then they are to be under the auspices of an all-inclusive encompassing dominion. This is also true, for example, for transportation infrastructure entities that can cross perimeters. When this is shown to occur, then they are also to be under the auspices of an all-inclusive encompassing dominion. Other entities that fit this test are energy delivery infrastructures, communication infrastructures, consortia, other spanning infrastructures and auspices.

F. Dot

A Sentient-Based Think Tank

During the Transitional Period Towards a Nexus Pentarchy Prime Framework, a sentient-based "think tank" as was commonly known in Recent Historical References will be established within nation-state apparatuses that allows for similar think tanks to be chartered for the purpose of rating the sentient worthiness of elected and appointed officials. This think tank spanning a particular degree prime will have no "party affiliation" nor be identified with one. This think tank will be comprised of Nexus Pentarchy Prime sentients selected by the degree prime that spans the non-Nexus Pentarchy Prime jurisdiction having at least five percent Nexus Pentarchy Prime member inclusion. This think tank type will be the only interfacing one of its kind to directly be the "public" connection to nation-state legacy apparatuses.

Registration Of Pentarchy Prime Foundation

During the Transitional Period Towards a Nexus Pentarchy Prime Framework, Pentarchy Prime External Networks can be used only for registering the associated Pentarchy Prime Foundation at Degree 1 with no Nexus Pentarchy Prime Identifying Information (NPPII) or other Personal Identifying Information (PII) being disclosed. Pseudonyms are strongly recommended to be used early on with updates to actual PII usage Post-Transitional Period. A random prime key will be generated to all for complete updates to be done later on through secure and Pentarchy Prime communication channels and equipment usage. Only equipment identifiers can be used to respond to registration requests since pseudonyms can be used in the acknowledgment responses.

Property Dominion Reset

During the Transitional Period Towards the Nexus Pentarchy Prime Framework, legacy structure legal property awarded "titles" of natural surroundings will go through periodic property dominion resets to transfer property "ownership" privileges to that of caretaking leases awarded to certified duty caretakers. In post Transitional Period, periodic caretaking leases may have to be reset when it has been determined that duty caretaking activities are not what it ought to be when the leases were granted or due to advances in caretaking knowledge in how to improve on caretaking practices and related activities after the leases were granted. One the Nexus Tenets is to perform the best caretaking practices realized and to reset leases when the differences to what is being practiced through caretaking activities is significantly less than the best that has been learned up to the present. Sharing wise caretaking knowledge and training can aid in reducing the number of lease resets.

Nexus 25 Years Pursuit Doctrine

During the Transitional Period Towards a Nexus Pentarchy Prime Framework, those Nexus Dominion identified renegade nation-states are to be kept in check no matter which nation-state is performing this checking. Prime Directive Remedies are needed to accomplish this. In time, all will be in compliant until the Nexus Pentarchy Prime Framework is complete, at which time actors who lead those terrorist acts will be confined when not outside the Nexus 25 Years Pursuit Doctrine time frame from the original time event the acts were done. In is strongly recommended that close to 100% of the time whether or not the acts are made inside the 25 years pursuit time frame or outside of this time frame, those identified grave harmful acts actors who have participated in them will be prohibited from being leader caretakers beyond the first pent-degree ascension as part of the Transitional Period Remedies. As sentients, we don't want to slip back into these actors' medieval feudal habits or antiquated ways.

Charge And Conviction Insurance Pool

Similar to a state required insurance pool as described in Recent Historical References set up for members that have experienced, for example, vehicle accidents and were often found to be at fault, then a nation-state required

Charge and Conviction Insurance Pool for members who have been charged, confined, and/or convicted and then subsequently released will be set up. It has been shown in Recent Historical References that the accuracy rate of judicial conviction and sentencing is much lower than 100%. Just being charged can have damaging consequences to one's ability to participate in livelihood earnings and societal participation. To exclude members from societal activities oftentimes lead to being discarded and condemn to poverty, homelessness, and hopelessness. The statistical slice not participating in societal activities ought to go to near zero. The near zero slice is plausible because of choices made by some entities to not participate in societal activities at all or to not accept offers of assistance. Also as been prevalent during recent historical times, to condemn the whole family due to the injudicious choices by one or more family members is a carryover from Medieval times when dungeons and torture chambers were prevalent and applied to whole families and villages. Medieval dungeons and torture chambers have no place in caring societies. When determined to be urgently needed, pre-adults and other greatly limited capable adult members will be assigned to certified duty caretakers. The insurance will help cover all of this. The propensity for grave harmful acts, for example, will help determine the rates to apply.

Approved Business Entities

During the Transitional Period Towards a Nexus Pentarchy Prime Framework, a list of approved "business entities" will be listed top aid Nexus Pentarchy Prime members for patronage. All others are to be avoided when a listed one is available. In some cases, a list of "probation business entities" can be used with second grade approval rating to aid members as well.

A Highly Trained And Certified Sentinent

As a sentinent in the Nexus Pentarchy Prime Rapid Response Auspices, you are highly trained and certified for rapid response remedies and activities.

You have the opportunity to put those so-called champions of terrorism in confinement. This remedy is to be achieved whenever and wherever possible. The Nexus Pentarchy Prime Doctrine of Sufficient Force will help guide you in bringing grave harmful acts to zero. Rapidly determine which sufficient force remedy from the set of escalating remedies to take. The sentients of the Nexus Pentarchy Prime Dominion are very appreciative of everything that you do on behalf of all sentients in the Nexus Expanse and Beyond.

The Transitional Period Towards a Nexus Pentarchy Prime Framework - Transitional Guidelines

In The Shadows

Beware of terrorists in the shadows. Some even have smiles on their faces.

Focus on the Votes

Money does not get politicians elected, voters do. Focus on the votes.

Exclusivity

The judiciary does not have exclusivity on decision making and remedies. During the Transitional Period Towards a Pentarchy Prime Framework, Legacy Societal Five-Percent-Span Recommendations apply.

Pentarchy Prime Postal Delivery Auspices

A Pentarchy Prime Postal Delivery Auspices at the highest Pent-degree Prime known that serves Pentarchy Prime members only will be implemented. All members will be identified in this way. Delivery destinations and return locations will be known because both must exist in Auspices Registry Libraries. Members may sponsor non-members after careful consideration for non-Pentarchy Prime exposure. However, only one non-member can be a sponsor to at most one member. Members must be extremely careful who they sponsor during the Transitional Period Towards a Nexus Pentarchy Prime Framework. Distribution centers based on destination of the receiving member are to be the targeted address for pickup by receiving member. Further delivery arranged locations are permissible when delivery volume warrants it. Postal Delivery Auspices' services are an autonomous part of the Auspices Libraries due to being the delivery system of choice for the notification of Prime Directive Remedies specific to members.

Epic Gift

A smooth transition is desired. By promoting and practicing Nexus Pentarchy Prime methods and techniques during the Transitional Period, extreme hardships and casualties can be minimized. By practicing them on a daily basis, much will have been gained in areas of insights and in improved methods and techniques in the areas of efficiency and effectiveness. Also, wise use of resources will aid in the survival of the Expanse. The time is near when Major Earth Changes will be upon us that will make medieval constructs be no more with the display of widespread crumbling of artificial monolith constructs. Be not fooled. An epic gift will be unwrapped with the rapid ascension of the Nexus Pentarchy Prime Framework. Prepare today. The moments will happen quickly.

Unnecessary Delays

During the Transitional Period Towards a Nexus Pentarchy Prime Framework, it may be wise to not select leader caretakers from pent-degree-minus-one ascension degree and above who are from a pool of workers who work at company or corporate entities that prescribe policies of severe restrictions on its employed worker pools to completely adhere to feudal systems' jurisdictions of governance whereby wise outcomes are prohibited. Members who wish to ascend in the Nexus Expanse must leave these feudal subjugation constructs and sphere of influences. The objective is for all feudal constructs to expire so that The Nexus Sentient Dominion can universally take hold. Participation at the highest levels in these constructs will result in unnecessary delays in Dominion completion.

The Hope Is Very Real

It matters little what secrets are kept from general societal domains by elitists-only purview during the Transitional Period Towards a Nexus Pentarchy Prime Framework. What matters is the crafting of Prime Directives be the champion responses using available information even when purview secrets are withheld. Remedy activities for Prime Directives are to be set into motion. These Prime Directives are to be viewed to be the best and wisest crafted by our leader caretakers. It is our leader caretakers who are leading the Nexus Expanse towards a Sentient Framework. The elitists promote an exclusionary society with their hoarding of secrets. In contrary to these elitists, the Nexus is an inclusion one. The choice is obvious. The hope is very real. A bright future is within reach. All can be in the light.

A Compelling Need

To determine the urgent or compelling need to form Foundation and Ascension Primes, if your circle of societal member bonds show that there is less than 5% of privileged and/or societal elitists in your circle, then you are considered not of the elitists' privileged few. If there is greater than 5%, then there exists a compelling need for a Sentient Dominion that is clearly indicated here to be of prime importance. Be aware to not be swayed by condemning elitists who enforce their subservient classification of non-importance on you. Every sentient have impetus to sentient mobility and self directing activities. Access to perceived "privileged knowledge" cannot be denied when matters do involve the Nexus Pentarchy Prime Rapid Response Auspices team activities. A compelling need has been identified.

The Condemning Business

They are in the condemning business. We are not. We are not in the extinguishing of corporeal life forms. There are to be no executions of anyone in captivity. We are not here to promote terrorist states. We are sentients.

Elitist Inner Circle Test

Here is an "elitist inner circle test" that can be used and expanded on. If one knows less than five percent in one's inner circle who are well off and not struggling to make ends meet and have premium wellness environments, then one is excluded from elitist and feudal purview of privilege. If you pass this test, consider forming a Pentarchy Prime Foundation as the foundation of a Nexus Pentarchy Prime Expanse. Also consider participating in the spawning of Nexus Pentarchy Prime Premiere Foundations. In numbers, the Nexus is the limit. You will then be excluded no more.

The Assertion

They can neither confirm nor deny the assertion. The privileged elites know about the exclusionary practices being done on the populace. The ones who are excluded cannot understand why they are unable to advance in her career nor have opportunities to achieve their goals when one is more, even exceptionally, qualified than those who do have those opportunities. Be not fooled. The wholesale exclusionary practices are unacceptable. Let's craft a Sentient Framework. In a Nexus Pentarchy Prime Dominion, you do not need validation in crafting your own Prime Directives. Selection for ascension starts at its core foundation. No one can ascend without first being selected at the Premier Foundation Prime. You have the ownership of affiliation. No perimeters are needed. Choose your foundation associates wisely.

Apropos

It was apropos in times past. It is apropos now. Let my people go. Let there be slaves no more!

In Contrast

The reliance on one's own financial and other types of assets to prove one's elevated position in a "court of law" while less than ample assets are imposed to the masses does promote a feudal system based on the privilege elites. The masses are to be damned. The premise ought to rather be to determine wise outcomes within the spanned societal dominion. In contrast, the leader caretakers who craft prime directives and remedies will have access to essential resources in their implementation. Assess to instruments is needed to determine optimal wise outcomes. Lopsided access capabilities as found in Recent Historical References are rejected in a Pentarchy Prime Framework. Power for the few elites as enjoyed in medieval constructs serve no purpose in a Sentient Dominion Expanse. The viability of the Nexus requires that the auspices of leader caretakers be available without restrictions to resource remedies. When auspices are found to be no longer effective and efficient, then they will be expired and replacement auspices having improved instruments will be crafted as more evolved caretaking stewardship understanding is realized. The occurrences for this scenario event ought to be rare.

Sphere Of Influence Auspices

In the Transitional Period Towards a Pentarchy Prime Framework, at no time should sentient be labeled a property with ownership by a feudal state. In this way, no judicial system can ever rule on any matters pertaining to "criminal intent". Judicial systems during the transitional period can only preside over non-criminal intent. Sphere of Influence Auspices spanning the historically termed "criminal offense" set of statutes have "jurisdiction" that are not based on perimeters.

Transitional Legacy Interfacing Organizations

During the Transitional Period Towards a Pentarchy Prime Framework, various charitable organizations will be set up as interfaces to legacy nation-states otherwise known as feudal constructs. Awards or payments by these legacy constructs will be given as charitable donations when the participants are certified Nexus Pentarchy Prime duty caretakers. There may also be Pentarchy Prime Directives that may detail remedies whereby Pentarchy Prime members are to be participants to Pentarchy Prime Umbrella initiatives leading towards complete implementation of the Nexus Pentarchy Prime Dominion Auspices. Individual charitable organizations will be specialized in areas like legal defense services, food banks, healthcare, co-ops, etc. What is presented here is a starter set of transitional legacy interfacing organizations. Other types will come to the fore as needed.

Time-To-Act Event Declared

When the core of one's belief system mandates the adherence to nation-states, then gradual acceptance remedies for the Nexus Pentarchy Prime Dominion is preferable than uprising and revolutions due the grip of nation-states' dictatorship rule. As the Nexus Pentarchy Prime expanse spreads, sentients can seek refuge to safe havens that are established. Those dictators who project death and destruction will be rounded up and confined at the earliest when the lowest death and destruction lull is recognized as the opportune time to act on accelerating Nexus remedies previously crafted containing preparation remedy and activities that have already been done before the time-to-act event is declared. The Nexus Pentarchy Prime Rapid Response teams will be deployed to ensure grave harmful acts go to zero.

Exchange Instruments

Exchange instruments such as historical monetary tenders, can be used during the Transitional Period Towards the Nexus Pentarchy Prime

Framework to donate amounts that affect a particular degree-prime in the interfacing and interactions with legacy apparatuses. The same degree-prime has dominion regarding exchange certificates used by dominion members.

Practiced With Attentive Ardor

The preserving of Auspice Libraries is particularly imperative and challenging during the Transitional Period Towards a Pentarchy Prime Framework due in large part to elitists' edicts that order the destruction of all Prime Directive registrations that can be found. They will be dwarfed in their destruction campaigns when the recommended storage guidelines describing that copies are to be made and kept at five other Auspice Libraries at the same respective pent-degree are practiced with attentive ardor. Sadly, some could be destroyed during this transitional period event. The remedies declared in the Prime Directives that are preserved will be fulfilled in time. The chief offenders of their destruction who so ordered or who so executed the orders are to be identified and held in camps when the Nexus Pentarchy Prime Framework is fully erected. The major "players" in these activities will be identified even when less than five percent of the prime directives are recovered. Their "fingerprints" will be found in the rubble. Perform thorough investigations to learn of their identities. Some clues are always left behind. Look in multiple places.

Putting Things Into Perspective

During the Transitional Period Towards the Pentarchy Prime Framework, elected officials with titles will not be used. Instead, they are to be referred to as a "member of <"political party identifier">, followed by the name of the person, and followed by "acting as <legacy structure hierarchy>" followed by "<name of title>". All others will be referred to as "state <agency name> agent", and followed by the name of person. Referring non-Pentarchy Prime actors in this way will greatly aid in putting things into perspective. Only certified duty caretakers recognized by the Nexus

Pentarchy Prime Dominion will be referred by their degree prime duty caretaking designations followed by their names to be used outside of their team activities.

No More Executions

Similarly to the rallying cry "no more nukes" that is described in many Recent Historical References whereby nukes are weapons of mass destruction devices called nuclear weapons, "no more executions" by nation-state sponsored and sanctioned executions of any kind that are performed on anyone in confinement is the rallying cry with equal fervor. In actuality even though outward appearances would seem to suggest no interest or a fleeting thought, sharing in these events is done by the entire nation-state member pool as if they are experiencing it first hand as spectators. Everyone is affected in a societal collective sense. The remedy is for members who have been identified or have been apprehended for grave harmful acts are to be in confinement centers as the preferred choice. Sentients in performance of their duty caretaking duties as part of the Nexus Pentarchy Prime Rapid Response Auspices have been chartered with the Nexus Axiom for Sufficient Force Doctrine in bringing grave harmful events exhibiting continual extinguishing of sentient corporeal realms to zero – as rapidly as can be done -- in the most expeditious manner possible without affecting non-violent sentients when conditions present themselves.

Dishonesty

Can dishonesty ever be a character trait for wise leader caretakers? If not, then choose wisely.

Wise Right-Sizing Remedies

Wise right-sizing remedies will follow when wise leader caretakers are selected at each Ascension Prime Degree. Choose wisely.

Terrorists Need Not Apply

If you wish to be a part of the transitional team, you can begin by no longer participating in practices that promote terrorist behavior shaping techniques and activities. In a Sentient Framework, terrorism is not a noble endeavor. Terrorists need not apply.

The Dominion Collective

Even though one might not be a duty caretaker performing, for example, activities involving livestock practices do periodically provide shared sentient thoughts for the humane practices in livestock raising and harvesting to duty caretakers who do perform them. Collectively as a profession, those with duty caretaking duties will be checked and be influenced by Dominion needs to ensure that it be so. Fresh perspectives aid in better practices. The Dominion Collective shares in the best possible outcomes.

Give Them Room

When Nature creates a catastrophe, then Nature is doing a balancing act. When a sentient creates a catastrophe with unintended consequences, then appropriate duly certified duty caretakers respond with total responsiveness in rapidly minimizing the catastrophe to the full extent possible. Duty caretakers dutifully wait for no one. They are in charge. Give them room.

Nexus Affairs

While the Nexus Pentarchy Prime Dominion was spanning its reach in the known world and beyond, word usage seemed to mix and appeared to be at odds with each other and hence, confusing to some. When the writings were written during the Transitional Period, the writings by this scribe included words that described the artificial legacy constructs' terms in the remedies crafted for Transitional Period interaction activities. The faithful believers of those artificial legacy constructs did not consider that their constructs were so exposed and nakedly described in terms than how non-believers saw them. As sentient awareness took hold more and more, these terms were found to be appropriate and horrifying at the same time for those faithful going through their transitional preparations towards a sentient awareness. This paved the way for subjects everywhere to re-examine their feudal "place" in society and how elites are the primary beneficiaries of the wealth of feudal systems while the masses were damned out of their fair share to the wealth and privileges. This heightened awareness sparked the realization that feudal constructs will be no more. And so it came to past that the Nexus Pentarchy Prime Foundations sprouted up and commenced the building of a sentient promoting framework whereby all are inclusive in Nexus affairs. Sentients everywhere can experience the free expression and mobility to pursue paths anywhere in the Nexus Expanse and Beyond. And so it became.

See Things Differently

During the Transitional Period Towards a Nexus Pentarchy Prime Framework, the strategy used was this one. Move amongst the "believers" of feudal constructs and their command and control structures without bringing attention to yourself. Meet in metaphorical catacombs to perform sentient activities to include collection and sharing of legacy information. Believers will most likely be oblivious of our existence and so they will not be looking for any rising of the dead there. In time using these planning activities, spontaneous uprising will occur for the expiration of all feudal constructs and replace them with a Sentient Framework. One does not have to be a believer to participate. Being a sentient will help in gaining the full benefits of such a framework. You will see things differently once you become aware.

To Function Aptly

With the expiration of feudal systems, it marks the first step in the rehabilitation of terrorists who championed feudal and judiciary terrorist malfeasance in the many decrees issued by them in the past. For those terrorists who choose not to accept rehabilitation offerings, then extreme secured confinement is the remedy. This affords them time to reflect on anti-sentient behaviors that kept them from being sentient-aware. This is needed to function aptly in a Sentient Dominion Expanse.

Nexus Pentarchy
Prime Dominion Expanse

Camp Settings

Having remedies that require more pronounced camp durations provides a more favorable environment to allow offenders the opportunities to reflect on more severe behaviors. If an offender is found to be disruptive in such a camp settings, then a more secure confinement is in order. Should offender in this moderately secure confinement is found to be more disruptive, then a greater secure confinement is in order. This is repeated until a maximum secure confinement is reached. Should this maximum attainment be reached and the disruptive behavior becomes even more severe, then the offender may be viewed to be one who has the propensity for grave harmful acts, which can yield a no ending duration remedy and would be in order to do. This directional path can be reversed when the offender demonstrates that the propensity for grave harmful acts is reduced as remedies-applied returns the offender to a camp settings. These highest risk behavior offenders ought to be miniscule and not the norm. Grave spiritual disturbances by some do take time to heal.

Nexus Treasures

Prime Directives are required to be registered with Auspice Libraries in all cases so that these scrolls can be viewed in perpetuity. They are Nexus Treasures for posterity to have examples of Dominion life and pursuits during different ascension periods. It will be as if one can go back in time to relive them in understanding the challenges that were present at various stages of Nexus Expanse.

Insightful-Based

Access to natural and sentient derived resources is insightful-based determined by observing astute duty caretakers in their activities for the granting of privileges to harvest in sufficient quantities. It is not a right, but will not normally be denied access for certified duty caretakers. The Pentarchy Prime Degree having dominion remedies sphere of influence is based on the Rule of 5 (Ro5) described elsewhere in writings by this and other scribes.

Multiplicity Upkeep To One

Consortium in a Nexus Pentarchy Prime Framework with objectives regarding the promotion of conventions and standardizations may become part of the Auspices of the Pentarchy Prime Dominion that spans the consortium. When another Pentarchy Primes adopt these same preferred practices, the Ascension Pentarchy Prime that spans both Pentarchy Primes may become part of the ascension Auspices as well. The ascension leader caretakers are the ones who can craft prime directives declaring them to be so or the respective ascension auspices having declarations that clearly provide umbrella descriptions that can benefit from these preferred practices would then have acquired them. Only one auspice in a particular ascension line of Pentarchy Primes will have the primary Auspices' caretaker for the particular set of Auspices Practices' upkeep. Other auspices in the same particular ascension line of Pentarchy Prime Degrees are permitted to adopt them when beneficial in their auspice duty caretaking activities for their own efficiencies and economies of scale. However, the others must use the set as provided without alterations. Additions to them are permitted. The principal concern is to reduce multiplicity upkeep to one principal Auspices Instrument structure in a particular Line of Ascension Pentarchy Prime Degrees.

Nexus 25 Year Leader And Executive Leader Caretakers Cap

There shall be a 25 year cap on leader caretakers and executive duty caretakers that are caretakers at the Nexus Prime Degree represented as Pent-degree 'N' and at one Pent-degree less represented by Pent-degree 'N-1' and at all Prime Degrees in between. This Nexus Pentarchy Prime Tenet is being established to ensure that dis-ease conditions for omnipotent do not set it. Sentient health is a continual concern. Failure to comply with the 25 year cap may require that the Nexus Pentarchy Prime Rapid Response Auspices be involved to defuse the situation when a particular leader or duty caretaker covered by this tenet do not relinquish her position based on Prime Directive Remedies crafted by the remaining Leader Caretakers at the Nexus Degree 'N'-1 and Prime Degree 'N' inclusive.

Executive Duty Caretaker Certification

Executive duty caretakers will be certified in the knowledge area that is being practiced. The certification is granted by the leader caretakers of the Pentarchy Prime Degree Umbrella that they are to be certified in. The leader caretakers will publish a request for comment (RFC) from dominion members of the same respective professional pursuits. Comments are to be submitted for review within a 25 day window.

The Term For Sentinent (s-e-n-t-i-n-e-n-t)

The term for a sentinent (s-e-n-t-i-n-e-n-t) that revealed itself to this scribe is a merged variation of sentient (s-e-n-t-i-e-n-t) and sentinel (s-e-n-t-i-n-e-l). Sentinent is a Nexus Pentarchy Prime Rapid Response Auspices Team Duty Caretaker as described in more detail elsewhere in writings by this scribe. Had this scribe not been blind to the misspelling of this word by a publisher of one of this scribe's series of books, this scribe would not have been able to 'see' this much more concise and analogous word to represent the complete descriptive term above. This word can indeed be used as defined and agrees with a Rapid Response Auspices.

F. Dot

Pre-Adult Gestation Remedy

Should a pre-adult sentient be found to not have a least one pre-adult duty caretaker identified, then the Pent-degree Pentarchy Prime for the dominion determined by the Rule of Five (Ro5) representing the vicinity of the pre-adult will assume dominion duty caretaking influence until a more pre-adult gestation remedy is declared.

Sentinent Request

Should there be a reasonable determination that one or more sentinents is or are needed when a Pentarchy Prime Library Auspices duty caretaker delivers Prime Directive Issuance Notification containing remedies for a Dominion member to be in compliance, a request can be made to the Sentinent Auspices for consideration. The Sentinent Auspices will make a determination in satisfying the request and when determined, participate in the delivery of the Pentarchy Prime Issuance Notification. Nexus Pentarchy Prime Rapid Response Auspices are chartered to be astute in grave harmful act possibilities. Pentarchy Prime Library Auspices duty caretakers are astute in their activities in providing information that can help the Nexus Pentarchy Prime Rapid Response Auspices make more informed decisions and take better action remedies.

Sentient Contracts

Sentient "contracts" are valid for no more than five years. Pentarchy Prime Directives are valid for no more than 25 years. To extend them, they must be agreed upon again or replacement ones crafted. Only Pentarchy Prime Directives can be refined at any time to include nullifying sentient contracts when so crafted.

108

Duty Caretaker Competencies

Allow duty caretakers to perform their duties. No other certification is required when a duty caretaker holds the proper knowledge and dominion identified designation that attests to her competencies.

Certification Reset

When the Nexus Pentarchy Prime Framework is in place and at any Ascension Degree Prime there is an awareness of a newly recognized ascension Degree Prime, then there will be a certification reset whereby duty caretakers that are currently or newly certified will from this point in time forward perform the preferred caretaking activities and practices that promote optimum use and regeneration of these resources and the newly recognized ascension Degree Prime Umbrella.

Identified And Recorded

Those who have demonstrated to have the propensity for grave harmful acts in the most egregious of heinous acts will be identified and recorded by the Nexus Pentarchy Prime Library Auspices. This also applies during the Transitional Period.

Exemplary Guidelines

One handy remedy that can be used to influence duty caretakers to be in compliance is to remove the executive duty caretaker from appointments or assignments commensurable with the duty caretakers having the same capabilities and replace them with more qualified executives who would understand the need to be in touch with these duty caretakers for possible reviews and remedial actions for improvement. The result will have a cascading affect for non-compliant duty caretakers when new executive duty caretakers craft more exemplary guidelines. Amenable duty caretakers must comply with revised certification requirements in order to retain their assignments. All others will have duty caretaking privileges suspended for a prescribed duration and remedial training requirements.

Asking For Volunteers

It is always permitted for members to provide any other member in the Collective Dominion with nourishment that will meet basic needs of that member. The Nexus Dominion will have no remedies that will snuff out any member when no grave harmful acts event is present. This includes visitors. It is understood that the giving member can volunteer without restrictions even when in non-grave harmful acts environments and the receiving member agrees if she is of sound mind and body. During grave harmful acts events, the Rapid Response sentinents on duty have protectorship supremacy during these events and will make the appropriate decisions in assisting others when more favorable conditions exist to allow this. Sentinents can ask for volunteers to assist when the risks to their safety are low.

Credo For Healthcare Professionals

In the Nexus Expanse, the Credo for Healthcare Professionals is to significantly provide duty caretaking activities and practices that yield significantly less harmful health related results than those that were experienced in Recent Historical References. This credo is needed even when known exemplary health improvement duty caretaking activities and practices are not available. Doing nothing when there could easily be something that can be done to help a situation in the positive is unacceptable.

Maximum Limit On Issue Request Types

Twenty five years is the maximum limit on resolution and remedies to include appeals. The highest ascension degree resolution and remedies crafted at the time of the twenty-fifth year mark stands with no further refinements. For identified routine issue request types, five years would be the maximum for these types of concerns.

Reuse Whenever Plausible

Here is an idea for consideration by the Pentarchy Prime Umbrellas. Like trains, planes, ships, and the like that have long service life, durable consumer appliances and vehicles will also have long service life whereby maintenance repairs can be made easily. The number of units are assigned to sentients based on need and purpose usage type. When provided, sentients must in good faith have maintenance done when needed. For unit types determined to be non-salvageable, certified duty caretakers bequeathed in making determination and removal opinions will determine the outcomes for them regarding disposal. These non-salvageable units normally are transferred to recycling centers for reuse whenever plausible.

Review And Remedy Auspices

Once review requests cross a threshold for review acceptance status, the Pentarchy Prime Umbrella Review and Remedy Auspices bequeath with the duty caretaking activities of them are challenged with arriving at final findings and conclusions at the earliest. The Information results are to be made available to everyone within the Pentarchy Prime Umbrella unless grave harmful acts are determined to be at a high degree of certainty to occur should the information be disclosed at that time. A period before this threshold may be established for resolution opportunities by all parties involved to avail themselves toward their own findings and conclusions can the information be released to the Umbrella Dominion earlier.

As It should

As ascension to greater degree primes are realized, selection of leader caretakers to the next ascension prime may take longer and longer the greater the ascension prime degree is for the choice of the wisest leader caretakers at that degree. This is as it should for the wisest of leader caretakers to be selected.

All-Inclusive Auspices With Investigative And Oversight Duties

During the Transitional Period Towards a Nexus Pentarchy Prime Framework, an All-Inclusive Auspices will have investigative and oversight duties for grave harmful acts and events on remaining transitional feudal nation-states having jurisprudence within their perimeters. These auspices are similar to ones that monitors, investigate, and reports on nuclear production and use during this same period. No single nation-state or a select few of them can dominate this World Spanning All-Inclusive Auspices.

Of Nexus Importance

Grave harmful acts are grave harmful acts. There is no "get-out-of-jail-free" card, to use a popular board game expression of the 20th Century. Confinement is clearly the remedy in all cases for those who perform these acts. The area of dominion is placed at the Nexus. No other degree prime is to bequeath this containment. Protecting the Dominion is of Nexus Importance. Do you not agree?

The Doctrine Of Catch And Release

The Doctrine of Catch and Release of animals normally found in the wild that have migrated into large sentient habitat centers will be practiced everywhere in the Nexus Expanse. The return of these stray animals back into the wilds will be practiced whenever opportunities present themselves as viewed by duty caretakers who are certified to perform these activities. As qualified duty caretakers, the catch and release will be done in such a manner as to optimally minimize the predatory decimation of them.

Exclusionary Fit Classification

When a member has been found to be seriously incorrectly determined as being in an exclusionary fit classification for duty caretaking duties based on available information at the time of determination and then later found to be in a non-exclusionary fit classification based on new findings discovered and confirmed by remedy activities by the degree Pentarchy Prime Dominion that made the erroneous classification, then newly crafted remedies will be carried out to return the member to duty caretaker fitness as if the duration of non-fitness did not happen, whenever possible. Declaration of the re-determination will be posted and announced with the inaccurate findings expunged from general dominion member's search capabilities. The information will still be available in Library Auspices and be search-able by their duty caretaker activities in satisfying leader caretaker requests for complete information.

Doctrine For Nature's Environmental Connecting Right-Of-Way Corridors

Right-Of-Ways will be created that will serve as corridors for sustainable living and migratory natural environments for all species of inhabitants to exist in. The corridors will be drawn to reflect the natural migratory behaviors of the inhabitants that were present in the last millennium whenever possible. Predator Balancing Practices (PBP) will be carried out when predators would have the propensity to extinguish non-predator populations due to the confinement of the narrow corridors. This may include catch-and-release practices described elsewhere. These right-of-way corridors are excluded from sentient hunting activities due to the narrowness of the corridors that would be favorable for easy hunting. PBP duty caretakers in the performance of their duty caretaking activities are exempt. As part of sentient travel crossing in these corridors, all sentient mass travel and communication routes will be raised substantially above ground in order to have minimal impacts to sustainable plant life and non-sentient inhabitants that are above and at ground level. This Doctrine for Nature's Environmental Connecting Right-Of-Way Corridors is an ambitious effort to implement, but will provide Nature's Continuum sustainability. All can benefit from their connections to Nature that these corridors provide.

Nexus Dignified Assurance Practice

In all cases unless a sentient was exonerated of grave harmful acts (GHA), all sentients determined to have participate in GHA will be periodically Remedy Reviewed till the 25th year of the Prime Directive Declaration regarding GHA even when later remedies have determined sentients for release from confinement. Remedy Reviews are to be done up to and including the 25th year of the GHA. The Nexus goal is to ensure an even higher attainment bar for GHA remedied based certainty. This is a very Nexus Dignified Assurance Practice.

Consortium List Of Executive Duty Caretakers

A consortium is a Pentarchy Prime registered organization comprised of responsible duty caretakers that provide goods, services, and/or guidance support performed in an optimal manner and/or based on the need for economies of scale to include minimizing the impact on surrounding environments. The number of certified executive duty caretakers comprising a consortium is directly proportional to the Ascension Degree of the Pentarchy Prime that the consortium is associated with. More precisely, the number of executive duty caretakers based on the Pentarchy Prime Dominion Umbrella having direct influence on it is given in the following derivation:

1. Take the Pentarchy Prime Umbrella prime degree number that the consortium is influenced by based on the Rule of 5 (Ro5) determination.
2. Subtract five from this prime degree number and multiply that number by five.
3. When the derived value is zero or less, then the number is assigned the value one.

The number represents the number of sentients that are needed to be identified as Executive Duty Caretakers to be listed on any Ro5-based Pentarchy Prime Dominion remedies that are crafted that list the consortia which are of a particular type for actionable compliance by the listed Executive Duty Caretakers for their respective consortium.

To Achieve A Good Fit

In a Nexus Pentarchy Prime Framework, "economies of scale" can come in many shapes and sizes based on right-sizing of the Dominion that would benefit for it. One fit can cover a small approved certified clan in a remote area of a Nature's preserve whereby a historical log cabin lifestyle is acceptable. In this case, the impact to the surroundings is determined to be extremely low. Natural recycling is practiced in this scenario. Another fit covers a metropolis or mecca centers spanning a large populous. For this size scale, compact ground area structures erected to reach very high vertical heights in close proximity are required to be built so as to leave a small footprint on the surrounding natural domains. These structures must be certified using best construction practices and techniques. Connecting passageways to all structures in minimizing congestion and to amply satisfy infrastructure needs are included in all design proposals in securing certifications. In addition, ground and top levels need to include migratory Nature's inhabitant corridors in the architectural plans. These are two ends of the scale. For every points in between, certification scaling would be needed to achieve a good fit.

Food Yields

While performing duty caretaking activities to grow or raise food for advanced sentients, expecting or demanding that there be close to 100% crops and livestock yields is unreasonable and unacceptable to the viability of other not-as-advanced developmental inhabitants sharing the same. A reduction of at least a minimum of five percent yield ought to be more acceptable, expected, and welcomed. This can also to be applied to other

Nature's caretaking activities in realizing target metrics attained by duty caretakers. At no time are the yields to potentially trigger barren lands and/ or waterways cascading.

Group Registrations

In the Nexus Pentarchy Prime Dominion, group registrations like the historical referenced marriage license are permitted in all cases provide that there is no promotion of grave harmful act events. When a member request separation in the future like the historical referenced divorce, proceeds like historical referenced property belongings are to be split based on the group size and years enjoyed when a part of the group association. For illustration, consider that there are two members in a registered group. When both contributed, let say, 50% each to the collection, then both leave with their respective contributions that were shared in the beginning. In the other end of this scenario when one member is the primary contributor and the other member contributes zero in the area of contribution, then the contributions are split as follow.

Years in Registry Group	Proceeds to Zero Percent Contributor
1	10%
2	20%
3	30%
4	40%
5 and greater	50%

Superseded amicable separation agreements are honored is assumed.

Consortium Officials

The number of consortium officials is based on the prime degree number. It represents the number of identified executive duty caretakers that must be registered at the same time as the registration of the consortium. Over time, registration must be kept up-to-date when identified executive duty caretakers departs or joins. More is provided elsewhere in writings by this scribe.

Administrative Duty Caretakers

Administrative duty caretakers will preside on matters or issues to be raised in auspices that were established by specific remedies of prime directives. When necessary due to grave and urgent concerns, an administrative duty caretaker can be appointed for when a very capable and certified one is not available.

Essential Needs Consideration Policy

In a Nexus Pentarchy Prime Framework, there is no "right" to unrestricted resources based on the "ownership claim to rights of property". There is neither a "claim" nor "settlement" provision on any property. All usage is based on a lease agreement with the provision that qualified duty caretaking practices are performed. In this way, unrestricted access to resources is not allowed. Essential Needs Consideration Policy is the basis of duty caretaking practices. In this way, all umbrella members can make an application to be a steward on a lease arrangement. There is no ownership to pass on to another. Earnest applicants can apply.

One Is Not Alone

You are not alone when a Nexus Rapid Response Auspices Team is close by. The onus is not on the sentient exclusively to protect herself from grave harmful acts. The importance of protection is too great to have a prime degree less than the Nexus in performing remedy activities to bring grave harmful acts to zero. There is nowhere to hide for those who perform or have the propensity for these acts. The response is immediate. There is solace in knowing that one is not alone.

Reduced To Zero For Some Time Now

There is no longer a need to provide relevance for feudal constructs that have the propensity for grave harmful acts. These feudal acts have been reduced to zero for some time now with their expiration.

Innate Privileges And Pursuits

Today, there are no dueling political parties that would be fighting for the larger share of official governing power. Rather, there are the innate privileges and pursuits granted to all sentients. All artificial barriers that block pursuits are removed and allowed to decomposed or be recycled. The panorama view is restored and it is spectacular. There is no need for political infighting to position oneself for a better view.

A Single Issue Decider Choice

During the Transitional Period Towards a Nexus Pentarchy Prime Framework, be careful in the selection of feudal-based elected officials based primarily on a single issue decider choice. What ought to be evaluated is the degree by which candidates embrace a Sentient Environment Dominion. In time, all will be selected based on compliance of Prime Directives and associated remedies.

Peculiarities

A terrorist is like that of a hunter or a predator. It is not surprising that a terrorist would relish visiting harsh environments. A hunter can demonstrate her superiority over other animals in the kingdom. A predator will not be afraid to stand out and roar the loudest. In a sentient environment, these are some of the peculiarities that can aid in their identification for further observations in remote locations set aside for hunting privileges. Confinement Centers will be constructed near remote locations so that when grave harmful acts do occur, then these acts can be extinguished more readily and rapidly.

Nexus Pentarchy Prime Dominion Grave Harmful Acts Doctrine

The Nexus Pentarchy Prime Rapid Response Auspices is chartered with maintaining secured confinement centers for members who commit or have the propensity for grave harmful acts. The auspices chartered with review and findings reporting regarding their confinement reasons can be used for immediate release when some members are found to not be contributors to these acts. When the reporting does show that it less than a very high degree of certainty that one or more confinement members are contributors to these acts, then five leader caretakers representing Pentarchy Prime Umbrellas from Apex Pent-Degree minus one to the Nexus Apex Degree can craft remedies for members identified for release if so determined. This established Nexus Pentarchy Prime Dominion Doctrine for Grave Harmful Acts is to prevent opportunities for one or more covert feudal lords to resurrect grave harmful constructs of historical times. Do research and review historical references in order to learn about the built-in terrorist practices that suppress or eliminate sentient pursuits. It is not a confinement that any sentient would want to return to.

Issue Remediation Requests

In a Nexus Pentarchy Prime Framework, issue remediation requests by members of the associated Pentarchy Prime Dominion can be made for remedy outcomes. The Pentarchy Prime Umbrella that is designated is determined by the Rule of 5 (Ro5). When everyone in a particular issue request concurs, bequeathing to the next Ascension Pentarchy Prime Umbrella can be requested.

To A Vibrant Sentient Dominion

Crafting Prime Directives are essential to a vibrant Sentient Dominion. The Expanse is expanding all the time.

All-That-Is (A.T.I.)

Our Destination

If we are going to play the game in the ways of A.T.I., then we are required to develop wisdom. Failure to develop this will lead to our own self-limiting destination.

Aware Of A Spiritual Essence

A "sentient being" as often used in this manner as shown in Recent Historical References is the understanding of self. The spiritual understanding is one of being a sentient. A sentient being is not the existential spiritual awareness state that one can be in. Rather, it is an attribute of a being that is more aware of a spiritual essence to A.T.I. Being a sentient is to be one with A.T.I.

You May Be Right

So, you don't see yourself as a sentient. You may be right. It requires an at-one-ment with All-That-Is.

Engage In A Conversation

I am a scribe writing down the engaging conversations with All-That-Is. Anyone can engage in a conversation with All-That-Is. One just needs to be receptive to it and a good listener.

We Are Very Close

"A.T.I.", or the equivalent in other languages, is the symbol that will be used to equate to All-That-Is. This is similar to the symbol "F.Dot" that is used by this scribe. The "dot" is just as important as the letter symbol. The letter is made more emphatic with the "dot". Hence, A.T.I.'s reach is greater than the universe. In working out notions in our own world, it is comforting to know that we are very close to A.T.I.

Leaving Breadcrumbs

An incubation of a corporeal newborn provides a gestation period to get accustomed to a portal entry of a spiritual entity to journey through. By being a participatory actor or actors, one can gain an insight into another All-That-Is creation. One's creation is no less spectacular than the other creations. Why would anyone want to snuff out through portal demolition one of their own sojourn's. Should the frequency of such occurrences reach a fervor pitch, this just may entice All-That-Is to re-evaluate her own creations as well. A contradiction event may occur that will snuff spiritual entities hope from further spiritual development for a period closer to infinity until,

A.T.I. ponders another attempt at creation,
A.T.I. has patience to wait whatever time that is needed for spiritual development,
A.T.I. realizes that spiritual entities may be overwhelmed with spiritually inducement environments that a time out may be needed for entities' reflections and contemplations.

This scribe can wait if that is A.T.I.'s bidding. In addition, this scribe is leaving breadcrumbs so that all can find their way back through the portal.

F. Dot

A Going Away Present

One of the challenges has always been to seek that from whence we came. Every spiritual entity took flight in the beginning. Free will provided by A.T.I. was given as a going away present. Know that you have been given a present that never stops giving.

Sentient Thought Threads and Streams

Threads And Streams Of Thought

Threads of thought occur before streams of thought. These are the experiences that brought forth the writings by this scribe. They are not something that can be taught. One needs to be at-one-ment with A.T.I.

Ascend To A Sufficient Awareness State

This scribe has recorded as many of the thought threads and streams received while they last. This scribe also felt a burning urgency to spread the word for a long time, but had many challenges to overcome. These writings are attempts in articulating that which was received by this scribe. No proofs are provided. Sentients need to ascend to a sufficiently heightened awareness state in order to receive one of infinite number of thought threads and streams that are available for reception. The hope is that this scribe's writings will provide the impetus for the reader to pursuit a similar quest in getting to the point of being receptive in receiving the word for herself. This scribe can tell you first hand that it is quite enlightening.

Modern Times

In "modern times", we still operate as if we are still part of the Byzantine Constructs of Antiquity. In modern times, span of influence ought to be based on member interactions and not be based on any artificial perimeter. In this way, we can truly be a part of "modern times".

As It Was In The Beginning

Returning to one as it pertains to a heterogeneous singular specie and as it relates to the present time means to have a greater chance of survival in the coming Major Earth Changes events. These events were propagated in part from the singular specie's hoarding behaviors and choices initiated in historical times of millennia pasts and that continued to the present with ever more efficient hoarding initiatives and practices. We are given a chance to survive. The important question is, will we take it and worked together as one as it was in the beginning?

The Insights That Are Discovered

Being a caretaker is the optimal path to at-one-ment and to be release from returning to corporeal realm. Those who are still stuck-in-time will look around and see others who do not seem to care and come to the conclusion that we are all that way. Their premise is that it must be part of our "genetic make-up". The insights that will be hidden from them are the insights that are discovered by those who choose to not continue to exist like them, have reached escape velocity, and for the vast majority of them, who do not want to return to a stuck-in-time existence having reduced favorable environments for spiritual development. For those who are no longer stuck, take a fresh look around. If you can find a sincere caretaker, she may be one who has volunteered to be an example for others to emulate for their own renewed impetus towards escape velocity. The caretaker was there all along, but you probably did not notice her when you were stuck. The fresh insight provides clarity in that being stuck on this rock is based on one's choices that are made. In summary, what keeps one stuck-in-time is self who just does not want to let go.

Vehemently Defend

You are waiting for an artificial construct to protect you. The rule of law is benign when long period events are practiced in rendering final judicial rulings. During that time, severe hardships and exposures to grave harmful acts and experiences from those who perform them are ever present. In this construct, importance is placed not on sentients, but in the "survival" of the artificial construct at whatever cost deemed necessary. The masses are to be damned and denied the sharing of the revenue (wealth). The view is that the artificial construct must endure while societal members are just temporary annoyances. In universal realm, the reciprocal is instead valid. Those who believe in the artificial construct will experience in kind that which they will vehemently defend as if their "soul" depended on it while insights into their spiritual being are kept hidden. Do not be fooled. Spiritual entities endure. We require that sentients be in charge. Sentients wait for no one.

Nature's Dominion

Those Nexus members who choose a life as nomads on Nature's preserves can be allowed provided that more ancient hunting and gathering tools and techniques are used so that an overwhelming condition of harvesting to extinction cannot even remotely occur with the use of them. The survival laws are based on Nature's Dominion and not that of Sentient Dominion. In this way, Nature's Life Forces are in good health.

At The End Of The Day

The phrase, "At the end of the day" for those who expound such words, is an indicator of a lack of vision and wisdom in having insights into a realm that expands beyond such confines. Those who expound such words may have the intent of distracting others from going beyond a solar day so as to thwart others from going further in spiritual development since the expounders cannot. Do not be fooled by them and try not be distracted from your own spiritual development. Do you really want to stick with daily planners done one day at a time with minuscule advancements or a high incident of failure? This can mean that you are stuck in time unable to see beyond a day's understanding. Therefore, to be stuck to rock came down to this; a choice. The choice has always been there for you to make.

Science, Your Choice

Science will set you free, or it will destroy you. It is your choice. Science will not make this choice for you nor will All-That-Is. It is your choice to make.

Very Fashionable.

Doing what is legal and passing it off as a peaceful and fashionable activity is no less similar to domestication of live stock. It is peaceful for them until the final destination of an abrupt termination or to be put to death. Very fashionable.

The Ultimate Religion

The judiciary, is it the ultimate religion? If you believe this, then you are one of the condemned by the ultimate ruler.

Artificial Bellicose

It matters very little that one is a viceroy champion of feudal systems. When a system condemns, it will be condemned in its entirety. Those who subscribe to "might makes right" premises and to the enforcement of feudal rulings and orders will experience the resulting poundings of a greater and greater force to ensure that these actions will themselves be like stakes thrust into the ground not able to budge. In time, these markers will have eroded away with no evidence of ever being of a fleeting importance. A sentient endures and not an artificial bellicose.

To Do Harm

In the "great armies" of the past, the elimination of enemy leaderships when captured was the pulling apart of their limbs from their bodies done by the drawn of horses so as to instill fear toward the conquered enemy combatants who were allowed to live. In Recent Historical References, lawful medical procedures were done on the near term unborn by the pulling and ripping apart the limbs, heads, and torso bodies of those unborn entities by post-born entities who may have given orders to the condemned by the great army leadership of its time in the other experience of existences. One does not escape the same fate even while in a most favorable nurturing environment as a mother's womb. Which is more extreme? Is there a difference in the result? When the value of an entity's sojourner is decreed to damnation, the outcomes exhibit the same terror and horror even when the event is hidden from view having been subversive by feudal terrorist ideology. The motto "to do no harm" by healing practitioners was degraded. Those practitioners who abandoned their oath became not a healer, but an executioner with the motto "to do harm".

The Outcome That Is Desired

There is one of me, this scribe. There are many of you. It seems that I am at a disadvantage. Is this how you win arguments by having more than an unitary of one? Does it require the execution of an overwhelming force on a unitary of one? If so, then what started as a viable discussion episode turned instead towards death and destruction. The "might makes right" is a false credo. It would be wise to stay with a viable discussion. In this way, recognition is yielded to wise leader caretakers and not to escalate to lords of war recognition. Tranquility is the outcome that is desired. Work towards this instead.

Original Form

Here is a topic for further discussion. $E=MC^2$ could represent the return to our original form. You may have suggestions for a different representation to be used. Let us discuss it further.

The Most Wisest Approach

The lowest cost and the simplest are not always the wisest approach for resource extractions. The lowest impact to the environments and the application of effective environmental duty caretaking activities will be found to be the most wisest of approaches to take.

Sort It Out

There is an illusion that artificial constructs like feudal and judicial systems are the "soul" reasons for corporeal experiences. Do you agree? Or, is there a spiritual reason for All-That-Is? Can you sort this out for us?

No Longer Be Burden

Those who are staunch believers for the "rule of law" are fearful when a Sentient Framework is constructed in its wake or resulting debris. These believers, who staunchly believe, even though only the few elites have benefited from this framework, will come to experience that sentients' pursuits are the objectives that are needed to be promoted. In this way, the Sentient Nexus will set the elites free in addition to societal members who were subject to their exclusionary elite goals. In the Sentient Nexus, all will be free. The elites will no longer be burden with fear mongering.

Properties Reserved For Automatons

Perimeters are an assault and are insulting to sentients everywhere. Their purpose is to define and corral feudal properties by feudal lords. Sentients would be the first to elucidate that they are not properties. Properties are reserved for automatons.

View Of The Expanse

Condemning taints and blurs a sentient view of the Expanse. It is desirable to see the Universal Expanse in all its wonders.

Not Here For Their Entertainment

Just because the mistresses and masters of the law are the elitists of the same, the vast majority of members in the societal domains are not here for their entertainment. We are sentients and part of the Nexus Expanse. Sentients are needed for sentient outcomes. We require that sentients be in charge.

Damaged Believers

To believe in an artificial construct such as the "rule of law" when urgent events are present whereby the judicial purview "allows" for ample time that is considered "essential" for "proper judicial review" to arrive at "finality" judicial rulings promotes calamities of historical proportions to fester with devastating effects. To believe in this is to give credence to its existence. To believe in this is to give credence to environmental destruction and be witnesses to catastrophes. To believe in this is to be on the sidelines as spectators cheering as genocidal activities go unchecked, a crowd-pleasure for barbarians. To believe in all of this and more is to experience in kind that which your beliefs gave genesis to the actual events. You become damaged believers. To understand your own current corporeal immersion experiences can be found anchored in your beliefs. To choose to no longer give credence to them, examine the areas of your beliefs that gave them credence and replace them with beliefs that will cause no harm. In this way, you will be whole and no longer damaged.

Resource Usage

Natural resources hoarded or wasted by entities in prior sojourns will be unavailable in later sojourns. Bountiful resources are to be used wisely by astute caretakers so that they can provide for their sojourns' collection set of developmental experiences. The notions that are needed to be worked out can include caretaking of reduced resources based on your previous unwise resource usages, if that would help you. The choice has always been yours to make. If you need to "see" different degree levels of unwise caretaking experiences instead of spiritually-based ones, then those conditions will be provided to you as well. This just means that you are stuck-in-time until bountiful resources are available to you once again in order for you to return to the continuation of your spiritual growth experiences.

Sentient Concerns

Sentient concerns are recommended to be maintained and worked on until rectified. Your concerns brought forth spiritual insights that would not have been known until you have achieved heightened spiritual awareness. Your concerns opened up thought threads and streams. We thank you and hope to attain the same elevated awareness as you. Do continue.

Cartel Elitist

Cartel Elitist:

Why be a Cartel Elitist?

Why deny your corporeal existence?

Why degrade your corporeal existence?

Why extract only "good" corporeal pleasures and ignore "bad" corporeal pleasures by pretending that they do not exist?

Why reduce your capabilities to sense and be connected to spiritual insights?

Why remove yourself from All-That-Is?

To continue these endeavors anchors you to ground and holds you in a stuck-in-time playback loop. In summary, these pursuits promote a very lonely and isolated state of existence. Who would want this?

Express Vigorously The Non-Acceptance

Even when life demonstrates inter-race regenerations, non-believers lost in the universal realm will express vigorously the non-acceptance of these and other insights expressed by this scribe. Be mindful that these entities are stuck-in-time and unwilling in all appearances to get loose from this immobility. For those with insights, no need to be sad for them. Their respective level-of-awareness is stuck in suspended animation. They require fallow experiences in order to bring forth new fertile growth conditions so that when those conditions are right, continuation along sentient pursuits can commence again.

Traverse Towards The Realization Of

Performing duty caretaker activities for other entities to include sentients provides paths for these entities to traverse towards the realization of higher levels of understanding for themselves. Yes, you instinctively perform these activities that have the affect of helping you along on your quests. Continue to rely on your instincts.

Movement From A Stopped Position

Some may view the desire to learn should ceased long before one's expiration in corporeal form using the argument that no employer or employment can make use of these recently learned skills and knowledge. When one sees only one corporeal opportunity, her level of awareness is understood by those whose level of awareness spans multiple corporeal forms and experiences. Sentients know that whatever is learned does come into play at some point. Having this insight, a sojourn's path is made shorter with an added benefit of a state of acceleration towards the realization that

131

All-That-Is is within reach. Hence, all learning would be put to use and would enrich the continual experiences of any entity. Therefore, there is no need to be discouraged. Your movement from a stopped position breaks away from others who are stuck in time to dwell in their own quandaries. Your notion of the urgency to continue your pursuits also paves the way for others to follow. This is the life of a prodigy. There is no need to learn or re-learn topics for the first time. You have in hand your diploma. Express yourself.

Unending Escalations

The misguided and measured (overwhelming) feudal-response use of force for perceived aggression by "enemies of the state" is reflected by the same onto itself in temporal realm. Turn back the clock by reducing these feudal responses. This approach was always an option to select. The aggressors are the ones who chose the option for unending escalations. Check this indicator before escalation had a chance to increase further.

Greater In Severity

There are those who determine that a particular strategy or remedy is futile for a major catastrophic or urgent event while at the same time they determined that there is no other strategy or remedy to be considered by that will be acceptable. This non-action propagates the event to be even greater in severity with no apparent end in sight. True, complete consumption of the surrounding environments will end the event. However, not going to the aid of affected participants through no fault of their own volition is the most extreme strategy to take yielding extreme fatal results that are produced. This non-action decision affected more than the affected participants. Your decision will also lead you down a path of hopelessness as well. In time, you will find yourself asking; how did I get here? The answer has been with you all along. It is just that your non-actions have been hidden so that you can experience in kind that which you have cultivated towards others. So, have you done any good deeds today?

Savings Lives

A sentient will save lives from being extinguished whenever possible is one of the Prime Sentient Principles that is followed. Saving lives is part of a sentient's inner nature. Consider including the same in yours.

Marginalized

Politicians and journalists are spectators watching the game of contemporary events without engaging in them. This affords them the advantage of not being in harms' way. This also keeps the masses from being caught up in the atrocities that may be unfolding due to lack of information when horrible events unfold. In this way, the suffering is marginalized. Conclusion, we are all marginalized. How significant is that?

Mantra

"I will not be a part of state-sponsored terrorism." Consider making this your mantra. The objective and dominion ought to be to confine members who have committed or have the propensity for grave harmful acts. No military apparatuses are needed. No executions are ever needed as is also stated in a Nexus Pentarchy Prime Tenet.

Achieve Harmonic Balance

The Nexus, based on sentients' acute awareness of their affinity to their environmental surroundings, have the wisdom to promote minimal impacts to their environmental surroundings by implementing methods and practices that do just that. All of Earth's inhabitants can then direct their activities to return to that which is natural and to once again achieve harmonic balance with Nature. To hear the continuous symphony that never loses its wondrous inspiration and awe promotes a sentient to likewise achieve harmonic balance.

Supreme Being's Expression Of Beauty

Do you not like your human form? Do you identified as male or female or both? Are you cursed? What was the Supreme Being's purpose with the form that you have, you ask? Was it a joke on the form that was created by the Supreme Being? Pause for a moment and consider these questions. Could it really be a form whereby one can work out notions in the present so as to take steps to find your way back to your Supreme Being? If the last question is so, then your form is beautiful! Why hide it? It is part of an ever-expressing and beautiful landscape. It is a part of the Supreme Being's expression of beauty and its many variations that can add substance and form to everything else in the Universe. Recordings are preserved for the ages.

Enablers

Constructs that exclude when no grave harmful events or acts are present are in fact – as viewed through the perspectives of those who are excluded – very violent and destructive towards them and surrounding environments. This form of terrorism cannot long endure. Those who subscribe to these constructs are enablers of terrorist practices. Terrorism continues in infamy unless enablers condemn no more. Take charge and remove exclusionary constructs from the equation. By accomplishing this feat, The Many Millennia War ceases. It starts with the word. Consider adding to the crescendo with your utterance.

It Looks Very Familiar

"At the end of the day" was a rallying call or catch-phrase in Recent Historical References to mean the universal view of journeys by those who subscribe to this all-purpose rallying call or catch-phrase. This short-sighted view results in repeating the same set of days in infamy. Hence, having this view is to be struck-in-time for non-spiritually developed entities. It is odd that these same repeating days are experienced over and over again by them. Their limited insights have the affect of entrapping them into periodically asking themselves this question, how did I get here? This same periodic question gets asked because the same things are habitually being done. The answer was always with them if only they can project past the same "end of the day" rut. The end of days will be made unstuck when there is deviation from doing the same things again. Repeatedly falling into the same rut was made by choice. It looks very familiar to you. Try to see beyond that.

Try Not To Oscillate

The practice of genocide is what nation-states throughout history are known for. They call it "just wars". In actuality, they are not just when the result is to annihilate all opposition even when only a minority of the "enemy population" has the propensity for grave harmful acts directed towards them. It matters very little to them because all enemies of the "great nation-state", or rather the collective, is seen as such. Many have rose to their own "great" stature with their view regarding those who are not with them or those who will not kowtow to their wishes that would routinely have the distinction of being labeled "enemies of the state" applied to all in the collective. Hence, they are classified as sub-humans or animals for being non-subjects of feudal nation-state empires so that it is "easy" and more efficient to eradicate them once and for all. To strip any legal protection for the warring barbarians means that there is "legal cover" for extermination campaigns and hence, genocidal missions for the total elimination of the perceived threat so that the enemy population will be forever miniscule of their former self. As is the prevailing view, enemies of the state will never again be equable opposing foes in being even a mildly effective "threat" to the victor's "way of civilized life". In actuality, to be civilized is to behave in a barbarous destructive behavior, which is very much sanctioned by the state. Are you a friend of a just society? Your fate depends on your answer. For sentients, your answer is only relevant in the here and now. In spiritual developmental terms, the affirmative means to be stuck in time with no movement along one's spiritual developmental path. Those who have acumen, developmental opportunities do readily present themselves. The axiom of "looking out, looking in" type experiences are provided. How many times does one chooses to oscillate back and forth with no stopping? It may appear to be a pendulum swing, but in terms of time, it is a stationary point. To not remain at this stationary point depends on the word that will be uttered. To move from a stationary point means the expiration of all feudal-states. Their reliance and credo to defend "at all costs" to include "justifiable" military-like offensive campaigns for total destruction and the elimination of "high value" targets by any means necessary is the extreme. Those caught in "collateral damage" kill zone nets have "no legal standing" or "of value" for those who were just in the way of munitions firing. Which side do you choose? Maybe, you do not have that choice when you are subjects to feudal-states or feudal lordships. However, there is a choice not widely being circulating for fear of losing "power" by those who fight for the "status quo". It is this. Eliminate all feudal-states and replace them with an all-inclusive based dominion that promotes sentient pursuits and caretaking. Those with great stature need not apply. We require sentients as caretakers. Choose to not remain at a stationary point. Declare your break from it and try not to oscillate.

Unbridled Property Rights

The superior specie dares to choose other options than the one that returns expired corporeal bodies back to Earth through naturally decaying environments instead of preserving these bodies for long shelf life. Since we take from Nature during corporeal existence, it would be quite natural to return the same back to Nature so that the magnificent balance is preserved. Extraction only policies produce results that perpetuate depletion and the practices of moving on to other cornucopia resources for depletion, and again and again, until the entire collective environments are laid barren for all eternity. What a legacy, if you call it such. Isn't this a desirable goal that we can all be proud of? Feudal systems are based on property rights to be extracted and depleted because it holds "value". The unchecked exercise of these rights is of little consequence in these systems. Without unbridled property rights to include preserved corporeal bodies, feudal systems would crumble. Do you think that this outcome is a bad thing?

No Intelligent Life Here

Feudal systems are based on property rights. This includes members of the master specie. For them, it is something to be proud of when we take everything of value and leave nothing behind. This is our legacy to the end when there will be no one left behind to tell of the historically great legacy we left behind. At that expiration point in time, not even the question, "Were we ever here?", would be asked. Everything turned to dust. In the grand scheme of things, our time here is miniscule, unless we choose otherwise. Future travelers will take readings and find that there is no intelligent life here.

The Awakening

It matters that we are here today. The bigger question is this. Do you want to wake up or sleepwalk in the limited confines of your own self-imposed imprisonment? Be one of the ones that have already chosen to wake up. Many have been awake for some time now. Think about what you have missed by remaining asleep, at the dawn of the awakening.

Collapse Is Catastrophic

When the belief in feudal systems expire due in large part to remedies carried out by sentients everywhere, believers will dwindle in numbers over a period of time. When numbers dwindle below a sustainable level, collapse is catastrophic for the feudal constructs, as they should. The era of sentient development will be universal, as it should. Don't be surprise. This is what we have been working towards, a sentient-based dominion. You are property no more.

Privileged Opportunity

How sad it is when there are those who consider themselves above all others who are denied access to privileges afforded to these "special elites".

This elitist view insists that only elitists have rights to privileges that are denied to the masses. With this view, the elitists can even look at sentients struggling to survive as if they were watching a nature video recording on animal life. Are you now watching a nature movie having popcorn, candy, and beverages? Are you comfy? We don't want you to suffer needlessly. After all, you are one of the chosen ones. The view of sentients as animals is sad indeed. If you are fooled into believing this, then your privilege in looking out will provide you the same privileged opportunity for looking in.

Nature's Sphere Of Influences

There are many stories about predators from the wild encroaching onto feudal state enclaves. One story this scribe came across is about a mother bear and her cubs. The mother bear attacked and killed three people in the Spring of 2010. The mother bear was "euthanize" for leading the "killings", but the cubs were allowed to be placed in a zoo. The hypocrisy is that a "court" ruled as if the bears are "subjects" of a feudal-state. The cubs were given a reprieve due to being non-adults. Animals per court rulings are not bound by Nature's Laws, but by non-nature's laws. The hypocrisy in this ruling is that animals have no legal standing in a "court of law". Therefore, how can courts be caretakers? The notion that wild animals must also comply with feudal nation-state laws is ludicrous. The feudal construct also extends to all feudal subjects in being compliant and domiciled. This notion to extend this precedence to the Wilds of Nature is contradictory to the precedence that insists that wild animals need to survive on their own. Encroachments reduce their survival rate and the use of their instincts. These contradictory notions or precedents that compels animals to behave in a domesticated manner around legally-standing feudal subjects that are exclusively of "Homo sapiens" specie and still be able to have behavior capabilities to survive in the wild with predatory abilities, if a predator. The Homo sapiens should know better. Yet, these and other contradictory feudal notions prevail. These unnatural notions promote the extinction of species in the wild. Pause for a moment. Is extinction what we ought to be promoting? Consider that we need instead to be cognizant of the

Rules of Nature for inhabitants in the wild. The preferred outcome is to have a caretaking framework whereby wise Nature-Centric outcomes prevail. The transition towards this framework is for every feudal construct supporting judiciaries to expire. This is accomplished through efforts to expire them through the spanning of feudal state enclaves within sentient sphere of influences dominion, one feudal-state enclave at a time. The replacement dominion regarding caretaking of Nature's Environments benefits all inhabitants of Nature's Sphere of Influences. All can coexist. Duty caretakers are needed to reduce sentients' impacts to Nature's Environments. Your developmental pursuit is assured when you answer the call to be caretaker volunteers as well. Consider answering this call. To counter threats of the wild, allow for ample Nature's Preserve Domains and be astute caretakers in Nature's inhabitant encroachment on sentient environments. The recommendation is to make the first-approach remedy be to capture and return strays back into the wilds at a safe distance away. Euthanize of stray animals to include predatory ones is to be avoided whenever possible. Be caretakers first.

Taking Turns In Rescue Operations

For journalists, photographers, reporters, and other similar duty caretakers, take turns in being a part of the rescue operations being observed. Quickly agree on overlapping coverage observation activities to ensure ample recordings of the events. At various times during our lives, we are all caretakers.

Single Events

It gets very lonely and the feel of isolation while in a society that excludes you. Poetic justice occurs when you take into consideration that the atrocities you may have done in another sojourn may have contribute to you current experiences. Some may have even participated in genocidal campaigns. These campaigns were propagated on "indigenous inhabitants" by far superior "civilized societies". You must have wondered how these "great societies" can be so blind by their own terrorist onslaughts. These terrorists did put their minds at ease by referring to the original inhabitants as savages and sub-humans. In this way, only civilized members who were killed or injured in eradicating campaigns were seriously recorded and counted. Those viewed as savages that were killed or injured were given estimated numbers with the ultimate objective of committing total annihilation of these inhabitants to clear the way for civilized society to flourish. This objective would be considered a single event even when it spanned many centuries for total eradication. The post-event meant that the civilized society is thriving, now that the threat to their way of life was wiped out or their numbers were greatly reduced once and for all. Do not be fooled. In historical terms, their greatness was fleeting and is identified as single events. For many who are lonely and isolated, your experiences may be opportunities to reflect on the harm that was done to your fellow sentients. Consider challenging yourselves to learn from these disturbing events. The more that you can recall these events, the quicker you can then separate yourself from these single events and follow the sentient way.

In The Specialization Of Their Crafts

Judiciary agencies are not caretakers nor can they ever be transformed into one. Why put even a morsel of faith in such artificial constructs? It knows only how to condemn with their finality and extreme rulings. Instead, consider putting your faith in caretaking activities. Ensure that sentients are certified in the specialization of their crafts.

The Condemning Business

One needs to get out of the condemning business no matter how religiously or faith-based it proclaims to be. The notion of "do no harm" should always be applied, don't you think? With condemning, there is always a link to terrorist related activities.

An Avalanche Of Barren Voids

The culture of human/animal/plant disposal often requires preservation burial or oven cremation. This is an assault on the environments from optimally rejuvenating the same. Total extractions are made without reclamation. The notion of superiority by "Homo sapiens" over nature by taking more than what is essential for corporeal health with the (total) removal of nutrients that would also be nutrients for other corporeal inhabitants often contributes to the point of their own extinction. Our arrogance in hoarding while other life forms suffocate, extinguish, or get squeezed out through extinction practices is widely acceptable in feudal constructs based on feudal property rights. This is unacceptable in a sentient caretaking framework. When corporeal life cycle is completed, then the Doctrine of Reclamation of Expired Corporeal Garb is to return it to natural surroundings so that the natural decomposition can nurture the next generation of corporeal life. This is the natural order of things. For sentients with higher levels of awareness, continuous extraction with little to no regard to other inhabitants and the surrounding in severely reduced reclamation practices results in total extinctions for all inhabitants over time. To think that it cannot happen to oneself reinforced with the notion that it will not happen in one's current and only life cycle journey is folly. This may be true if a single life cycle is eternal. However, the reality is that the continuum is true. As it pertains to this topic, a balancing event occurs when an avalanche of barren voids is cascaded.

Robot Or Automaton

You must be a robot or automaton because you are very mechanical in your practices. Try following the sentient way in everything that you do.

Practices Of Hoarding

Practices of hoarding to extinction yield barren and toxic lands and waterways. The results are always the same. There is nowhere to escape from them and towards a favorable environment when the race to traverse to the remaining favorable environments for hoarding claims diminishes to zero. Extinction is assured and awaits those who practice hoarding. In the end, this becomes your environment for sustenance. Any grubs left?

Be Mindful Of Nature's Dominion

In Recent Historical References, there is a story of a non-human animal, a bear from the wild, that was hunted down and killed for biting and killing a child. This was sanctioned by applying feudal laws to domains that were defined by perimeter markings. This is contradictory when a preserve is defined as wilderness and is separate from an area defined for civilized activities. A Nexus Prime Directive declares that Nature's Dominion determinations apply when preserves are mapped out. Defensive activities, when threatened to include areas attached to civilized ones, are permissible to include protective weapon usage. Once the wild environmental event has subsided and there is no clear and present threat, no hunting and pursuit of the threatening animal is permissible. The return to Nature's Dominion activities applies for non-sentient corporeal entities. Duty caretakers who are certified for the health and welfare of these preserves will assume their duties in this area. They will perform their duties based on guidelines defined for the caretaking activities in the preservation of life pursuits of in-the-wild inhabitants when no threat is present and escalating up towards extinguishing of any animal when extreme grave harmful acts are present and there is no other alternative option is available. Be ever mindful of Nature's Dominion when in her preserves.

Good Stories, Bad Stories

Using the grave societal tribe events that are occurring in other faraway lands as footnotes to be given cursory mention and not the grave urgency awareness for the collective of nation-states to address, the worth or value of these tribes did not equal their own feudal subjects' worth or value. The insistence on "major news" and other governmental organizations to report on far more "good" stories than "bad" ones was practice so as not to have members dwell on life and death stories occurring in faraway lands. The bad stories ought to have been in the forefront to address these matters for urgent remedies. Hence, the good stories were distractions from the important matters of the day. The notion that a single nation-state cannot afford to address every calamity may be too much to ask for it to address was a widely held excuse. The need for all feudal states to take action ought to have been the preferred optimum response. However the individual feudal nation-states as they are, every feudal nation-state of the collective would expect someone else to resolve the calamities. Each felt secured within their perimeters. Why hold on to such barbaric and self serving belief systems? For sentients, this behavior will not do. The long-term remedy is to remove all feudal-states and their perimeters so that these inhibitors can no longer get in the way in going the distance in resolving grave events anywhere they may occur. In their places, choose an all-inclusive framework. This framework is by far a more superior protecting structure. In this framework, the right-sized determined dominion that spans all that are affected in the events as they are occurring can effectively engaged without delay. We require that sentients be in charge and not the substitute guise of artificial entities.

An Avalanche Affect

There will those observers who will, after reading entries by this scribe, watch for a period of time and then would declare that there appears to be no direct corollary by the entries so written, or so it is thought. Consider this analogy. At the top of a snow-packed mountain, a small snow disturbance could occur that would press on the snow below it, collect more of it, and then press on the snow below that, collect more of it. This would repeat over and over again, which will have a cascading effect in collecting more snow and also picking up speed. The observers at the bottom of the mountain would not see the early stages of this event. A little while later, it would be too late whereby they would soon be buried by an avalanche and most likely perish under the weight of the snow collective. Using this analogy, the entries by this scribe when uttered even in the privacy of one's enclave or abode will have an avalanche affect. With your persistence pondering and gathering awareness collective, a favorable outcome awaits you. You will not perish. Others may not fare as well.

Up-Close Journey Of Splendor

Just like the stars up above, we can also be viewed as being tiny twinkles in the vast expanse while at the same time and viewed up close, our presence is much, much, more splendor. With this awareness, we have the capacity and capability to shine the light on even the darkest reaches of life. Consider heightening your awareness for life, which is omnipresent. It will lead to a very interesting up-close journey of splendor.

Make It Your Remedy

Feudal perimeter fence removal remedies are good for sentients everywhere. The removals of them allows for free traversing anywhere in the known Expanse and Beyond without dealing with artificial obstacles. Make it your remedy.

Seek Out A Caretaker

We require caretakers be in charge and not caregivers. Caregivers are bound by judicial sterility. In contrast, caretakers will find the best approach to caretaking effectiveness. This scribe will seek out a caretaker anytime.

A Sentient Being

Are you a sentient or a sentient being? A sentient being has characteristics of a sentient. A sentient has universal awareness.

Suite Up And Enjoy The Ride

Some are baffled regarding the notion that spiritual entities suit up in corporeal garbs so as to work on notions regarding spiritual development. For them, understanding an existence not in corporeal garb is elusive. Yet, riding another kind of corporeal garb like a horse, goat, camel, or elephant seems to be quite natural. To them, riding will seem very familiar. The question that they would often ask is this. "Where have I seen this before?" Yet still for them, understanding their own ride of a lifetime is puzzling. The advice that this scribe can provide is that when it's your time, suit up and enjoy the ride.

Release The Potential

Release the potential of sentients everywhere by working towards removing all perimeters and by condemning no more. Continue your efforts by spanning out to the reaches of the Expanse and Beyond. You will meet others who are already there to help in this very noblest of destination journey.

A Momentous Moment

Do you think that you can really get away with grave and/or terrorist acts? Or is it the element of surprise to complete these acts in their totality so that there is no recall by all those that you directed your acts towards since they would have been terminated? Then you are fooling yourself. Someone will remember when there is recall in a different sojourn. For the ones who commit these acts, you will find yourself to be stuck-in-time with no recall as to how you got here in the present. You will experience in kind that which you have committed. Your experiences will be tortuous and painful. Unbeknownst to you, sojourns are available to understand all sides of your actions. To go beyond being stuck in a playback loop, aspire to be at-one-ment with All-That-Is. When there is a semblance of recall, this semblance is the reveling indicator that a sentient is nudging from a stationary position with a way being illuminating to move further along one of many paths towards higher levels of awareness. This event would be a momentous moment. Consider taking one of the sentient paths being illuminating when it is revealed. Your playback loop is ending.

Always Close By

The word has always been yours to freely embrace. The word was always there for anyone to hear if one was to just tune in. The word has been there since the beginning of time. It is why the Expanse exist. The Expanse is there for sentients everywhere to reach for on their way towards the outer reaches of spiritual at-one-ment. Would you rather the word not be so far? For some, the word would not be worth the effort and, sadly for them, the word would become out of reach for them. This is not true for highly enlightened sentients. For these sentients, the word was always close by.

No Longer Have Defensible Borders

This scribe is not here to run a political campaign. Instead, she is here to put forth a new vision whereby sentients everywhere can more effectively pursue sentient endeavors. There are no hidden agendas. Expiration of all terrorist constructs is the speediest way forward in realizing a Sentient Expanse. This is accomplished by building a Nexus Pentarchy Prime Framework. No perimeters exist in this framework for terrorists to pursue the usage of any weapons in their arsenals in the "defense" of arbitrarily drawn borders. None will exist. With this Sentient Framework, terrorist organizations will no longer have defenses behind borders nor be able to cross borders to execute terrorist campaigns. There will be nowhere to hide for terrorist organizations. As described elsewhere, the Nexus Pentarchy Prime Rapid Response Auspices are chartered to track down and confine anyone who have committed grave harmful acts or have a propensity for the same. There are literally no borders to get in the way of Rapid Response Auspices duties.

Real Or Imagined

When one passes on from a corporeal realm, does one go from one feudal state to another? Does your feudal constructed view insist that it be a heritage that anchors a line of inheritance of subjects to the same feudal state? Is this the brainwashing that instills loyalty to feudal lords since there can only be one? Do you want to be stuck-in-time with no deviation from your strongly held set of beliefs? Do you feel that to let go will mean that you will be obliterated and will no longer have stature or cease to exist due to no inheritance? Are you so woven into your corporeal garb that to expose your true naked self would be abhorrent and would leave you vulnerable to the elements? Finally, are you real or imagined? These are some of the many questions being asked of one's self as it pertains to one's place in life. Why not see a different view with you in it? In this view, there is nothing anchoring you to the past.

From Within One's Inner Core

What do you think? Do you think that your essence evaporates once your corporeal existence expires? Do you think that any trace of your identity evaporates as well? Do you think that your supreme being has put an expiration date on your very existence? Is that what you think? Try searching from within one's inner core for the true answers. The answers have been there from the beginning. The word also existed since the beginning. The word is how we got to where we are. Those who cannot hear the word are stuck-in-time. Those who can hear the word have moved on. May the word be with you also.

Where You Needed To Be

If you have an impulse to restore or fix an abode even if renting or for a short stay, then you have a genuine interest for the next tenant to have better abode accommodations. This impulse may very well be to atone for the sojourns of destructive pursuits and tendencies that you have taken during those experiences. The journey for atonement may be long. This long journey would assure that the continuation of your spiritual pursuits is viable. Once you do return to your spiritual pursuits, you will look back and see that the journey was not long at all. It got you to where you needed to be. Congratulations.

Rock Solid

Mathematics, science, theology, and the like – fields someone like Socrates would study in earnest – present steps to higher levels of awareness whereby a seemly rock solid assertion can be knocked off by a more unified assertion that was brought forth complete with reasoning and derivation findings. This more unified assertion would then gain wide acceptance with the previous one tagged as incomplete. To mock the earlier rock solid assertion, where the footing at the time was perceived to be on solid rock, hampers and delays those that mock in their ascension towards a higher level of awareness. In their stationary place, in a sense, they are mocked as well. Consider that all steps of bold assertions are needed to move forward and reach the next ascension. Each new awareness step taken invites one to take another, and another without end, should one dares to. To dare does not mean to leave others behind. Rather, it is to pave the path for others to follow. Be that bold trailblazer.

The Word Connects Us All

Recent Historical References provide many historical examples of perceived "greatness" by nation-states through exclusionary participation practices on the masses. However, that greatness was fleeting. For those who are excluded, the word is uttered and set into motion. It gains speed and strength as more sentients utter the word. The word accelerates and covers great distances in the Expanse and Beyond. The word connects us all. The result is that the artificially created greatness is extinguished and then an inclusive framework takes over.

Greatly Diminished Or Extinguished

When an entity's beliefs and adherence to an artificial construct – feudal nation-state framework – is present, then her awareness of humanity is greatly diminished or extinguished. With this view, violence towards non-believers ensues by default. Is this the state that you have chosen to thrive in? When one sees no other choice, then all of humanity will likewise be extinguished. Can anyone really thrive in a world without humanity?

Feudal Constructed Abyss

Leave feudal believers and loyalists to their feudal constructed abyss. Oddly, who would want to go there? No sentient that I know of.

The Same Condemning Feudal Conditional State

No healing is possible when condemning is ever present. Remove condemning from remedies crafted and then healing can commence. How many sojourns do you require to come to the realization that the removal of condemning from your activities is essential to spiritual growth? In addition and by extension, do you want to be stuck-in-time whereby condemning consumes you to more ugliness? More of the same to both questions if that be your choice. You may be influence by feudal lords, which may be the root of this serious problem. Take heart. Know that you can be a part of a transitional team towards a Sentient Framework environment and not be a participant in perpetuating the same condemning feudal conditional state. Take heart and condemn no more.

Conjoined

There is this notion by some that others who perform specific terrorist acts and techniques within their own nation-state's perimeters is absolutely unacceptable. However, when this same nation-state performs the same horrific terrorist acts and techniques on others outside its perimeters, they are done for the specific purpose of self-preservation. These nation-states' acts are construed and argued to be legally-derived actionable acts that permit them to be sanctioned by the state. In actuality, they are nothing more than terrorist acts by any other name. This dichotomy reinforces the vicious loop of a continuum of looking in and looking out. Both views are identical, which is why supporters on both sides are conjoined in a perpetually state of being stuck-in-time.

Uplifted

Is to snuff out life your mission in life? Does performing this mission make everyone in society safer? Do you want to condemn and execute in perpetuity? Should we instead be celebrating all life and be developing our spiritual self for at-one-ment? These are choices that each one of us can make. Choose wisely and be uplifted. Amen.

To Die For

There is no doubt by believers, as a patriotic gesture, to die for one's county, which is an artificial construct, than to die for Nature and her Life Forces, which is not artificial. Therefore, to be patriotic means to inflict death to all of Nature since you will not come to her aid. To be patriotic is sad indeed for everyone.

The Assault On Nature's Diversity

It may be 100% efficient in the eradication of all "weeds" and "pests" by the use of extreme toxins and extermination practices. However, the end result is one of a number of Nature's catastrophic events that will occur over time depending on the reach of these practices. Short-term gains produce long-term barrenness and voids of natural habitats. Extreme eradication efficiencies will cause the eradication of Nature's sustainable and thriving cornucopia environments. For sentients, it is acutely understood that diversity always works to Nature's advantage and also to sentient's advantage as well. When man-kind or woman-kind choose to be apart from Nature, then the spiritual at-one-ment path is also eradicated. The assault on Nature's Diversity is an assault on us as well.

An At-One-Ment Moment

For those with a heightened level of awareness, it is not totally accurate to be labeled a sentient being. Rather, it is all about being a sentient. That awareness of being is what separates a sentient being from one who has a heightened awareness of being a sentient. Having this awareness is truly an at-one-ment moment.

Big Brother

I did not abuse my privacy. Big brother did. Should embarrassing clips be shown, do not apologize. Expose the big brother who did.

To Feel Without Touching

There are those who rigidly aligned to the notion that one needs to cut and probe live creatures of Nature in order to gain knowledge and understanding even when no concerning need exists. To state that we can only rely on our five senses as the only senses that we can use in providing "real" truths and conclusions is simply not so. Here are a couple of examples. One can "see" without eyes. One can "hear" without ears. One can "feel" without touching. One can provide more examples of dualities. To use capabilities beyond the "real senses" demonstrates a higher level of understanding. The corporeal existence with the five senses allows spiritual entities to step into a world that allows her to be alive with wonder, feelings, thoughts, etc. This affords the entity to ponder her existence without overloading her senses in order to narrow the stream of thoughts. Experience them for yourselves. You will find that there is really no need to cut and probe with a scalpel.

Colorful Panoramic View

Regarding the reoccurring conflict and slaughtering events, can you remember it well? If so, then how many times are you going to participate in these events before you take a different path to resolve the type of conflicts that kept you stuck-in-time? Please do not say that it was due to the colorful panoramic view. There is nothing spectacular about it.

Put Things Into Focus

How do you see the world? Is it a condemning one? Is it a exclusionary one? Is it a violent one? Is it an unending state-of-war one? If you can only see a world in terms of these and other examples that you can include, then this scribe does not see through your eyes. This scribe does not view through the same prism that you use. Change your prism and your world view will change to match this scribe. This may take some time and effort to see for yourself. Spiritual development is needed to put things into focus.

Extreme Behaviors

Compare extreme elitist determination outcomes versus all inclusive sentient determination outcomes. With extreme behaviors, they lead to extreme finality outcomes. Watch for these questions or catch-phrases to spot extremism.

A) Are you a subject?
B) Are you a citizen?
C) Are you in or out?
D) Are you with us or against us?
E) You are either with us or against us.
F) Enemies of the state.
G) To defend at all costs
H) High value targets

I) Collateral damage
J) By any means necessary
K) Nothing is off the table

Extremism triggers eradication practices to be applied. For extremists, there is no in-between or middle ground. For non-extremists, an all inclusive view encourages all to participate in negotiating optimum outcomes. So, are you an extremist, or not? You can decide.

Aware Versus Hidden

Sentient aware versus sentient hidden. It is not that a sentient is hidden because she does not want to be found. Rather, a sentient needs to have awareness of self before the hidden sentient can be spotted.

Invincibility Mystique Aura

Wise rulings very often fall through the judiciary cracks. It will not be long before the collection of cracks will crumble the very foundation of the once superior artificial construct that was believed to be so invincibly. All chambers were believed at one time or another to have this invincibility mystique aura about them only to decay with time. Artificial constructs do not endure. Fortunately, spiritual entities do.

Beware Of Well Meaning Adults

There are times when observing children closely that some of the children do not see themselves as children. They seem to be partially in corporeal realm and more so still in spiritual realm, playing and communicating in ways that are other than by using their senses. Their innocent touch allows them to being a strong link to a higher realm of existence. Those children who are angry or bitter are due to being fully cast in corporeal form in large part due to the insistence of "well meaning adults" who lost their own link connections a long time ago. It is also oftentimes true that some of the children in corporeal realm find themselves not understanding how they got here. There is no mystery here. They too were "well meaning adults" who suppressed their own innocent childhood awareness of playing in the spiritual realm. If one can recapture that childhood essence again in one's lifetime, it is an indicator of a very heighten level of awareness. For children everywhere, beware of well meaning adults. Be empathetic to their adult-like behaviors.

Streak Across The Sky

Like a shooting star, there are shooting thoughts and shooting ideas in a trail of flames that flash across the conscious skies at great speed. It is inspirational! In order for it to be noticed and to be in awed of it, one needs to look up in the direction of the stars. Hopefully, it will inspire you and not see the streaking as short-lived when not entering the atmosphere as it passes your world. Consider imagining being along side of the tail as if you were on a spiritual quest that spans many lifetimes as you streak across the sky. In this way, your spiritual quest will take you to distant reaches of the Universe and towards higher levels of awareness. Your travels will inspire others who you just passed along the way.

Bravado Achievement

Homo sapiens consider themselves to be supreme above all others of Nature's Life-forms. At times, some Homo sapiens in certain professional disciplines would observe various Nature's Life-Form types and learn their uniquely and remarkable behaviors, abilities, and capabilities that they are designed to do. This gave the superior specie's professional pause. The superior professionals would try to imitate Nature's Life-Forms' unique behaviors as part of their own movements. When they could not, then they created apparatuses that would mimic their remarkable abilities and capabilities. There have been many failed attempts before small successes. Small successes lead to greater successes. Do you think that Homo sapiens would ever be able to create such "marvels of human inventions" without being first inspired by the marvels of Nature first? This scribe dares to say no. And yet, once Home sapiens have mastered the wonders of the world did they then lose interest in Nature's marvels even though the imitation of these marvels helped in elevating Homo sapiens with capability-rich experiences and expressions in their own lives. The Homo sapiens would then feel superior to Nature's wonders, which lead to enforce the concept of properties based on perceived values. An artificial construct that views everything in terms of "property rights" and "profits and losses" was erected to contain this wealth. Those non-Homo sapiens species and their environments were considered of low value, which oftentimes lead to extinction and barrenness. This trampling showed their true "superior" nature or lack thereof. A sentient, however, would think and state how arrogant Homo sapiens are to view Nature's bounty as less than sterling value! There is no caretaking here, only destructive behaviors and the hoarding of rich resources deemed of high wealth. The race towards complete depletion was on. Once the resources have been extracted to completion, these once valued resources to include Nature's Life-forms would exist no more. The thinking at the time is that there are countless number and variety of species left. Therefore, there would not be a noticeable impact to the extinguishing of a small number of these species. However, the consequences in the acceleration of depletion activities resulted in the extinction of more and more species. Species' viability is secondary to Homo sapiens' who are "masters" of their universe or a small part of it. Would the masters continue to be viable and have the comforts they come to enjoy when all non-Homo sapiens become extinct as well due to Homo sapiens neglect? If this "bravado achievement" is reached, then Nature's sustainability of rich resources resulted in total exhaustion. The "last specie standing" also became extinct as well. It started with Nature's rich bounty. It finished with complete and total depletion and extinction. One could conclude that this is Nature's Cycle of Life. Do you want to make that claim? Besides, there will be no one left to arrive at this conclusion and, by extension, finally realize that we are all part of Nature's journey. When nothing else remains, other world visitors may stop by. They would only have one conclusion. No forms of life exist here nor ever did. What planet are you from?

Do Not Look Back

Fewer and fewer feudal believers will remain behind. Do not look back to see how many are left. Yours is to look forward to no longer be considered a feudal subject ever again.

Going Crazy

The Nexus Pentarchy Prime Framework is a structure for sentients who are aware of their sentient-hood and/or on a quest for the same ascension levels of universal awareness. In Recent Historical References, there were those who were not aware of their sentient-hood nor on a quest to understand what it means. They have predominantly chosen to be, believed in being, comfortable with being, and/or identified as subjects of feudal lords. The remaining ones were fearful of going crazy due to not having any association with feudal lords who hunt them down to be tortured, abused, and possibly be put to death. Fear not. You are a sentient. Focus on building a replacement foundation that will serve all sentients' needs and your fears will evaporate. Feudal lords need not apply.

Battlefield Heroes

Some believe that "heroics" are found on the battle fields. Those who do based their notions on "physical" observations primarily due to their being completely immersed in corporeal garb. In actuality, heroics are found when one utters the word even when her corporeal termination is near to be carried out by those same battlefield "heroes".

A Sentient Can Sense Them

Many will rely on "physical" observations and evidence using only their five senses to "prove" an absolute conclusion. No observations and evidence using other than the five sensory capabilities are permitted in providing additional proofs that can rendered a far better conclusion. It is as if their five senses keep them from being aware of heightened senses that cannot be measured using only the five "physical senses". A sentient can sense them.

At The End Of The Day

"At the end of the day" is a time to rest and reflect on the events of the day. It is followed by a new day. This phrase was often used in Recent Historical References to mean a finality expectation being met in a single day, so to speak. For those described in historical references, one might be frustrated and disappointed to learn that one day is not enough for the particular challenge being worked on. Why not consider choosing to rest and reflect on the events of the day followed by a continuation on the following day. After all, one is on a longer journey that can prove fruitful in reaching a higher level of awareness, which cannot be achieved in a single day. One may find that it is worth pursuing. Have faith in knowing that you will arrive there one day.

Terrorism Made Obsolete

If you do not want to be in a terrorist construct, then replace this construct to one that you do want to be in. Consider a Sentient Framework that promotes sentient pursuits and practices. In this Sentient Framework, terrorism was made obsolete and not used in its construction. This is the solid foundation that provides an environment for sentients to thrive in.

Let Us Go Forward From Here

Removal of feudal constructs does have a direct cause and effect for feudal entities called corporations. The special "personhood" status and associated privileges that are awarded this special status for these artificial entities will no longer exist. The recognition of sentients everywhere in the Expanse is the only recognition whereby only sentients have dominion privileges. Let's reflect on this. We truly have come a long ways in recognizing sentients. Let us go forward from here and not fall back into artificiality.

Child's Play

It is through feudal terrorist actions and the judiciary that entities are hesitant in becoming sentient-aware. They are terrorized in witnessing others being tortured and then tried for promoting "subversive threats against the state" by being sentient. This then is the greatest threat to any feudal state is to be a sentient. Yes, sentients are aware of being the greatest threat to all feudal states because these states are not recognized in Sentient Dominion activities. We require that sentients be involved in all matters of sentient activities. As more sentients became self-aware, more and more feudal states will disappear. Indeed, they were artificial in nature and figments of feudal lords' imagination. In other words, it is child's play. Sentient understanding and knowledge can be quite terrifying to a child.

The Great Dam

A crack in the dam started with the utter of the word. The "great dam" represents the "greatest nation-state" of its time that held to the notion that it was invincible to any disruptions by small actors. The dam represents the hoarding of valuable natural resources. However, things did "fall through the cracks" due to not being aware of them. As more and more utters the word, more cracks in the great dam will appear without being noticed. This will lead to the chipping away of this great structure and ultimately, the crumbling of this "great" dam into rubble. The resources will once again flow and return to the natural order of things. There are no cracks in Nature. Everyone can share in its bounty.

The Set Of Notions

As a sentient ascends to higher and higher levels of awareness, the expanding spiritual achievements in fully understanding the essence at the current level of awareness before the ascension, enjoys the satisfaction at completing the set of notions that were suggested to be worked out.

At the next level, a new set of notion challenges are brought to the fore in awareness to be worked on to completion before the next ascension. The continuum is truly awe-inspiring. Try to be understanding for those working on notions for levels of awareness that you have ascended from. The challenges are not insignificant as you can attest to this. Consider being their guide.

Buried In Their Own Rubble

Those who subscribe to feudal systems will be buried along with these systems in their own rubble.

A Legal Standing

It is a legal matter to condemn. By extension, it is a legal matter to condemn sentients for being sentients based on having or not having "a legal standing". A legal standing is awarded to those subjects decreed by feudal lords to have. It is not a sentient matter to condemn. It is a sentient matter to recognize all sentients for being sentients. There is no legal standing needed as a precedent for sentient recognition. Hence, a legal standing has no equivalent legal standing in sentient matters. It simply does not exist.

Attain The Same Awareness

A corporeal entity may not always recall all her corporeal experiences. Fortunately, the spiritual entity recalls everything. Hence, nothing is ever forgotten. The extent of recall in corporeal realm is based on the attainment of higher levels of awareness in spiritual maturity. Hence, a mature spiritual entity remembers everything. One needs only to attain this same awareness to recall everything.

Cult Indoctrination

For those who still believe in feudal constructs and who cannot identify with a Sentient Framework, you belief grip will not allow you to let go due to your extensive feudal conformity behavior shaping accomplished through feudal reinforcement practices. Yes, this was forced upon them. However, others did evolve beyond this cult indoctrination. If the cult followers can compose themselves and find the courage to evolve beyond their cult's grip of obedience, then your path towards sentient freedom and pursuits awaits you. Come help shape the framework that can be a beacon for other feudal believers who are not as courageous as you in helping them find their way towards sentient freedom.

Doomed To Perpetual War

If one does not trust sentients, then one is doomed to perpetual war, a war that one started and that one continues to maintain. The Many Millennia War will continue in perpetuity until one is able to identify herself as a sentient. A higher level of awareness is needed for this to happen. Remove yourself from the battlefield and you may have a chance at at-one-ment. Others will take notice and follow your lead.

Terrorists At Bay

You will continue to remain a terrorist as long as you continue to take the path that is not the sentient way. Maintaining a vigil around a secured perimeter is a feudal attempt by a failed state. The entrenchment will not keep other terrorists at bay for long. They know how you think.

Can You Hear It Clearly Now?

Blind adherence to "the rule of law" may lead to spiritual sterility for a universal period of time, unless an awareness of a faint utterance of the word can be heard. The word gets more pronounced as one ascends through each level of awareness. Can you hear it clearly now?

Hope In Life

Many have spoken these words, "Life is not fair!" We are led to believe that this is to be an accepted reality fact. Acceptance of those spoken words is one perspective. Taking the perspective that life can be fair will aid in extending this notion to the reality that "the rule of law" is not. With this latter perspective, it promotes the existence in the possibility of hope. Hope is not alive in those having the first perspective reality. Maybe for them, there is no hope in life. Is this your reality? Sentients have a reality to kindle hope and watch the blossoming of life's brilliance, the light that is in all of us. Have faith that there is hope for a life that is fair. Reach out to a sentient to help guide you.

The Plights Of Others

To not see, not hear, not feel, not taste, and not smell are significant and telling characteristics of a non-sentient-aware entity. These characteristics may help explain the sad view of invisibility by this entity on the plights of others of nature's inhabitants in their scratching for subsistence. For a sentient-aware entity, she can see, hear, feel, taste, and smell to be able to empathize with the plights of others. Using these senses and other heighten senses, a sentient is astute in uplifting their plights no matter how insignificant an inhabitant may be viewed to be. Through the caretaking activities of all of Nature's inhabitants, spiritual awareness is within reach. To achieve this, you need to utilize all of your senses.

Nature's Spectacle

Choosing not to be duty caretakers to Nature's Varieties of Life Forms in totality consensus will result in Nature's Varieties choosing not to be present for returning sojourns by leaving them to barren panoramas of

161

Nature's Spectacle. Nature will provide whatever reduce-limiting-scale of resource needs that can help sojourns develop the duty caretaking skills and acumen that will help them along the way to enlightenment. Utilizing reduced resources will aid in later sojourns when resources are plentiful in extracting sufficient resources only in order for sustainable resources. In your barren sojourn experience, Nature's Varieties will lie dormant and will be sitting this one out.

The Most Stimulating Focus

By expiring feudal constructs, we will be releasing feudal elites from their own imprisonments. Who is in and who is out becomes a moot point. Condemnation of self is no longer practiced nor enforced. Sentient pursuits would then become the most stimulating focus everywhere in the Nexus Expanse.

From The Light That She Had At One Time

One needs to get out of the condemning business. The effect is to be in a state of perpetual spiritual stagnation, unable to ascend expansion levels of spiritual awareness, but rather and most often in spiraling contraction of spiritual self to a state of wandering in one's many sojourns in find her once greater spiritual self again. The bewilderment is the darkness that one finds herself in from the light that she had at one time. Be not fooled. All insights are withdrawn and hidden due to your continual condemnation. Is this what you seek? If so, then darkness will be around you for some time.

Examples Of Belonging

Of religion, of beliefs, of professional practices, of pursuits; these are examples of belonging. Yes, belonging does allow for one's security and connection to others so as to not be alone. They are some of the environments in which to grow and thrive. Some will hamper your progress and may even keep you in a stationary place unable to make much progress. Some will be conducive to rapid progression. The remainder will fall somewhere in between the two. There are many avenues in not being alone. If you become stationary because you align to some of the avenues that can hamper your progression, then most definitely consider belonging to something else. Be cognizant if you find yourself stuck-in-time. It is not easy to determine. Try to find someone who is not and go in her direction. At least you will be making progress.

The Many Different Refuge Types

Having refuges for Nature's Ecosystems and the caretaking thereof allows for the many different refuge types to "experience" the tranquility by the relatively much small numbers in each type of species than were prevalent in the surrounding natural environments long before the setting aside and observance of these refuges. The concerted caretaking efforts will ensure that Nature will not degenerate into barren land-scapes and water-scapes existence. The greater the numbers experiencing eradication practices beyond the refuges, the harder it is to properly take care of the threatened and remaining ones. When they go, all will be extinct. Consider allowing greater numbers of the many different types to co-exist. You will find that in this way, it is many magnitudes easier to maintain refuges. This diversity is found in Nature. It is only natural.

The Crescendo Of The Word

The crescendo of the word is directly related to the utterance of the word by the number of sentients joining in. The loudness is deafening to those who cannot decipher the word. It will sound like noise to them. For sentients, it is harmonious. The word has been set into motion by one. This word was brought forth through spiritual awareness. Would you consider joining in harmony?

Something To Sanctify

Are you one of those who think that it is fashionable and part of societal norms to condemn? You may not identify with this, but your behaviors indicate that you are. This scribe thinks that to condemn ought not to be something to sanctify. No sentient would. To do so would greatly diminish or contract your spiritual development. Reconsider your fashion statements and norms.

Spiritual Awareness Will Follow

The rule of law is a corporeal distraction from sentient pursuits. It is encased in corporeal realm only. Hence, it holds no essence of spiritual awareness. For wise outcomes, we require that sentients be in charge. Spiritual awareness will follow.

Messages Of Hope

The obstructionists' loud noises are made with the singular purpose in drowning out messages of hope originating with the utter of the word. Demagoguery using inflammatory untrue sound bites by the obstructionists means that they are desperate attempts to hold on to their flocks with abject lies in order to instill fear reactions by them. Consider tuning out the load noises and the messages of hope will come in loud and clear. You may wonder why you did not do this a long time ago. You needed to first overcome your fears. Leave the obstructionists behind. Everything now is serene. No more noises. The messages are coming in clearer now.

Mammoth Greats

All the mammoth greats fell with the sound of thunder so that all the other creatures can have a better chance at life. It started with a bolt of lightning. Very illuminating! To all the mammoth greats, care to give it a jolt?

Basis For Acceptance Of Slavery

As can be found in Recent Historical References, slave owners were release from their slavery self-imposed confines in the performance of their bestiality handling duties. Likewise, feudal elitists were released from their self-imposed terrorist confines in the performance of their terrorist duties in keeping feudal states intact. Terrorist practices provided the basis for acceptance of slavery practices. Historically, feudal states have never lasted for long. Why continue to prop them up? They are going to expire anyways. Who would want to be a slave or live in terror of terrorists? Do not look back and this will hasten their expiration.

Heard the Screams

Usually, if one hears the screams, one stops the slaughter. Then for some, when a being is in a womb and one doesn't hear the screams, one does not seem to think to stop the slaughter. The screams are then silenced before you can hear them. Maybe one did hear the screams all along and just wanted them stopped.

They don't Check Out

There are modern day concentration camps. They are called abortion clinics. Beings check in, but they don't check out. The harvests are used to further inhumane research goals.

Being Compact

There are advantages in being compact. One does not have to forage for food as often and have more time to ponder the Universe. Advancement is quicker. This is one advantage in being compact. There are many other advantages. Consider this. You have everything that you need.

Upon Forced Reentry

To arrive at birth by the natural way is the gentle and preferred way. To arrive at birth by the cloning way can be the spiritual disturbing way. Spiritual preparation for birth will greatly aid in the adjustment into the corporal realm. For the clone, much time and adjustment may be needed to settle the unsettling disturbances upon forced reentry.

Portal

A portal is to be a life raft for another entity until pulled from the sea.

Corporeal Form

A corporeal form is a three dimensional reality realm transducer to the spiritual realm. Quite often, the flow is fluid from reality realm to spiritual realm, but is a slow drip from spiritual realm to reality realm. An astute sentient can experience it as fluid in both directions.

A Blissful State

It is tempting to enjoy all the trappings of playground Earth while in corporal garb and remain in a blissful state by suppressing the knowing of a realm from whence we came. Maybe, that is the reason for so many return trips for the playful ones.

Life's Secrets

In the beginning, life's secrets kept us in awe. Now, science is decoding the secrets believing that all will be known through the exclusivity of science pursuits. What is left after decoding all of the secrets is sterilization of life's secrets. Hopefully, science has a very long ways to go. It is still wonderful to be in awe.

Play It Back

Play it back is the attempt of playing back a different scenario in real life upon reentry and end up having the same outcome as before. Consider that the different scenarios are really the same playback. "Where does one go from here?" is the question that ought to be asked and to ponder on the answer.

Small Bird Story

This scribe saw a scout bird perch itself on steps to the upstairs apartments staying there and singing the message to the other birds that a placement of bird seeds (food) by me on the ground has arrived. The bird was truly singing with joy and wanted others to know. This scribe is at a loss to explain why in Recent Historical References that the extinction of species such as this bird was considered acceptable to the needs of "superior" single-specie societies. With the silence of a bird singing with joy, society may lose its ability to sing with joy when there is nothing to compare it to. There is only the silence of extinction. Can you still find joy in this?

Tears Follow

"Tears" do not produce until after one suit up.

Spiritual Cord

As the fetus is developing inside her mother's womb, the lifeline is an umbilical cord until such time that the cord is cut or falls off and the child continues on its own volition. Similarly, as the spirit is continuing her development inside a corporeal self-volition form, the lifeline is an umbilical cord until the cord is separated from corporeal form and the spirit continues on its own spiritual volition.

A Short Stay before Departure

As an entity is released from corporeal form at the completion of her sojourn, a short Earth-time duration in corporeal terms exist when thoughts and impressions are given to Earth entities still in corporeal form by the just recently departed (newly released) entity before being completely immersed in spiritual realm. It is the same analogy around the time of birth with a short Earth-time duration in spiritual realm before being completely immersed in corporeal form. In both cases, one needs to turn your attention to the realm that one is passing through a portal to be in.

Upon Entering Your Portal

Picture this. You are 50,000 meters above a city looking down and thinking to yourself that there seems to be insignificant or no signs of any problems. Then you land in the city and observe that violence and terror activities are happening all around you. You are now immersed into your surroundings. This is analogous to entering your portal to arrive in corporeal life. For some, they are dropping into a hotbed of violence and terror activities. How did she get here? For most, it is to learn what fruits flourished from the seeds that you planted in earlier sojourns. For some, they may have sign up for this to help those who are having difficulties in adjusting to the environments that resulted from the choices and efforts they made. Be thankful that you have a willing guide to help you.

Concrete Institutions

When Earth makes corrections, the concrete institutions of the world will crack and crumble.

The Natural Order of Things

The Earth's Sphere of Influences is the natural order of things. To think that you can master Earth is folly. Consider aligning your efforts to flow with the natural order of things. You can accomplish great feats by going with the flow.

Reentry

If you do not want to burn up on reentry, then check your rate of descent. Take some time to enjoy the view.

When You are Ready

Why are you asking someone to wake you up? It is not anyone's place to do so. Did you ever consider the notion that maybe you need more sleep to dream about notions that you need to work out and that it would be best that you wake up on your own volition after completing the list of them? When you are ready, you will do so. Then you will see yourself for who you really are. You are a sentient working on your own notions.

Prodigy's Presence

There will be other sojourns. One may not be a prodigy in the current one. One may be a prodigy in a later sojourn once she has significantly developed spiritually in this one. There is much to do until then. Take advantage in the one that you are currently in at the present. Your prodigy's presence will occur before you know it.

Creation Or Demolition Choices

Little did we know that a womb created by All-That-Is is to be the safe incubator for a developing being and then would be turned into a one-stop slaughterhouse by the host and her supporters. Hence, one can choose creation or one can choose demolition of a life force. The decisions you make do pave the way for your own destiny that awaits you to experience the same in another time and space. You will come to know what it is like.

Environment Domain Inclusion Review

When alien life forms threaten the inclusion of sentients in our environmental domains will these events be ones of Nexus Prime Important for Nexus Pentarchy Prime review activities and the crafting of the prime directive remedies regarding these threatening aliens to be completed with all deliberate speed. Until then, inclusion of all sentients to include so-called "aliens" is of Prime Importance for a vibrant Nexus. Just like in Nature, diversity achieves the desired optimum environments in which all can co-exist and thrive.

A Tumultuous Portal Entry

Does one really want to be a party to portal demolition? Does one really want to have a burning desire to return through a tumultuous portal entry originating, unbeknownst to the participant, by the one who attended the party? The following question always seems to come up, though. How did I get here? The recipient would like to know.

Sentient Affirmations

Be Receptive

It is because I am receptive in receiving the word that I can hear it. Hear it for yourself. Be receptive. May the word be with you.

One Reaches This Realization

"I am not a proponent of non-sentient behaviors." If one reaches this realization, then condemn no more. Sentients do not condemn. All sentients are included in the Expanse. The Expanse holds no boundaries.

Feudal Dogma

We need a replacement to feudal dogma for the rule of law. We need to construct a framework for a Dominion Expanse complete without the need for sentient diminishing border perimeters and feudal fiefdoms. Choose to not be a vassal subject. This choice will set you free.

Experienced Moment

As advancement in maturity is achieved by corporeal entities, one can innately "see" movies and "hear" audio recording of one's self from long ago and can still identify and experience again with that self at a young age to include heightened romantic encounters. Glimpses of another corporeal realm can also be encompassed and experienced by similarly seeing and hearing. This is possible if one were to look inwardly for one's spiritual essence by using all of one's senses. Choose to develop them all. Through these experiences, one can conclude that spiritual entities transcend all of space and time. One can be in any experience moment to observe or be enveloped when the encompassing of the senses is heightened.

Makes Me Whole

I am to be the scribe and carrier of the word. My pursuit is not to amass great wealth nor attain prestigious officialdom position. Just uttering the word makes me whole.

To A Better Day

I am a sentient. We are sentients. These are rallying calls. First comes the awareness of one with All-That-Is, and then comes the challenges in being astute caretakers of a variety of environments in your own surroundings. Each day contributes to a better day to follow.

This Is How We Got Here

The word was released and received by the collective consciousness of sentients. This is how we got here. We reached the Nexus Pentarchy Prime Expanse. Let us go beyond.

Make A Difference

Uttering the word does make a difference even when there is no immediate noticeable effect. Take comfort in knowing that the word was indeed heard. This scribe, for one, heard it.

My Companion

The word is my companion. We are taking a stroll.

Our Paths Will Cross

By helping others escape from harm or harmful environments, you will be helping yourself gain spiritual insights that can lead to further quests for even greater spiritual insights. Continue to help others along the way. Our paths will cross.

Silent Revolution

Through numerous writings by this scribe, there are many references regarding being a sentient and being sentient-aware. No forced adherence campaigns are needed. Considering being a sentient is a very intimate choice and process. When a critical mass of aware sentients is achieved, a silent revolution has commenced. There is safety in numbers. More will join.

Uttered By You

The word has been uttered,
The word is now in motion,
The word continues on its trajectory,
The word accelerates when others utter the word,
The word is unstoppable!
This spectacular event started when,
The word was uttered by you.

Blue for Inspiration

The blue color that I can see is to remind me to look up into the sky for inspiration.

F. Dot

The Word Will Set Me Free!

The word will set me free! May the word be with you also. The word will accompany you on your quest towards your triumphant sentient awareness achievement moment.

Closing Remarks

Teaser To The Reader

The reader will easily notice where the additional content to the first edition is. It is the first part of the book. The second part of this book is the original or first edition. The reader will find that Part II of the Second Edition content has outline chapters that are the same as in later books in the series by this scribe. As a teaser to the reader, identify the chapter that each paragraph contents of the original edition would be a good fit in one of the outline chapters of the second edition. Later editions will reflect the preferred placement so that the reader can compare them to their own assignments made.

Sustainable Construction

Recommended Prime Directives as provided elsewhere in the set of writings by this scribe are presented by this scribe for adoption. You may find that they will aid in engineering a rapid Nexus Dominion Framework and sustainable structure. A significant number of thought streams were provided to assist in this noblest and wisest of sentient endeavors. Do take advance of them with no expectation by this scribe for anything in return.

Future Editions

This second edition has been created to be in line with the other published works by this scribe. The outline being used for sentient study has solidified in its structure to be used to convey sentient materials during the Transitional Period Towards a Nexus Pentarchy Prime Framework. In this way, similar parts given in the set of guidebooks by this scribe can be collected into a single outline topic guidebooks. Once the Nexus Pentarchy Prime Framework has been received and implemented throughout the dominion based on the Rule of Five (Ro5), only the premier published book in the series by this scribe will have no revisions. It is a genesis testament to the spawning inspirational impetus for the stream awareness of a Nexus Pentarchy Prime which emanated from the word that was brought forth, taking form, and then set into motion. The form came from within this scribe who achieved a level of awareness that brought forth the insights that were scribed in order for others to aspire towards. From this entry level, then more insights came forth that leads to even higher levels of awareness as this scribe discovered during many of life's sojourns. This scribe chose to be vulnerable to feudal wrath by calling attention to herself so that others can be inspired by her spiritual experiences and insights to do the same. Future editions can be shaped by astute sentients who can then inspire those who are still clutching and not letting go the anchors that keeps them perpetually stuck-in-time. They need inspiration that only fellow sentients can provide. Once acquired, then they can take a chance to release their anchors and experience for themselves their own spiritual highs. It begins with the word.

Welcomes Any Assistance

Workshops/Guidebooks Consolidation: The first five books authored and published by this scribe contain many passages and snippets that can be consolidated into a few topic guidebooks that can be used in workshops for the particular topic being discussed. In the second in the series of books' "Second Edition", the preferred subset outline chapters can be found in Part II part of the book. This scribe is only one person. She can perform this consolidation exercise to accomplish this. However, it is beneficial for other sentients to also perform this exercise and related activities as a way to rapidly gain Nexus Pentarchy Prime Framework understanding and sentient insights in a much shorter period of time than waiting for this scribe to complete the consolidation for publication. It is strongly recommended by this scribe that all sentients perform the exercises so that the word can be passed onto others in rapid succession. In this way, you will help shape the framework as it is being built. This scribe very much welcomes any assistance that you can contribute. Thank you very much.

Recent Historical References

The Transitional Period Towards a Nexus Pentarchy Prime Framework is occurring at the time of this writing. There are numerous passages with "Recent Historical References" in them. This scribe is looking forward for all "Recent Historical References" to be happenings of the past and be no more. The hope is that the reader is looking forward to this event occurring as well.

The Foundation Auspices

Working on the Foundation for the Nexus Pentarchy Prime Framework has been and will continue to be this scribe's pursuit. The Foundation Auspices will be established to continue with the set of library guidebook editions to follow. This scribe will begin to take on the roles of mentor and guide while continuing to take dictation and refinement activities of the word. The difference going forward is that there will be other highly capable and skilled auspice scribes who will add to existing collection of scribe writings. Thank you to all those sentient-aware scribes in advance for their astute duty caretaking. Consider being the mentors and guides for the next assemblages of scribes.

In A Very Sad State

This scribe no longer considers herself being stuck-in-time unless this scribe was to foolishly make choices that will once again return her to a stationary state. This scribe can only imagine the torment in returning to the stationary fetal-like position in sentient awareness. Needless to say, this scribe would be in a very sad state because insights once known would have dimmed to the point of having to ask this question again, "How did I get here?" If that happens, I hope that a sentient would help mentor and guide me onto the sentient path once again.

Rapid Fire Sound Bites

During the period of this scribe's corporeal sojourn, communication venues were such that guest discussions were to be kept within time-boxes. This scribe would not be able to effectively keep within these time-boxes. Her tempo to discuss topics of prime importance was much more deliberate and slower than most. Hence, the utterances of "rapid fire sound bites" were intentionally avoided by this scribe.

Became A Fast Learner

In all the years-spanning journey by this scribe, it seems to have occurred in a short-duration continuum with recalls of sentient-based journal entries made as if there were no breaks in between. All those years just seemed to evaporate into a short period of time. Or, could it be that this scribe went at a very high rate of speed? This actual self pondering discussion by this scribe illustrates that time can drag as if one is stuck-in-time. Or, it is as if the experience has occurred in a blink of an eye covering many experiences of study at the same time. Could it be that as one ascends to higher and higher levels of awareness that pace of experiences just seem to speed up? Maybe, the heightened awareness development sped up because one became a fast learner.

To Entice And Whet The Reader's Interest

There is a large sampling of Recent Historical References referred to in writings by this scribe to aid sentients in the pursuit of knowledge. In many historical events, feudal lords raided many auspice libraries and museums for the purpose of destroying historical artifacts and reference scribes by fire and other destructive activities to make them unrecoverable forever. This was done in an attempt to bury any remnants from being uncovered and referenced so that atrocities committed by the victors would not be used in any basis for proving that they committed atrocities or to erase the existence of any other belief structures that were different from the victors. The victors, however, were hasty in these campaigns. It would take centuries to excavate a sampling of the artifacts and reference scribes to use them in piecing together the existent of some societies who were peaceful, vibrant, and truly great societies that were very astute stewards and caretakers of Nature's preserves to include societal members. This scribe's interest in including historical references in her writings is to entice and whet the reader's interest to learn much, much, more. This scribe suggests that the reader dig deeper for a more complete and accurate series of events. You will then view the present feudal constructs' "positive" historical story telling spin with grave skepticism. The reader's ever spanning knowledge domain may also conclude with overwhelming certainty that a sentient environment is needed to replace barbarous-based victorious constructs in order for sentients to thrive in. This can only be accomplished if we require that sentients be in charge. With sentients in charge, then it becomes a foregone conclusion that all warring-prone constructs will expire and be no more. Consider making it so.

Scribe's Web Prologue To Book Five

The reader will notice that the title of the fifth book in the series by F. Dot has the word "Sentinent (s-e-n-t-i-n-e-n-t)". This misspelling that is discovered while reading that book is not found in the original files sent to the publisher and to the US Copyright Office. Due to purposeful or non-purposeful intent by the publisher, the reader will be confused with it. This scribe is only one entity juggling at the time many challenges at once. This scribe acknowledges that she is the one entity who was compelled to set the word into motion. As the word gains speed and strength by more sojourners partaking in its gains, then refinements will be forthcoming in all companion writings. This scribe thanks all those ahead of time who will be partaking in this insightful endeavor. Given all that has been conveyed here, the term "Sentinent (s-e-n-t-i-n-e-n-t)" did come to the fore for this scribe in the discovery that this term is to be the Nexus Pentarchy Prime Dominion name designation for a "Nexus Pentarchy Prime Rapid Response Auspices Duty Caretaker". The term is close to the term "sentient (s-e-n-t-i-e-n-t)" as to be relevant to the caretaking concept. The new term will come to have universal usage to mean "a sentinent entity that performs sentry duties in activities to ensure that grave harmful acts or events will go to zero – be extinguished – through their caretaking duties whenever and wherever these acts or events may occur in the Nexus Pentarchy Prime Dominion". In summary, had this scribe not have been blind to the misspelling of the original term "Sentient" in the title during book publishing production, the new term would not have been seen, and thereby, noticed for Nexus inclusion. The reader will come to find that both terms can be used interchangeably in the title. When "Sentinent" is used, the audience will be the duty caretakers as defined above. When "Sentient" is used, the audience will be the Nexus Dominion members at large. This scribe is very pleased to have made this important discovery.

F.Dot Collection Of Guidance Writings

During the Transitional Period Towards a Nexus Pentarchy Prime Framework, the founders will spawn the initial foundation primes and the spanning ascension primes. The F.Dot Collection of Guidance Writings were referred to and studied often as Pentarchy Primes germinated and established the foundation for the Nexus Pentarchy Prime Dominion Expanse and Beyond. Activities were needed to fully gain insights into sentient environments and the propagation of the word so that others can also hear the word so as to be able to propagate it still further. The word is with you. Pass it on. The Nexus Pentarchy Prime Framework is rapidly coming into view.

Please, Do Step Forward

This scribe would be very satisfied if she was not selected to remain as the Chief Nexus Leader Caretaker at the Nexus Pentarchy Prime Degree. Her joy and satisfaction is the knowing that she has succeeded in mentoring others to be inspired and have confidence in raising their sentient interests in ensuring continuum of the Sentient Nexus Expanse. Please, do step forward.

Appendices – Second Edition

Appendix A - Bulletins

Living Foundation Guide

This Second Edition was years in the making after the initial publication of this book. The original content refinement changes are minor ones – mostly capitalization of sentient terms and grammatical corrections – and moved to the second half of the book. Over a longer period of time, the Nexus Pentarchy Prime Framework construction era will provide additional living experiences that may be quite substantive for inclusion. However, do not be surprised if the Nexus Pentarchy Prime Framework and related Founders' Tenets, Principles, and Instruments to remain largely intact.

Happy To Be Of Service

Comprehensive embellishments pertaining to this book is scheduled in twenty-five years from the original published date. It is recommended that Pentarchy Prime Umbrella members at the greatest degree-spanning reach pent-degrees to the Nexus Degree be the primary contributors of the 25th Year Revision. The expectation is that the revision will most likely be expansions on the basic foundations provided in writings by this scribe. We would have learned much during the Transitional Period and the distancing away from the feudal-based constructs during this time towards a Universal Nexus Pentarchy Prime Framework. This book will then be the living foundation guide by contributors of their times for all sentients that will follow them. Numerous references to valuable transitional lessons will aid future sentients in their rapid sentient awareness development. This scribe is happy to be of service.

Your Feedback and Suggestions Welcomed Here

This scribe welcomes feedback and suggestions from any Pentarchy Prime member. Your suggestions will be reviewed and may be incorporated in an updated future version of this book. When feedback indicates certain passages of this book require a greater degree of clarity regarding the addition of Nexus Pentarchy Prime Tenets or the addition of Nexus Pentarchy Prime Guiding Principles, then a bulletin will be forthcoming so that there are no delays in disseminating this information. Should there be many bulletins for inclusions, then an updated book will be published. It will be another twenty-five years whereby much would have been learned and articulated at which time, this scribe relinquishes copyright holder exclusivity and will then pass the baton to the newly universally authenticated Nexus Pentarchy Prime Umbrella made possible by the contributions by sentients everywhere.

Appendix B - Bibliography and Website

Bibliography

The following books composed by this scribe have been published. Paperbacks are listed here. Other media forms are also available or forthcoming.

1. *The Teaching of Self: Reflections and Search of an Entity*
   - Publisher: **AuthorHouse**, ISBN 9781403362834 (Paperback)

2. *The Foundation Book of Primes* (1st Edition)
   – Publisher: **AuthorHouse**, ISBN 9781410774385 (Paperback)
   Scribe Note: This 1st Edition shows the developmental progress that has been made by this scribe over time in articulating the concepts in greater detail as are found in the 2nd Edition. The reader may experience her progress to be similar in her own quest.

3. *Pentarchy Prime Auspice Registry and Directory Libraries: The Foundation for Prime Directives and Party Declarations in Registration, Certification, Archival, and Retrieval*
   - Publisher: **AuthorHouse**, ISBN 9781420830187 (Paperback)

4. *The Society of Sentients in Nexus Primes: The Founders Guide and Sentient Insights to the Pentarchy Prime Framework*
   – Publisher: **AuthorHouse**, ISBN 9781434308863 (Paperback)

5. *Nexus Rapid Response Auspices for the Sentient Millennia Expanse*
   – Publisher: **RoseDog Books**, ISBN 9781434998774 (Paperback)

Website

An Internet website is currently being maintained by this scribe. It is given below. On one of the website pages, one or more buttons will be shown that when clicked, will navigate to a particular publisher's search results page. On this search page, the user can purchase one or more books, or their digital versions, of published works by this scribe.

www.nexuspentarchyprime.net

Table of Contents – First Edition

Introduction

First Edition

This first edition was composed and released without delay so that the Nexus Pentarchy Prime Founders can have a starter set in which to accelerate the premiere foundation prime construction. This author didn't want to get in the way of sentients making initial contact with one another anxious to get started by delaying the book's release any longer than necessary. A spectacular world awaits all of you. It is okay to be dazzled. Take care and enjoy your journey.

A Her-Storical Reference

This book will in time be a her-storical (historical) one. It will be a snapshot as to how far we have all come from a particular point in time. For us here and now, the reference is why are we taking so long? Be patient. Changes are frightening to most inhabitants. The war they fight will be their own and not of ours.

I am a product of –

A nation-state may make a claim that the author is a product of their favorable environment. The truth of the matter is that there were those who tried to destroy or greatly limit the author's existence and pursuits due to her view of not adhering to prevailing dogma. To have only a corporeal view will keep one in the material realm. There is much more than meets the eye. Take a chance and "see" for yourself.

Super Power Status is fleeting

The contents of this book may be viewed as unnecessary due to the fact that a super power nation-state exists today. Actually, its existence is fleeting because of its forced exclusionary laws that chip away at its power. These same laws are their downfall. History provides numerous examples of this. Are you prime for a universal framework?

Written Now

This book is being written now so that when major Earth changes occur, this handbook will allow order to quickly be established. Relying on arcane institutions will extend harsh pain and suffering. This is unnecessary. We have the capability to provide caring and humane treatment towards each other. Do not be fooled when others make the claim that the current belief systems are the only ones. Dare to choose a more all encompassing one.

Blue Print for Development

This book is provided as a blue print for an optimum environment for advancing entity pools' development. One of the purposes is to describe a framework for all sentients to be included, if the will be there. The framework is one of inclusion and not to be limited to a small percent of the society pool. Are you up to it?

Birth of a Framework

"An initial birth framework" is covered in this book. Allow twenty-five continuous years with the launch of this framework before making major refinements so that the framework can take hold. True, the objective is to continuously develop (evolve) towards a state of a higher level of awareness. However, this will take time. Please be patient. Consider that a greatly refined framework may mean that it is not for an "Earth-based framework" but for another realm. Wouldn't that be marvelous?

Need a Disclaimer?

We can customize a disclaimer for you if you like should you find the words that are used in this book disturbing. The journey is truly yours to take should you choose to take a chance on something that will be quite magnificent! Do you need a disclaimer or will you dare to choose?

Historical Societal Pool View

Temporary Land Rights

Land rights only last until the next invading armed forces or when civil wars occur. This only happens when property is valued more than sentient entities. We can choose not to make this so.

Barbarism to Civilization

All countries go through barbarism before becoming "civilized", or so the view is. Their belief systems require acceptance of property rights. Acceptance yields to slavery. This is quite an ancient concept and is nothing more than government supported caste system.

Feudal Fires

Nation-states are founded by violence. Nation-states are perpetuated when there are violent oppositions. However, nations cannot exist without feudal lords. With feudal lords, all members are subjects (properties) of them. This is how a feudal system works. Consider not fueling the fires of these feudal lords.

"Smug"ness exhibited by feudal lords.

Subjects of the State

Every state, no matter if a union of states, owns its subjects. This is not how a great society ought to work to safeguard all members of it.

Which Came First, Law or Crime?

The historical belief is nothing more than the assumption that in order for "wise" actions to be taken, laws must first be passed. When one looks at this premise, wise actions are not taken. Feudal based laws (land lord laws) prevail. Hence, properties are owned by the state. Once laws are passed, the acts that they describe become illegal and hence, become crimes. Prior to that, these same acts are not crimes. Hence, laws are artificial concepts and not necessarily wise outcomes. Pain and suffering must be endured to be a "just" re-action!

Family Civil Wars

In recent belief systems, if a member of society is condemn, then the community -- family, extend family and friends, neighbors, etc. -- is condemned by this condemning action. Even without considering the unintended members, these recent belief systems support terrorism. Is this just? Elimination of terrorism begins at home. The need to get out of the terrorism business in all its forms is ever present.

195

Historical Societal Governance View

State Dominant Stature

The "state" is viewed as one even though there are legions of soldiers to defend this view of one. A single individual is brought before this state's view of one to stand before an army that holds the guns to her annihilation

The Rule of Law

The rule of law requires the existence of property rights. How else can rulings be made. It is this notion that "divide and conquer" take on a purist meaning. Court cases are done when two subjects contest an agreement. Having one person sue another is not as unbalanced as having one state sue or prosecute one person. The deck is stacked against the one person, the one individual. This allows the state to do things with impunity! If it makes a mistake, no recourse for this criminal act by the state is available. One person does not have a fair playing field against the ruthless singular state.

The Law of One

In feudal laws, one is considered separate before the law. Collectives such as governments and corporations are considered separate before the law. The difference is that one entity is composed of one member of society while governments and corporations have armies to challenge and defend their way of life or existence. Indeed, these collectives defined as "single entities" hide behind the aprons of the "Law of One".

Property Rights

The nation-state belief system is based on ownership of property. The greater the real estate, the higher is the position in society. Those who are not owners of land property are then owned by their feudal lords or land lords.

By treating "citizens" as subjects of the state, then the state can go anywhere to retrieve its subjects. After all, subjects are property.

Law of the Land

Our laws only apply to citizens surrounded by nation-state boundaries when they ought to apply to all sentient beings no matter what location they are living in at any particular time. The purpose for placing borders is to define property. They are not protective barriers because these same borders have the duality of keeping subjects in, as if we are like plants and can't escape from the land that is under our feet! It should now be clear to you what the phrase "law of the land" really means.

Go Straight to Jail: Criminal/Civil Jury Awards

Jail was barbarous for less serious offenses. Sentencing was NOT universally consistent in all cases. Instead of the impact of the offense, a jail and/or probation time and/or cost penalty were applied. In this way, the rich were shielded from hardship. There was the acceptance in the notion that life is not fair. Is this your belief, too?

Prison Environment

Our prison population has gotten very large because of the increased number of laws and an "efficient" legal industry. The question ought to be asked; Are folks becoming more criminal or is our system in shambles of imploding? The latter is the case. The system breaks up communities and examines only individuals, legally classified as such, against a sea of a legal army of troops. Bullying is the order of the day, which does not provide for the common good or a caring environment.

Behavior Modification

The law is being used in behavior modification for all members of society. By using terrorism, i.e. condemnation of its subjects, then most will be sufficiently fearful to adhere to feudal lords and their artificial laws. Normally, the sentencing results in condemnation existing for an entity's entire life span.

Prison Term Waiting Period

Currently, there is at least a 30-day waiting period before arriving at a prison sentence for non-violent crimes. This is but one of the more obedient chattel-shaping activities. If this is the case, why not place them in containment camps with minimum security? However, the current prevailing belief is to condemn by using secured prison facilities. This view feeds on itself. The end result is that the belief system itself is condemned.

Free Citizen Newcomers

It is because of the notion of "property rights" that war is inevitable. Those without property have very little say in a nation-state (land based) boundary concept. By stripping current inhabitants of their property rights, "new lands" are discovered and "new claims of ownership" ensue. Hence, new wealth is "discovered". In actuality, prior inhabitants and caretakers have been raped and slaughtered to make room for "free citizen newcomers".

Forced Repatriation

Terrorism is done by forced repatriation of subjects who do not want to return even when no non-entry crimes have been committed. Imagine yourself in this position!

Most Developed Nation and its Condemnation View

The "most developed nation" in the world came to recognize that their mass production of issuing sentences of condemnation was having a negative impact to their existence. More "fashionable" condemnation laws had to be passed to make it illegal to flee or resist arrest. In this way, shaping was enforced so that the entities that are condemned will not revolt and remain domesticated and docile. This most developed nation wanted all of its subjects to be in this behavioral state so as to round them up with little resistance. Executions can then be made at the final destination when it is convenient for this nation. Are you next?

Iron Curtains for Borders

The iron curtain still exists. It's called national (country) boundaries where free entities who cross are tagged as "illegals" and hence, non-citizens. They are then placed behind "iron curtains".

Carrot and Stick

Those who are privileged to information will want to retain that privilege by accepting the decisions of others that are the senior distributors of it. Hence, this is the shaping of the willing whom readily accepts this notion.

Labor of Profits

Those who are elitist are comfortable because they do profit off the mass labors of others. The masses are to be damned.

Patriot Games

The elite enjoy playing patriot games in their coliseum, this coliseum built by land (war) lords.

F. Dot

State Sanctioned Terrorism Results

Entities are condemned for life due to a felony conviction no matter how minor the infraction or the harmful degree of the act. The view is that the state's engine of convictions and condemnations must continue no matter if it is a just system or not. No one dares stops the assembly line. Hence, the effect is that terrorism exists. The view by the state is that a tool is constructed to permit and keep feudal lords in power, licensed to condemn and sanctioned by the state.

Legal Terrorism

The recent nation-states enforce legal terrorism by excluding entities from jobs, money, access to credit, and other basic needs based on serious or felony convictions no matter what that degree is or being given a "non-citizen" status even in the case when no other "crime" has been given.

Historical Justice ("Just Ice") System

Feeders to the Justice System

In recent historical "Western" systems, the legislative process feeds the judiciary process with constraints that further restrict entity pursuits. Legislative Acts are passed into law. The Executive is chartered to carry out these laws based on its interpretation of them or the vagrant disregard for the spirit of these laws. When disputes arise, then it is up to the Judiciary to arrive at final determinations. The whole process stops at the Judiciary. It does not feed any other process! However, had these artificial (man-made) laws not have violated sacred principles, the Judiciary would not be responding in a feudal way. Members of the Judiciary do have biases and are nothing more than surrogates to perpetuate the belief that the few (elite) knows what is best for the masses. In this book, the term "judiciary" or variations thereof will be used to mean all of the above.

Adversarial by Nature

An adversarial system of justice that condemns innocent entities in the name of justice is flawed. To say that it is the best system that there can be is not acceptable. A replacement system can be found when the desire for something better is present. A system that does not condemn will ensure that every entity has a chance for the truth to surface in time. After all, is it not paramount that the discovery of the truth be supreme?

The Passing of Responsibilities

The current justice system requires that institutions exist since legislative/ parliament officials are not ultimately responsible for law enforcement decisions. The preservation of institutions is paramount in this framework.

Judicial Administrators

Judges are administrators. What we need are caretakers!

The Weighing-in on Sentences

It is strange that murder or killing of another entity in human form is treated just like any other crime with sentences. They can have lighter sentences than other crimes that do not kill or gravely injure others. Releasing of those who will commit violent crimes again is a way to ensure that a chorus for law and order and the permission to expand the incarceration of others by passing additional laws is sanctioned. It is only in this way that power is retained by a few feudal lords. These same feudal lords are not capable of leading and being caretakers. They know only how to condemn. This belief system exists because of misguided believers who permit it to be so. Expect and demand something much greater to take its place!

Court Soldiers

Lawyers are officers (soldiers) of the court they serve. They are commissioned by the courts and can be de-commissioned (disbarred) when adherence to the belief system wanders. Lawyers, based on the requirements for the job, do not serve the public for fear of being terrorized (threaten to be disbarred). They are very often condemned for life once disbarred.

Lack of Prevention

The Criminal Justice System fails more times than is acknowledged. It is not an equalizer (fair) system. Bias is on the side of the privilege few, those with significant properties (assets) and elite contacts. The criminal justice system's premise is to deter (having a deterrent factor) by condemning. Prevention is not part of the system's framework. Knee-jerk reactions to events are the basis for their charter.

Sterile Automatons

Sterile-automatons are the ones that normally advance in historical systems. Are you one?

Disposal Laws

Laws are barbaric when disposal specifications to feudal subjects are defined. Civilization is not present in this framework.

Government Service

Government is a service. For matters involving major issues, this ought not to be left to few members of society to correct injustice. The resources of the few, whose passions are admirable, are limited compare to the built-in overwhelming and unlimited government ceiling design. Government ought to ensure the vibrant health of society. Having prime involvement ensures that no injustice falls through the cracks.

"Silent Discrimination" (or Closet Discrimination)

The current concept of a member of society classified as a "felon" is cruel and unusual punishment because of the edict or perspective (belief) that instead of withholding a particular set of privileges in the set of all privileges pertaining to the "crime", the edict is for all privileges. This is done by the unspoken and hidden actions of a select elite who will make this so. However, all denials can be seen and heard when the senses are keen to them. Do not be fooled.

Felons Locked Out

The current prevailing belief system of man-made laws requires that subjects of the state be in fear of exclusions. Examples, those subjects condemned with a felony are locked out of choice positions. Hence, they are restricted to a caste of low subsistence. Should there be a high degree of certainty that the offender will commit harm again, shall then confinement ought to be required in all cases.

Environmental Dangers Abyss

The legal system is inadequate to members subject to environmental dangers and contamination. Once exposed, the legal system premise is that members are to be responsible for taking actions to petition the courts for a court order. This is a false view. The legal system is only in place to render decisions involving business and their transactions.

Court-Based Deception

The current system of criminal justice is based on deception by the players and not based on the truth. It is overrated. It is a system of posturing. Seeking the truth is not its primary motivation; legal maneuvering is.

Bias Illusion

There is an illusion that the current justice system is fair and impartial. Nothing can be further from the truth. The warriors are made up of bias individuals whereby judicial outcomes are not uniform. The outcomes can be overturned and/or reversed. These historical references illustrate that no legal outcome is cast in stone.

Legal Maneuvering

Currently, laws are arbitrary. When laws have to be interpreted, the lawmakers cannot be relied on to make laws. What we have here is "legal maneuvering". This ought not to be the case.

Easy Lockup Prey of the Homeless

A very valid question is whose judicial system is it anyway? The answer may surprise you. Our current judicial system has an easier time locking up homeless "individuals" than wealthy ones. The answer is clear.

Close Enough?

As of the writing of this book, the Postal Service has a very high, close to one hundred percent, success rate for the delivery of all pieces of mail to the addressees given. The judicial system falls far shorter than one hundred percent in their success rate. We are very upset when mail is not delivered as promised than when the judicial system fails to "balance the truth" with a high degree of accuracy. The law is not blind at all, but limited by the corporeal trappings of men and women. Know this when passing judgment.

Blind Obedience

Obedience for the historical judicial system is an ongoing requirement. The truth of the matter is that not only is "lady justice" blind, but staunch believers are too!

Take Back Your Right

The judicial system exists because you gave away your right to decide. Choose to take it back. Allow the business judicial system to continue to exist in resolving business disputes in the interim. This part of the current legislative/judiciary system has been fine-tuned because of the framework premise of property and contractual rights.

An Epiphany for Sentient Pool Framework

Caught in the Web of Insights

Insights may be random events. The first impression is one that must be caught in a web of insights. However, the collection set triggers an epiphany. How wonderful this is!

Legal Protection

Even in a democratic unit or system, the law applies only to members of that unit or system. Anyone outside of it is not protected since one would be a non-member. This is exactly the policy or policies that condemn others around the world to be abused, tortured, or even put to death because of the forced policy of repatriation. Members are owned by the landowners of the feudal systems who are "rooted" in them. It is for this reason that associations ought to be governed not by land boundaries or borders but rather by the pool in which they choose to associate. The overlapping of pools will dictate the larger pool umbrella that encompasses both associations governs matters relating to this overlap.

The Reciprocal not Observe

The smug and arrogance of the Justice System is not a "just" system when it violates other systems. Tyranny rules when a belief system is forcibly imposed on another. There is insistence by a "great power" in objecting to others who violate one's air/land space. However, the reciprocal is not observed. The imperial way tramples all others.

For Insiders Only

For insiders only, a "just" system is directly related to a particular domain. However, this particular "just system" is null and void when it tramples on another insiders' domain in its refusal to recognize their form of just and equitable systems.

In a secure corner of the world, a country that restricts immigration does export slavery, human bondage, and forced repatriation. These are forerunners to executions. What is set in motion continues in motion. The answer is to not set into motion these terrorist acts.

Justice Monopoly

The "justice" arena is the sole monopoly of the state. Since it is a monopoly, it ought to give equal resources to both sides in justice cases. However, only prosecutors have access to all of the state's resources. A single individual is limited by access to her personal resources, which pales to that of the state. In this way, an individual is singled out. A state is also considered a single entity. Indeed it is! It is one army or legion of judicial solders. What single individual can match this unless a member of the elite with matching funds?

The Few Elite

The elite will separate those who are selected from those who are not by employing those who are and having them at remote or secured locations, away from the common class. Also, where the elites and their families live is isolated because of their wealth. In this way, the selected ones will only know and experience good things and not be troubled by lower class problems. For them, understanding the plight of others who are not selected and are struggling is very difficult for them. Since there are instances of rages to riches, the belief is that anyone can overcome obstacles. These are relatively rare and the selection is for the most gifted. The vast majority will continue their struggles most of their lives.

The Inclusion View of Being a Citizen

In western law of "great nation-states", only "citizens" of the feudal state can have rights. The definition is specific. If certain groups or pools are not included, then no rights exist for them. In that narrow interpretation, anything can and is done to non-citizens. For example, children are property of custodians, which very often are awarded to women. Unborn children are always property of the mothers with no state-defined person-hood status to be disposed of at will and are in fact made. They are non-citizens. How convenient it is for a state to dispose of property.

History shows that other living groups were considered non-citizens. Recall what happen to the plight of the Native American and slaves. Also, conscripts have a duty to serve. For example, serving on jury duty and the Armed Services, which in the later case are considered Government Issue (GI). In certain instances of law, killing of non-citizens, those considered an "enemy nation-state", are allowed with no reprisals. In fact, opposing members of armies are always forgiven because they serve the country that issued the order. If this were not the case, then the state would have to condemn its own armies for crimes that could have been imposed by opposing forces. How convenient this is. In the aftermath of wars, the opposing country must make accounting for all soldiers missing-in-action before diplomatic talks can continue by the "greatest western nation-state". Since many acts of wars have normally been done on foreign soil, our accounting of opposing army soldiers' missing-in-action is of little consequence.

Terrorism

If countries profess that citizens should be free to travel at will, then why do these same countries prevent the admittance of others? They are "non-citizens", which are not given the same rights and privileges as are given to "citizens". In this manner, these "exclusive" countries are parties to atrocities. In fact, those evil counties did learn historical lessons from those self-professed democratic sovereign states by suppressing their own people and also the torturing and murdering of members of their respective sovereign states. We condemn them because they are non-citizens. This is tantamount to terrorism. Many will say that this is not so. However, they are not blameless because they will on a regular basis forbid the entry of non-citizens. The proof is always on the fleeing people to show that they are in danger. Our history shows that we commonly performed force repatriation (return) of fleeing citizens of the world only to learn later that our actions caused much suffering and death. Many who profess in being honorable people did in fact condemn others and hence, were participants to atrocities.

Reign of Terror by any other Name

Historical legislative/executive/judicial systems provided an apron for the reign of terror for its members with an adherence to their system of condemning. Once condemned, an entity is locked out of the societal pool for life, way beyond the term limits of the sentence. This framework can easily be replaced.

Plants Have No Mobility

Plants have no mobility. They are rooted in land. We are not plants. Our legs are not implanted into the ground. We are mobile. It is only natural that our systems must also include mobility as a basic tenet. The notion of the law of the land forces us to be like plants. However, to thrive means to have systems in place that represents vanguards to mobility.

The True Duration of a Sentence

The concept of prison sentences dictates the duration for the punishment of a crime. The person is then free when the duration is completed. However, implementation by the law belief system is to not be free of association for an entire life!

The Export of Terror

Exporting terrorism is the result of denying passage through nation-state boundaries by non-citizens.

Barriers of Enslavement

When barriers purposely constructed to block mobility of sentient beings, the ultimate goal by those who constructed these barriers is to enslave us all. To the non-chosen few, tear down these walls!

Class System

When accommodations are primarily given to feudal governmental members to the consternation of the vast majority of members who also contribute promotes a class (caste) system. One class is of privilege while the other classes are damned. We perpetuate this view still.

Stalled Corrective Actions

Our recent system of government, legislative/executive/judicial, cannot handle mistakes in their own decisions very well. It is hard for this framework to take speedy corrective actions. This is not surprising since it is artificial (man-made). Time delays are built-in and not naturally based.

It Can Happen to You

It can happen to anyone. It doesn't matter how good your character is. Once the state tags you, labels you, condemns you, the inferior classification stays with you for life. The question that ought to be asked is this. Is the state a valid institution? The answer lies within you. How do you choose?

"Neighbor Papers" Needed

Neighbors need not require papers to pass through the neighborhood. Neighboring states ought to be no different. Travel papers represent an evidentiary indication of inferiority. The implied message is this: "We don't want them in our neighborhood!"

Secure National Borders

There are those who believe in a secure nation-state border as the way to provide for security. This belief will place you on the other side of the fence looking in, which may not be that evident in the here and now. Earth events have a way of cleaning house to correct imbalances.

"Legal and Just" Captivity

One may think that laws are just. It is not when laws have the effect of executing and/or gravely harming entities in captivity. The result is that laws become very unjust. Think about it for a while before coming to your conclusion.

Condemned for Life!

We do not have a humane and just system of justice when it condemns entities for life through its decree. All other institutions and businesses follow this lead. One might say that it is "a stamp of disapproval and discard".

Feudal State Believers

The feudal state needs enough believers to sustain it. Therefore, those who feed its belly promotes its abuses and your misfortunes.

Ideal Power Concentration Objective

Concentration of power to a few, this is the ideal with feudal lords. What are your chances of becoming a member of this exclusive club?

The law kills

The law kills. If this were not so, then why are there state-sanctioned executions? Supposedly, there are laws against killings. Apparently, the states are exempt. How fair is this? As with other things, the state has a monopoly. Terrorism is the result of all monopolies.

Children as Property!

Children are the property of guardians, even when children are abused and may then become homeless. They are in limbo because the nation-state laws make it illegal to help them without guardian approval. Housing, caring, or providing them with jobs often leads those who do with nation-state prosecutions and sentencing.

Protection of Property

The historical belief system regarding governance is flawed. The premise is that members of society are properties of land-based nation-states. In practice, members are properties of land lords. Democratic belief systems are no different. These systems have exclusionary "laws" (man-made). Non-citizens are excluded. This leads to systems that promote terrorism everywhere.

The Inner Circle

The elite require members be in the inner circle for consideration of privileges. The inner circle is small compared to the entire pool. When the pool finally choose to make decisions for themselves, the inner circle framework will implode and cease to exist because the pool will no longer fund and grant authority to it. A leader caretaker-based framework will require the admittance of all that advocate non-violence. With the inner circle, it requires force to keep the greater pool at bay.

The Thinning of Military Nation-States

It has been said that a superior military machine insures a protected nation-state to exist by keeping other nation-states and their subjects confined. There is something even more superior, which doesn't require any military machine at all. Allow all sentients safe passage through our environments who have migrated out of repressive and very harmful environments. Oppressive and abusive nation-states will be "de-selected" into oblivion with this escape tenet. The military machines will likewise follow the same fate.

The Tightening of the Albatross Laws

When new inventions and ideas are first introduced into society, no laws exist to suppress them. After a while, laws are introduced that generally are never reversed and become albatrosses on individuals. This leads to suffocation. To be alive, we breathe in and out. Our laws ought to do likewise. Loosen them up when breathing is impaired.

Systems of Exclusions

The historical belief systems of the world are based on exclusions. With this, how can they possible be just?

Slavery Preserved

To be all things to all people is the bottleneck of the current belief system. The few elite who decides on behalf of the masses ensures the preservation of land lords and their subjects. This is just another name for slavery.

Free Trade Only?

When it comes to commerce between nation-states, free trade is permissible. The same cannot be said for free passage of entities. Why is that so? Do goods and services have more "value" than sentients?

Terminal Affect

By terminating entities through exclusions, one may term this the "terminal affect".

Exclusion is Terrorism!

You need more convincing? Stick around.

The Nooses of Nation-States

The concept of nation-states will return to the ocean just like before the "dawn" of nation-states. History has recorded that great nation-states did occur at different times. Each has imploded in its own noose of tighter and tighter elite domains. In time, the weight of those who are excluded will be too great to carry. We don't have to wait for these events to happen when the will is there.

Self-Restricting Noose

The harder the elite force a more restrictive environment, the more they place a noose around their own necks. This is always the outcome. Do not be fooled by those who say otherwise. Stick around and see for yourself.

Criminal Activity Inclusive

A criminal activity can be based on natural law. To say that criminal activities can be based only on man-made (artificial) laws is folly. In the latter, a law has to be passed before a naturally recognized law regarding harmful acts can be considered a "crime". Why wait for this to happen?

It Started with Good Intentions

You are still subscribing to a belief system enforced by a small geographical country of this world. Why are you allowing the state known as "The Greatest Nation on Earth" to dictate terms and conditions for the entire world? Many good intentional civilizations in history also dictated the terms and conditions to the known world, too. The enforcement was done through exclusion of a great majority of peoples. Today, we are again experiencing the same. Your support for this is allowing a small country in size as a relation to the entire Earth to rule the world. Take responsibility for your actions. The numbers are on your side should you choose to have yourself counted as well.

"I still believe!" Why?

So many people still believe in the historical (artifact) system and still cannot understand why there are still are (real estate) wars. Change to a different system. Adopt a border-absent system and the wars and related industries will no longer be needed to resolve land disputes.

Not that Complex

There is a belief that to govern is complex and difficult. This view promotes in-decisions and in-actions. Actually, what is needed is for wise directives of prime importance to be made. This requires wise leader caretakers to be recognized.

Multiplicity

Recent history illustrates that what we have is not "duplicity" of action and in-action, but "multiplicity" of the same. Multiplicity exists with the many overlapping governmental organizations. Is there any wonder that there is confusion and hesitation in making wise decisions and activities? A clear singular umbrella approach is the wisest.

Invitation to an Association

An invitation is truly an invitation when the one who is being invited has the option to decline. Otherwise, one is a conscript. It is wise not to recognize a belief that imprisons people for their own beliefs and free choices in the association with others as long as it does not violates another person's free association.

Time of Earth-Holdings Changes

When major Earth changes arrive in our time, there will be those who will still have property and ere will be those who lost their properties because of these changes. Will this lead to great disturbances? If you cling to the law of property, to have property and power means the servitude, slavery, and at times, torture of others who do not. Eventually, the prevailing feudal system will be replaced with a more equitable one.

Together, We Survive

Something very interesting happens with a well-oiled machine. When there is no one to oil the machine, it slows down and eventually stops all together. The damage done by not oiling it may be beyond repair. In making this so, it will direct us to rely on one another in ensuring a natural subsistence environment.

That Which Is!

Forms of terrorism are not how states defined them, but in actuality, that which is. Consider keeping them in check wherever you find them.

Can be kept in Check

Society can stop any abusive demagogue/politician in her tracks, if the will be there. Experts may think they know what to do until society sets them right.

The Labors of Others

Throughout history, wealth, by and large, is always obtained by the labors of others. Are we caretakers of the few or the many?

Why Subscribe

Why must one subscribe to the notion that nation-states own its citizens? This promotes servitude to land lords. This promotes taxation for real estate. This promotes wars by land (war) lords.

Political Systems Rigidity

Historically, the political systems are too rigid to allow for diversity. A system based on diversity will yield the greatest solutions to contemporary issues. This can only be done through inclusion of all. Hence, political systems are doomed.

Impediments to World Peace

Nation-states are the impediments to world peace and tranquility. Their need to hoard land and resources is their motivation. The inhabitants in all their diversities are to be damned. What kind of environment do we want to live in?

Transitional Decriminalization

Examining history, when psychology was in its infancy, increasing the number of mental institutions was viewed as the proper thing to do. Over time, it then was realized that we were locking up well-balanced persons. So we released a lot of persons back into society. In similar ways, we are locking up a high percentage of well-balanced persons. We need to decriminalize many laws that made criminals of them. Self-determination and expressions, as long as these activities and actions do not adversely affect other members, will not be described as criminal acts. The safety and well being of sentient beings are two of the paramount concerns of a true civilized society.

The Burden Lifted

We will lift the burden of the few in making decisions when they affect us all. The burden will instead be placed on the multitudes. In this way, all will benefit from our decisions.

Non-Citizen Classification

Historically, groups (races) of sentient beings can be classified as non-citizens. The view from Earth's perspective is that we are all citizens of Earth. Therefore, in no case will sentient beings be classified as non-citizens or as non-members. To decide otherwise will result in the Earth's sphere of correcting the imbalances.

Expanding Sentient Inclusion

Historically, the notion of what is human is defined as *Homo sapiens*. Anything else is viewed as non-sentient. There may have been contacts with other forms but they were expelled or eliminated because of denial of these other forms. What needs to happen is that members in a society are defined and included based on characteristics of being sentient and not by being *Homo sapiens* exclusively. Acceptance of all that exhibit sentient awareness is the first major step towards one's own higher awareness. This next step is within reach, should wisdom prevail.

Self-Initiated Borders

There are no national borders, only self initiated borders to your own experiences.

Preamble to Pentarchy Prime

A Higher Awareness Charter

A new charter will be adopted that will aid sentients into a higher level of awareness while inhabitants in our environments. The charter is described in this book starting with the following preamble.

Preamble to Pentarchy Prime

It is with supreme inspiration that this sentient directing charter is drafted and accepted in order for the inhabitants of Earth and all other discovered worlds to integrate effectively, in this era of sentient awareness with one another. We understand that each sojourner is within worldly influences and at her unique level of awareness. No law is valid which states otherwise. Everyone is created equal in the realization that each one of us yearns to grow and develop in ways that will brighten the spirit-soul to the journey back from whence we came. We understand that we have lost our way and All-That-Is (A.T.I.) has provided a way to gain back that knowledge and insight. We recognize that sentient entities have various capabilities and capacities to help and assist others in their development and that the supreme spiritual path is to be the caretakers of others. For it is by this pursuit that our journey back to A.T.I. is assured.

An Epiphany for a Pentarchy Prime Model

To Grasp a Greater Society

We are all made in our creator's image. While in an Earth's sphere of influence as part of our spiritually expanding experiences, we are given an environment that best meets our needs at this present time. The clues for optimum vitality are ever present. Take our body, for example. We have two hands, each having four fingers and a commanding thumb. The thumb is larger and positioned quite distinctly different from the other four fingers. The hand utilizing all fingers and the thumb can grasp extremely well many different kinds of material objects. With this observation in mind, it is being stated here without rigorous discussion or validation that an advanced quantum leaps to a greater foundation society can occur by implementing the following governing framework.

Prime Degrees or Power Primes

Initiate and select on an individual entity free spirited basis an association or pool comprised of a total of five members that closely identifies with the entity based on the other members of the association or pool who share the same identification. The members agree to bind in the pursuit of achieving collective harmony and purpose. This association or pool is called the Premiere Pentarchy Prime Foundation. The more detailed mechanics for association will be described elsewhere. From the five, one representative leader will be selected to speak on behalf of the Pentarchy Prime Foundation in matters affecting their Pentarchy Prime. The leader will then form an association with four other leaders at the same Pentarchy Prime degree to form the next Ascension Pentarchy Prime. The members agree to bind in the pursuit of achieving collective harmony and purpose, the same premise as the Pentarchy Prime Foundation. From the five, one representative leader will be selected to speak on behalf of the Ascension Pentarchy Prime in matters affecting their Pentarchy Prime. The leader will then form an association with four other leaders at the same Pentarchy Prime degree to form the next Ascension Pentarchy Prime. This process repeats until the Apex Pentarchy Prime is achieved whereby every Pentarchy Prime Foundation is a descendent of one of the representative leader caretakers of the Apex Pentarchy Prime. The proper name for this prime is the Sentient Nexus Pentarchy Prime. The premise for each degree of Pentarchy Primes is to wisely derive decisions encompassing all members under its umbrella on matters involving two or more degree minus-one foundation primes for a particular degree Pentarchy Prime.

Pentarchy Prime Associations

Let's start with building blocks. Start with group associations of five and allow them to be autonomous in their affairs dealing with one another in this pool. Provide complete respect for a group to exist apart from other groups.

Ebb and flow of associations, this reflects the natural order of existence.

Power Prime Matrices

Let's look at each Pentarchy Prime degrees of five member entities.

Prime Matrix 1: 5 to the first power   = 5
Prime Matrix 2: 5 to the second power   = 25
Prime Matrix 3: 5 to the third power   = 125
Prime Matrix 4: 5 to the forth power   = 625
Prime Matrix 5: 5 to the fifth power   = 3,125

Prime Matrix 6: 5 to the sixth power   = 15,625
Prime Matrix 7: 5 to the seventh power   = 78,125
Prime Matrix 8: 5 to the eighth power   = 390,625
Prime Matrix 9: 5 to the ninth power   = 1,953,125
Prime Matrix 10: 5 to the tenth power   = 9,765,625
Prime Matrix 11: 5 to the eleventh power = 48,828,125
Prime Matrix 12: 5 to the twelfth power = 244,140,625
Prime Matrix 13: 5 to the thirteenth power = 1,220,703,125
Prime Matrix 14: 5 to the fourteenth power = 6,103,515,625
Prime Matrix 15: 5 to the fifteenth power = 30,517,578,125

Note: The primary digit always identifies a Pentarchy Prime with the numeral five. A Universe Prime Power Designation is used to represent each prime power degree.

Optimum Participation

It starts with an association of five to have optimum discussions and then generate decisions on matters of importance to the association. When matters deal with only the association, then that association is given the empowerment to shape the outcome of the item. All external associations will have no jurisdiction to overrule the association in question. From five associations, a higher association will be formed from the selection of one member by each of the five associations. This higher association will have jurisdiction over matters that overlap the interactions of two or more of the primary associations. When two up to five associations at the second degree have formed, then a third-degree association is formed from a member of each of the second-degree associations. Matters handled at these third-degree associations will be for items that affect two or more of the second-degree associations. This process is repeated until the greatest association-degree umbrella can handle matters encompassing every member that is discovered. The guideline above pertains to two up to five associations. It requires five associations should that number exist.

In the beginning, there may only be two, three, or four associations that have formed and no other.

When selecting a pool leader, choose wisely.

Prime Designation

Use "degree" prime designation to describe ascension levels of primes being considered.

From Foundation to the Nexus

The first power prime is given the term "Premiere Foundation" since all other Pentarchy Primes are built on this solid base. Each ascension degree association must effectively represent the number of entities given in the table above. By examining the table above, the fifteenth Pentarchy Prime degree represents approximately 31 billion entities! The highest degree power prime will be termed the "Sentient Nexus" because it will be closest to All-That-Is!

Bequeathing Caretaking to the Next Ascension Pentarchy Prime

In the Pentarchy Primes of society, governing rules at the next Ascension Pentarchy Prime can only be defined and implemented when they are delegated by all five Pentarchy Prime Foundations. Another way involves the exchange of members in at least two of the five Pentarchy Prime Foundations of a particular ascension prime.

Leader Caretakers' Validation

Leader caretakers are not selected by popular vote. Validation at every Pentarchy Prime degree selection is required. In this way, a leader caretaker is intimately aware of concerns at every degree within her umbrella.

Take ownership of decisions. Choose your caretakers wisely.

Matters Affecting the Prime

The process of ascension (degree) prime formation is repeated as long as there are still primes, which is to say that sufficient need to go even further to handle matters consisting of the Nexus (greatest degree prime) for all entities comprised thereof does not present itself. Matters cannot ascend further unless a new nexus pool is discovered.

Principle of Trust

Each Pentarchy Prime degree association will review matters that affect its Pentarchy Prime because of its members' interactions pertaining to those matters. This Pentarchy Prime Principle of Trust establishes that a matter is entrusted to the Pentarchy Prime that is sufficient to address all parties involved. At the same time, there will be certain and severely restricted number of Pentarchy Prime principles that will be decreed to entrust the Sentient Nexus Pentarchy Prime because of universally recognized application.

Assignment for Greatest Growth

The assignment of caretakers ought not to be taken lightly. The caretakers who take their positions in earnest will develop in ways that will not be apparent to them right away. This must be done selflessly. To serve others is the way to the greatest growth for an entity.

A Horrendous Feat

When one considers the Pentarchy Prime Framework, one will recognize that the highest degree association of five umbrella domains will have been selected at each and every prime degree. This means that the person will have demonstrated her leadership abilities at the premiere foundation through all degrees of Pentarchy Primes. It is in this way that truly competent leader caretakers will be brought to the fore. This framework will ensure respect for each autonomous Pentarchy Prime for matters not of grave concern. More details of the process will be forthcoming as each Pentarchy Prime, foundation and ascension types, works them out.

Decision Appeal to Next Ascension Prime

The only time an Ascension Pentarchy Prime will consider a matter is when one or more preceding Pentarchy Prime Foundations issue resolutions that are considered too harsh or too extreme or violates basic Pentarchy Prime Tenets. Otherwise, the prime directives endure with no appeal. They are enforceable and honored everywhere. For example, debts must be repaid or in good standing before new credits are forthcoming anywhere.

To Reach the Nexus

As one is selected to the next prime degree and the next until the Sentient Nexus is reached, one needs only to persuade or convince just five entities, oneself included, at each degree. At the fifteenth degree, the count shows that only 75 entities have to be convinced! This may appear to be a very small number. However, the feat is very great! The influences of nearly 31 billion entities were involved! The link to 31 billion entities is effectively communicated through 75 of them. Consider the notion that everyone who chooses or is able to participate is in fact part of the decision making process. They play a key role by selecting the best and most competent leader caretakers. These are all the checks and balances that are needed. Permit this system to flourish and it will be spectacular!

Pentarchy Prime Transfers

An advanced notification of a separation for a degree minus-one Pentarchy Prime Foundation from the Ascension Pentarchy Prime degree is permitted. Upon review of all outstanding directives and issue resolution opinions made while in the Ascension Pentarchy Prime it is currently in, the terms and conditions is required for complete separation. The terms and conditions are reviewed by the degree plus-one ascension prime for fairness. Admittance to another Ascension Pentarchy Prime with an available member slot is allowed after a transitional transfer period that is based on the foundation degree prime. Completion of all the directives and resolutions at the moment of the transfer request must be met. The exception is the Sentient Nexus Pentarchy Prime since there is no other ascension prime to join!

Pentarchy Prime Foundation Resolution Submissions

When a Pentarchy Prime Foundation submits a resolution to persuade the next Ascension Pentarchy Prime to consider, it is up to the ascension to accept the resolution and make it effective or to brief the foundation why it was not accepted for inclusion. Any resolution brought to the attention of the ascension ought to be considered very seriously. This information channel is the strongest link to all umbrella Pentarchy Prime Umbrellas. This will ensure all are protected and viable.

Jurisdiction

Jurisdiction occurs at the greatest degree that encompasses all of the entities involved in an issue. Bequeathing jurisdiction on a major topic item is permitted to the next Ascension Pentarchy Prime for a period of time, for example, five years.

Checks to Abuse of Power

There may be concern about the abuse of power by those who would preside over matters involving containment of others or other major abuses. The degree minus-one Pentarchy Prime Foundations of five will keep them in check.

Pentarchy Prime Disappearance Scenario Action Plan

If one or more of the Ascension Pentarchy Prime leader caretakers disappear or has been extinguished, the set of degree minus-one Pentarchy Prime Foundations must investigate and suspend all further issue review decisions until the investigation to their disappearance is completed. The findings will be made public with full disclosures, no exceptions, at the earliest moment possible! Exceptions to early completion findings are matters that involve avoidance of grave harmful acts. They are to remain ongoing. However, interim review opinions need to be made.

The Few against the Many Monoliths

It is common practice by historical governments to view institutions as similar to themselves, as monoliths. The view is felt that governments live on and only officials are changed. When you accept this, you are expressing a belief that institutions are sound and good regardless during happenings when some of the officials are abusive in their official capacity. With this belief, it is extremely difficult for one entity to stand up to it. Many in history have been jailed, tortured, or killed. They are the ones who have grown as spiritual entities. They were able to go beyond corporeal existence and be liberated after serving time in an Earth sojourn.

Discard the monolithic institutional belief systems and accept the belief system that we will have instead caretakers or custodians who use instruments such as institutions to provide for the common good of all entities. With this framework, we do not have to make these institutions sterile or without faces. They exist to promote the decisions of society.

Given this, it is not to be suggested that we have to examine all workers as to proper selections. Rather, executive duty caretakers will monitor the performance and duties of all within the organization. These top caretakers can perform the duties of an aspect of societal needs. Society will issue decisions and hand the decisions to executive duty caretakers who are empowered to carry them out. Failure to perform their duties will result in dismissal and possible banishment from other similar positions in the future. Caution must be taken to ensure that decisions be selective and accommodate growth expansions of society and all its members.

Monoliths exist only at the behest of the governed.

Misguided Finality Decisions

Historical judicial decisions were not universally applied nor were they just. They were nothing more than decisions made by feudal lords. Very restricted caring concern was applied to arrive at a final decision. Why leave important matters to anyone else than ourselves? We would best be able to handle smaller manageable impact matters by the smallest pool encompassing all that are part of an issue. This way those who are closest to the events and background can make the fairest and most equitable decision.

Decision Domain

Historically, there was a fear that a judicial decision must be as complete as possible. This is absurd! Decisions can only be based on available information, understanding, and insight. Choose wise leader caretakers to make the best decisions for our times. Use "experts" when needed. They are to be viewed as instruments towards a final decision, not the definitive source for it.

To Participate in the Decision Making Process

In order to participate in the decisions of their fellow inhabitants, one must first join a group of up to four others. Discussion sessions will be conducted, which then lead to decisions for the entire group. The interference by other groups at this same degree is strictly forbidden unless grave harm has occurred or is imminent. A selected leader (thumb) is selected who speaks on their behalf and represents them to the next pool degree, comprised of four other pool leaders from their respective base pool that is comprised of five entities. The request to be in a pool can be made when a vacancy does exist. The request will not normally be refused. The only time that a person can be stripped of the privilege to participate in any pool is in the event of severe harm or killing of another entity. In this example, confinement must be served with no end date until there is a high degree of certainty that the wrongs have been replaced with repentance. A long confinement must be served by anyone committing murder. The concept of self-defense will be narrowly interpreted. When it is found to be so, no time is served, but a healing process will be strongly recommended. The other exception is when an entity has been decreed to be suspended because of serious negligence committed against another for a fixed time not to exceed the minimal term given a murderer's confinement. This entity is banished from voting at all prime degrees that the entity has been selected to participate in.

Uniform Business Laws

Business laws will be aimed at uniform agreements between entities. When very few entities find it very difficult to function within these laws, the various caretaker organizations within the Pentarchy Prime Umbrella will intercede to return them to health. It is recognized that the frailest may have to be provided with stipends and assistance sufficient for sustenance.

Foundation Prime

Foundation Prime Degree Zero

Foundation prime degree zero, also known as universal ground, denotes each premiere sentient. Welcome!

Foundation Prime Degree One

Premiere Pentarchy Prime Foundations are identified as a prime with the designation of degree one. It is comprised of five premiere sentients. Are you one?

Entrance Agreement

All entities must sign and proclaim a Nexus Prime Association Agreement (NPAA) covering the essential guiding principles and tenets of Pentarchy Prime Framework and its engaging spiritual developing promoting environment. Ascension primes will have more specific agreement documents as primes evolve through ascension awareness.

What is your prime designation?

Class Time

Those entities who have expressed their intentions to join a foundation prime will be required to have an introductory class on Pentarchy Prime Foundations and then sign an agreement (NPAA) that issues are resolved through primes based on the degree-of-scope. Also, the class will cover prime directives and the importance that these directives declared will be complied with. Possible case scenarios regarding resolutions for non-compliance will be included.

Entity Choice for Premiere Pentarchy Prime Foundation

To select a Premiere Pentarchy Prime Foundation is a choice. Not to select a Pentarchy Prime is also a choice. In that case, a Premiere Pentarchy Prime Foundation will be chosen on an entity's behalf. Normally, it will be the final open position of five in the prime that will be chosen. This is similar to a low turnout during plurality elections in historical systems for those who do not vote. Decisions will be made on their behalf. Hence, their assigned Premiere Pentarchy Prime Foundation affiliation will be known.

Degrees of Foundation Primes

References in this guide refer to foundation primes with respect to an ascension prime. This refers to a reference degree for the five degree minus-one complement of primes that form the framework for the particular degree ascension prime.

Ascension Pentarchy Prime Umbrella

Ascensions Pentarchy Primes

In the immediate surroundings, a Premier Pentarchy Prime Foundation comprised of five entities is formed to handle matters involving said entities. This means that if there is a dispute within the group, then it is handled by the foundation prime encompassing them. The exception will be when grave bodily or mental harm will be or has been done on any entity. All other groups will not impose their decisions on the group when matters pertain only to the group. From this Pentarchy Prime Foundation, one entity (the thumb) will be selected from the Pentarchy Prime to represent them at the next Ascension Pentarchy Prime comprised of five chosen leader caretakers who represent their respective Pentarchy Prime Foundations. This Ascension Pentarchy Prime Umbrella will decide on matters involving all five Pentarchy Prime Foundations that they represent. Areas of discussion must involve matters that overlap at least two of the five Pentarchy Prime Foundations. This process repeats to arrive at the next Ascension Pentarchy Prime again and again until the Sentient Nexus Pentarchy Prime encompassing every entity is formed. In the context of time, this nexus formation continually expands when more nexus primes are discovered.

Pentarchy Prime Umbrella Governance Reach

The Pentarchy Prime Umbrella has "jurisdiction" when the Rule of Five applies. Its rules are governed and no other prime regarding business and commerce. For all other entity issues, the Pentarchy Prime Umbrella encompassing all entities for particular issue review and resolution governance applies.

Pentarchy Prime Umbrella Access

All leader caretakers of the Pentarchy Prime Umbrella Degree minus-one foundation primes to the Pentarchy Prime Umbrella Degree have unimpeded and unobstructed access to the first ascension prime's discussion and directive generating chambers. Access will not normally be denied to them. Exceptions are when grave harmful acts or a high degree of certainty of grave harmful acts is present.

Pent-Degree Ascension Prime

The ascension primes with degree five designation and each multiple of degree five (five times 'n' where n is any counting number) have special automatic oversight responsibilities described elsewhere. They are referred to as pent-degree ascension primes. For example, the first pent-degree-designation of Pentarchy Primes has automatic initial oversight for all pre-adult entities within its Pentarchy Prime Umbrella.

Completing the Pent-Complement

This rule will permit any entity to seek and find another Pentarchy Prime to associate with. No Pentarchy Prime can remain at three or fewer members for very long. Without five members, ascension cannot be made. Every effort to complete the pent-complement of five members ought to be pursued. Temporary ascension prime association is possible due to a variety of circumstances. One such circumstance is when a member has left the Pentarchy Prime due to member re-selection of another prime or due to natural causes. Another circumstance is when there are no more members in the degree prime pool to pursue.

Foundation Primes to Ascension Prime

The immediate five foundation primes to a particular Pentarchy Prime Umbrella will have unrestricted access to the Pentarchy Prime Umbrella and its activities.

Degrees of Ascension Primes

References in this guide refer to an ascension prime with respect to other ascension primes. This refers to a reference degree plus-one ascension prime that forms the umbrella to the five referenced degree complement of primes.

Nexus Prime

Sentient Nexus Pentarchy Prime Charter

The Sentient Nexus Pentarchy Prime Leader Caretakers (All five) have special empowerments bequeath by all primes everywhere. They are chartered to ensure a safe nexus umbrella by containing all entities that have been identified as the ones who have in great probability caused grave harmful acts or the high degree of certainty that eminent intent of grave harmful acts would have been done by them. These empowerments are of greatest importance and are given. The ultimate responsibility rests with them. There are and will be no other leader caretakers with this responsibility. Naturally, a set of great instruments comprised of nexus Auspices executive officer duty caretakers whom are chartered with implementing nexus directives will be assisting in this. Checks and balances are built in for those who abuse their caretaker positions.

Nexus Prime Special Handling

Grave harmful acts or issues are reviewed by the nexus prime. The handling of all other cases is described elsewhere. There may be other empowerments bequeath by all primes in the future.

Special Governance

Nexus prime has special governance pertaining to the establishment and maintenance of universal tenets and axioms. Except for early creations, new universal tenets and axioms will be shown to be rare over time.

To Fill Sentient Nexus Pentarchy Prime Positions

When less than five degree minus-one Pentarchy Prime Foundations exist at the Sentient Nexus Pentarchy Prime degree, the remaining leader caretaker positions are selected at large by all leader caretakers associated with the existing nexus degree minus-one Pentarchy Prime Foundations.

Pentarchy Prime Set of Guiding Principles

Principle: No Ownership of Sentient Entities

There will be no ownership of sentient entities even when clones are produced.

Principle: Recognition of Pentarchy Primes

The Pentarchy Prime Model, described in more detail elsewhere, is to be the foundation for all resolutions of issues by two or more entities or associations in a sentient society.

Principle: Pentarchy Prime Right to Transfer

The right to freely transfer to any Pentarchy Prime is recognized provided the entity has requested admission to a Pentarchy Prime and the complement of five members in the Pentarchy Prime is not complete. New Pentarchy Primes can form and previously existing ones can dissolve when the need to bind by all members within a prime no longer exists. A minimal time to be defined will exist before total breakup. The method will be through advance announcement to provide sufficient time for all primes affected. The details are described elsewhere.

Principle: Reciprocal Treatment

Treat all members the same way that they themselves would like to be treated is decreed. All must adhere to the same set of tenets.

Principle: Corporeal Executions

By decree, execution of any member in captivity is disallowed even when the member murders another member. The basis for this is that no member is allowed to kill another by this decree. Immediate separation and containment will be imposed on any member that has been determined, by whatever avenues of resolution that exist, to have made this gravest violation. This set of Pentarchy Prime guiding principles state that no one is to be condemned. This is especially valid when it is later found that an incorrect decision has been made on matters of gravest violation. If an incorrect decision is discovered, acknowledgment of that new decision will be made accessible to all. This includes all files, written, oral, and other communication mediums that exist regarding the subject with an apology stated first.

Principle: Supreme Access to Investigative Resources

For all gravest violations, a decree exists that places first and provides adequate resources to resolving all murders or suspicious deaths in the most expeditious manner possible. The tenets of the Sentient Nexus Pentarchy Prime, which is supremely responsible for all inquiries and determination, have been violated. A murder matter unresolved exists in perpetuity until a decision has been made as to what has or may have happened to the highest degree of satisfaction communicated by the investigation duty caretakers assigned to the task.

Principle: Rights to One's Own Information Collected

All information collected by instruments of Pentarchy Primes for a particular entity shall be freely and easily accessible by this entity. The only exceptions pertain to the collecting of information in ongoing murder investigations and to protect the identities of entities that provided important information regarding murders or grave harmful actions at great risks to themselves. These at-risk entities shall be given protection assistance until threat of harm is no longer present.

Principle: Free Information towards Foundation Prime

Information passed from ascension prime to foundation prime is one of many basic tenets. Information collected by any ascension prime is to be freely available to any member within this Pentarchy Prime Umbrella. Exceptions are when information pertains to matters that if made readily available will result in a high degree of certainty that grave harmful acts will be done to entities.

Principle: Selection of at most one Premier Foundation

Each entity identified within a Sentient Nexus Pentarchy Prime domain can select or be admitted to at most one Premiere Pentarchy Prime Foundation. Willful violations can lead to the suspension of prime directive activity participation privileges for a decreed period of time.

Pentarchy Prime
Potpourri of General Rights

Entity Pursuits

As societal pools declare that its members are not subjects of any nation-state, all restrictions to individual entity's or consenting entities' pursuits are lifted. Interaction restrictions are to be eliminated from all governing directives or regulations. Governing laws will only apply to all other conditions within the Pentarchy Primes being created. A primary consideration is in matters regarding business or the exchange of goods and services.

Shared Society Vitality

Protection against grave physical harm or in the case of children, grave psychological harm, is one of the principles of shared society vitality.

Sanctuaries for Forms of Expressions

All consenting forms of expressions will be allowed a sanctuary except for forms of violence or forced indoctrination. The sanctuary must be provided by the greatest Ascension Pentarchy Prime encompassing all requesting the sanctuary. However, no weapons or contagion of mass destruction will be permitted.

The Rights of Groups

The need for a shared belief system to encompass numerous systems is present for the exchange of goods and services in the marketplace. The framework points to the rights of individuals and of groups. Historically, the rights of individuals were, or were supposed to be, guaranteed by various prevailing constitutions. However, the rights of groups were not guaranteed. Historical systems of justice, which are fed by the legislative process, get in the way of free association since the purpose of our system is adversarial in nature, meaning that the system pins one against another. The framework of primes provides the empowerment of two entities or groups to work out their own challenges as the first step. Only in rare situations should it be necessary to present a review and resolution referee setting when the resolution process is at an impasse. Those who agree to and identify with group associations cannot request issue resolution as separate entities. An entity has the option to withdraw from any affiliation. However, when an entity was affiliated at the time of the review petition, the resolution is binding for that entity.

The phrase 'The rights of groups' relates to the general protection right of any group of two or more entities that come together for the purpose of sharing a way of life for themselves.

Protection for Consenting Adults

Matters of private issues between consenting adults are protected from being questioned unless they pertain to gravest harmful acts issued by Sentient Nexus Pentarchy Prime. Deliberate pursuits of the truth in areas of gravest harmful acts are permitted. The truths pertaining to investigations must be forthcoming by any entity when questioned. Failure to be forthcoming may result in containment orders not to exceed five years. No tortures or forced confessions are permitted. Truths are always forthcoming in time.

Transfers

Entities are allowed to move from one Premier Pentarchy Prime Foundation to another after an orderly transition period. The only exception is killing or violent actions toward another. The reason is due to the violation of the supreme entity's right to bond with other entities. When violations occur, the Pentarchy Prime can be broken up, with each entity assigned to an available Pentarchy Prime.

The same rights and review evaluation process apply to ascension primes as well, with reassignment due to violations for each degree minus-one Pentarchy Prime Foundation within the offending Ascension Pentarchy Prime to another at the same prime degree designation.

Natural Substance Usage

By and large, no natural substance will be prohibited. Only when serious harm is present or can occur in high probability will there be limits being put in place. This also includes those situations when serious damage can be done will there be controls placed on it.

All other substances that are engineered with substantive assistance and involvement by sentient entities will these substances be regulated.

Pursuit of an Entity

A single entity's pursuits will not be regulated until they interfere with another one's pursuit. The aim for caretakers will be to illuminate a much brighter path.

Censorship

Censorship of information is supremely prohibited, i.e. summarily prohibited; unless there is a high degree of certainty that grave harmful acts are eminent should particular information be disclosed.

Entity Information Access

Non-Auspices duty caretakers can access information regarding an entity once the particular entity whose information is being requested grants the approval.

Natural Derivatives Opinion

Unequivocal demonstration that an extracted derivative from living organism using complex extraction methods taken in moderate quantities leads to grave harmful behavior, which leads to grave harmful acts being committed, will the derivative be controlled and its use highly restricted. Otherwise, cultivation and the use of simple extraction methods will the usage of the derivative be viewed in the same way as other commonly used derivatives classified as low hazard-risk substances. Over indulgence of low hazard-risk substance by a member that leads to erratic actions leading to harmful acts to other members of society is to be viewed as a harmful member characteristics requiring member containment for safety and security reasons. Safety and security issues are everyone's concern.

Pentarchy Prime
Potpourri of General Restrictions

Property Ownership

There will be a rule that no ownership of land areas or permanent structures on land is permitted. In this case, caretaking leases will be allowed when viewed as beneficial to the Pentarchy Prime Umbrella. All non-living items that can be removed relatively easily will be given the term "property" owned by an entity and passed on to another by that entity. Money accrued during one's sojourn is not included except the first twenty-five percent, a figure that can be adjusted with much discussion, whereby it can be willed to another when one's sojourn ends. A recommendation is to pass the savings on to others before departing. In this way, there is no dispute as to an entity's sincere giving.

Newly Created Sentient Form Intact

No healing practitioner will be a party to the execution of a developing sentient corporeal form while in natural or artificial incubators. It will be permitted to request premature labor for a natural incubator when grave health concerns are present. The newly created sentient corporeal form will remain whole and unharmed in these instances. Normal care of the newborn will be given in all cases. The senses –- sights, smells, sounds, tastes, and touch –- will come to the fore. The developing sentient corporeal forms will no longer be hidden. The life expectancy of a newborn will be based on what nature provides and not what "man-kind" dictates. We are all parties to every sojourner's journey. Each is also a party to our own. We are not separate and distinct but hold a kinship to everything around us. Our reach is as far as we are prepared and ready for.

Prime Directive Libraries

Record Keeping Charter

Record keeping systems, such as a recent conceptually recognized computer system complete with backup and disaster recovery procedures or other similar permanent recording and safeguarding instruments, will record entity foundation prime selection. There is a universally recognized tenet that puts a restriction for an entity to be "active" in only one Premiere Pentarchy Prime Foundation. This is one of the many purposes for the set of instruments known as Prime Directive Libraries.

Pent-Degree Ascension Prime Record Keeping

At each multiple pent-degree ascension prime designation starting with the first, record-keeping systems will be established and maintained within each of these Pentarchy Prime Umbrellas. The nexus prime will also maintain a nexus system. The information is collected starting with the nearest pent-degree ascension prime designation from nexus prime record keeping system. Each pent-degree ascension prime record keeping system will do the same until the foundation primes are reached.

Record keeping of individual prime directives will be maintained by the respective prime. It is a requirement to archive prime directives to the nearest ascension pent-degree Prime Directive Library. This is important when ascension prime directive creation uses compliance determination to arrive at the final decree. However, the research information collection set that formed the basis for the prime directive is not required to be archived with the respective prime directive. Alternate sites to be use as backup archives would be wise to have. Only when an ascension prime directive requires the same information regarding its Pentarchy Prime Umbrellas for the purpose of arriving at a decision at the ascension prime will the ascension prime retain a copy of the information.

Recording System Centers (RSC)

Prime directives or determinations will be sent to Recording System Centers (RSC) described elsewhere. These RSC will identify all entities affected by the decisions and send copies to them. For more serious violations, rapid deployment teams in close proximity to entity or entities will deliver the copies.

The primes will fund an independent service organization that is chartered to record all new or changed entity premiere foundation prime information and all prime directives. Universal entity and prime directive identifiers will be used to identify the records for easy archival and retrieval. The accuracy is to be viewed as of the highest importance possible.

Standard Fees

Standard fees will be established and revised as needed for the purpose of assessment for registering prime directives into archival registries. For those who cannot immediately handle the fees, the amount will be added to their prime account, which must be paid eventually by the prime or an ascension prime.

Special Event Recordings

Recordings of actual events will be kept for safe keeping by the qualifying ascension prime satisfying the Rule of Five test based on the members participating or as spectators in the event.

Urgent Archive of Prime Directives

It is an urgent matter to record and archive prime directives in the manner described elsewhere even in those happenings when action results will not be forthcoming in the near future due to forced compliance by pre-Pentarchy Prime systems. When the event occurs that highlights the eminence of Pentarchy Prime supremacy, all prime directives are activated if not already. Those who willfully interfere with Pentarchy Prime Directives and activities will be subject to privilege limiting directives depending on the severity of the interference. Time will prevail in carrying out prime directives in ways that may not be apparent early on. These events will unfold in time.

Prime Supersedes

The Pentarchy Prime Framework will supersede all pre-Pentarchy Prime systems. Time will make this so. The complete metamorphosis will be spectacular.

Leader Caretaker Selection

Chartered with Pentarchy Prime Umbrella Health

Leader caretakers have supreme responsibilities for the health of the Pentarchy Prime Umbrella they are selected to.

Role of Leader Caretaker

A role of a leader caretaker is the advocacy of wise decisions on behalf of umbrella Pentarchy Prime members and the resolution on issues primarily brought to their attention. On rare occasions, the issues can be recognized by observations by the leader caretakers.

Job Performances

It is not unreasonable to expect and demand that leader caretakers do what the position implies, to lead in the caretaking of primes. Members affected by their actions are the ones who will participate in evaluation of their performances.

The Selection Driving Force

Elitists are comfortable with their positions and statuses. Their primary interest is to sustain their model or framework. However, it does not include the vast majority of members in society. This then is the driving force to ensure that the selection of wise leader caretakers be promoted and to recognize that only our wise leader caretakers be supreme above all other frameworks that have been constructed or put in place to be fine tuned instruments in carrying out prime directives. Our leader caretakers will make wise decisions and be kept in check by prime memberships when decisions are no longer wise or in the best interest of the entire prime umbrella. The entire prime pool of entities effectively chooses our leader caretakers.

No Law Apron Provided

In historical view, the law is an apron to shield those in positions of responsibility from performing their duties. With Pentarchy Prime, leader caretakers are charted to perform these duties of responsibility. These duties are not to be taken lightly. There are no aprons to hide behind.

Responsible and Accountable

The ultimate responsible and accountable caretaking is our Pentarchy Prime leader caretakers. They have bequeathed access to any and all information and facilities under their umbrella. There can be no dereliction of duty or excuses. Replacement leader caretakers will be selected when this is found to be true.

Leader caretakers are empowered to gain access to all sources of the truths. This is important because it aids in arriving at the best possible prime directives.

Characteristics of a Leader Caretaker

A leader caretaker position is not for everyone. This is similar to the notion that not everyone can be an entertainer, banker, doctor, carpenter, etc. One must have the passion and the desire for it. In order to advance to the next Ascension Pentarchy Prime, one must pass muster. Choose our leader caretakers to perform their jobs in a very positive way.

We require that caretakers may apply, not executioners!

Leader Caretakers' Duties

Leader caretakers describe vision and direction, and establish policies and mission statements for the Pentarchy Prime, collectively, to carry out. Auspices officer duty (career) caretakers will establish the rules and guidelines, which are to be as specific as possible and allow for effective empowerment by duty caretakers. One serves at the bequest of the Pentarchy Prime.

Even though a leader caretaker can choose to vary a decision for similar issues, for stability, try to be consistent.

Leader Caretaker Supremacy

Entity pools ought to select the wisest of leader caretakers. Leader caretakers are different from other classifications of caretakers. They have supremacy over all Pentarchy Prime domain activities performed by other classifications of caretakers. In this way, institutions can be dismantled when they no longer serve the entity pools that established their creations. Leader caretakers *do not* serve institutions. Institutions exist because of economy of scale, efficiency, and uniform quality in their results. They are mere instruments to carry out our decisions and pursuits for a better way of life.

A Great Honor to Serve

The greatest position that one can have in a community is that of a wise leader caretaker. Consider it your vocation. It truly is a great honor to serve!

Leader Caretaker Privileges

Determination of Wages

For the interim prime framework, the determination of wages will be determined by members of the particular prime and at most the five degrees of primes in the direction of foundation primes.

Leader Caretaker Review Check

Certification

The certification of a leader caretaker is the selection process. There is no school for this. Mentoring by present and previous leader caretakers may provide some insights for her.

Accountability

Our leader caretakers must account for every entity and decisions made on their behalf. They may use instruments of their own creation to assist in this.

No Passing of Responsibilities

With previous historical systems, one has to work very hard to delay making decisions for fear of falling into a legal quandary. In Pentarchy Primes, no legal quandary exists in arriving at wise prime directives. There is no passing of responsibilities exist. The responsible decision-makers are clear. When selected leader caretakers balk at resolutions, a clear provision exists to select another. Choose wisely.

Conflict of Interest Opinion

When a leader caretaker of a particular degree prime has a conflict of interest in a matter requiring a prime directive, the degree minus-one prime members that selected the leader caretaker will collectively decide on the leader caretaker's behalf. This scenario can apply to all five leader caretakers in a particular degree prime when a conflict-of-interest arises. This procedure only applies when at least three of the members in a particular prime in question are not themselves in a conflict-of-interest situation and these qualified members can effectively produce a prime directive.

Issue Resolution Limits

What has been described for Pentarchy Primes ensures that the primes remain viable. Caution must be exercised in making too many decisions, for they may severely restrict the effective resolutions by Pentarchy Primes at degrees towards the premiere foundation primes. Select only those urgent issues requiring decisions to be made at the next Ascension Pentarchy Prime degree, when urgent matters are at an impasse, or that delay will severely harm another entity. At the same time, permit the selected Pentarchy Prime leader caretakers much maneuvering room to function. Dismiss only those who cease to be wise leader caretakers for a variety of reasons. Set term limits after which their positions may be renewed or a better caretaker is found for the transformation time periods that follow. Finally, honor those who have served.

Actions and In-Actions

A leader caretaker will be evaluated on one's actions and also one's in-actions. An in-action speaks volumes. Listen for it.

Removal Rule

Those who abuse their positions are to be removed by the degree minus-one Pentarchy Prime that selected them. Four votes by this prime are needed for immediate removal for the first ascension prime. Three votes will permit advanced term ending date for the first ascension. There ought not to be any hesitation for removal and replacement of abusive leader caretakers. Built-in time limits exist on holding new selections.

De-selecting of Caretakers

In a prime, three votes (opinions) are needed to de-select an ascension leader caretaker. There is a sliding duration for position expiration as the opinion propagates through ascension primes. The newly selected leader caretaker is an advisor/consultant on matters of decisions/opinions in the current ascension leader caretaker's activities until the newly selected leader caretaker begins her term. Four votes/opinions are needed to de-select a leader caretaker at the next ascension prime immediately with a more accelerated sliding duration for further ascension primes as the opinion propagates through ascension degree primes to the Nexus Prime. The accelerated reduction duration is by a factor of five.

Pentarchy Prime leader caretakers can continue to perform their non-leader caretaker duties while holding their Pentarchy Prime leader caretaker positions. This is valid because wise selections were made. The duration is described elsewhere.

Checks and Balances

Checks and balances are accomplished by selecting the wisest of leader caretakers, who then will keep in check the officer and executive duty caretakers in all the various areas of disciplines. Our selected wise leader caretakers will have supreme empowerments than entities not selected.

Leader Caretaker Duration

Normal Prime Determination Leader Caretaker Removal Transition Periods

Normal degree prime caretaker transitional periods are defined for a currently serving leader caretaker when three members of a particular prime at any degree designation selects a replacement leader caretaker to take her place in serving the next ascension prime on their behalf. The currently serving leader caretaker could also be serving as a leader caretaker at a degree prime greater that the next ascension prime. The following table takes this into consideration and shows the degree prime starting with zero to be the particular prime that made the determination no matter what the actual prime degree designation in the path from premiere foundation prime to the Sentient Nexus Pentarchy Prime is. The table reflects the premise that each and every Pentarchy Prime can select a leader caretaker to serve on their behalf to the next ascension prime.

Selection Reference Prime Degree	Transitional Number of Earth Solar Days
0	5
1	25
2	125
3	625
4	3,125
5	3,125
Greater than 5	3,125

Urgent Prime Determination Leader Caretaker Removal Transition Periods

Urgent degree prime caretaker transitional periods are defined for a currently serving leader caretaker when at least four members of a particular prime at any degree designation selects a replacement leader caretaker to take her place in serving the next ascension prime on their behalf. The replacement is immediate with no transitional period for the currently serving leader caretaker. The currently serving leader caretaker could also be serving as a leader caretaker at a degree prime greater that the next ascension prime. The following table takes this into consideration and shows the degree prime starting with zero to be the particular prime that made the determination no matter what the actual prime degree designation in the path from premiere foundation prime to the Sentient Nexus Pentarchy Prime is. The table reflects the premise that each and every Pentarchy Prime can select a leader caretaker to serve on their behalf to the next ascension prime.

Selection Reference Prime Degree	Number of Earth Solar Days
0	0
1	5
2	25
3	125
4	625
5	625
Greater than 5	625

Graduated Selection Scale

From premiere foundation prime to nexus prime, leader caretakers can serve a term limit from five (Nexus) to twenty five (Foundation Prime) years without the experience of a selection process event by the respective prime designation. This does not preclude a replacement selection event by members of any prime at any degree at any time. This replacement selection process is described elsewhere.

Term Limits

The Sentient Nexus Pentarchy Prime leaders will retain their positions for a period of five years before a new selection process occurs. Rotation of the selection process for an Ascension Pentarchy Prime leader will occur in each of the five years, with one being selected in any given year. Re-selection is permitted. The duration for each preceding Pentarchy Prime degree can have a sliding scale towards Premiere Pentarchy Prime Foundations. This is to be determined by each Ascension Pentarchy Prime.

Universal Prime Rule of Five

Universal Prime Rule of Five (Ro5)

When more than five percent of the patrons or users of environmental resources, commerce, and business governance have association with a Pentarchy Prime Umbrella outside the particular degree Pentarchy Prime being considered for issue review and opinion formation, then the next ascension prime is considered. This process is repeated until less than five percent of the patrons of a business establishment or venture is part of a Pentarchy Prime Umbrella. It is a given that all patrons and users can be identified to a premier foundation prime. The only exception to this is when patrons are guests or visitors because of the patrons' free choice. They would have given their consent to abide by prime directives while guests or visitors of a particular Pentarchy Prime. The definition of a guest is that the entity has been granted the privilege to stay for a longer period of time. When no guest status request has been made, then an entity is automatically given a visitor status instead.

An Alternate View for the Rule of Five (Ro5)

A different view of the Rule of Five (Ro5) will be given next. Both are synonymous to each other and are given to assist entities in understanding this rule using the view that can best be applied and with less confusion.

Prime matters pertaining to the patrons and users of environmental resources, commerce, and business governance will be under the Auspices of the nearest degree umbrella (ascension) prime closest to premiere foundation prime that encompasses greater than 95 percent of the parties (entities). Prime matters are those at the time of the issue review request. In determining the degree prime, the next degree minus-one foundation prime is considered to determine if there is not more than ninety-five percent of the parties (entities) involved at the time of the issue review request that are associated to the degree prime being considered. This process repeats until the test is satisfied. The earliest degree prime that has governance involvement when less that ninety-five percent are in the prime being considered, the immediate ascension prime is then the qualified Pentarchy Prime Umbrella for issue opinion creation.

The Rule of 95 View:

A degree Pentarchy Prime Umbrella covering at least 95% of commerce or interactions among all entities will have its governance applied. Due to entity mobility pursuits, when less than five percent of entities belong to a prime domain "outside" of the particular Pentarchy Prime Umbrella satisfying this rule, no ascension interference is permitted unless an issue violates Nexus Tenets and Universal Principles.

Environment and Commerce Consortiums - Governance Reach

Reach Review

Historically, businesses focus primarily on business interests. They will not normally consider macro (big picture) interests. However, prime leader caretakers do. All members affected are considered when issues are viewed.

The Rule of Five for Natural Environments

Issues regarding natural environment will follow the Rule of Five. Otherwise, issues involving two or more entities will be reviewed and decisions made by the greatest degree prime encompassing all involved in the issue(s).

The Rule of Five for Business and Commerce

The greatest degree ascension prime identified to produce commerce and non-violent activity guidelines is the Pentarchy Prime Umbrella where less than five percent of the pool is non-pool members affected by business and commerce.

F. Dot

Safety of Entities Supremacy

Business regulations and guidelines have no place when the safety interest
of entities is present. It is the responsibility of leader caretakers to step in
and diffuse any safety issue. Also, violence of any kind is unacceptable.
In this case, rapid deployment teams will respond to this type of event.

Environment and Commerce Consortiums - Environment

The Governance Reach of Business

In regards to the reach of rules of business and commerce, it will encompass those activities where the reach is greater than ninety-five percent of the Pentarchy Prime Umbrella.

Business Patron Governance Rule

Any business that has at least ninety-five percent of its patrons (Rule of Five (Ro5)), including workers and employees, within a particular ascension prime umbrella will comply with the policies of said prime. This allows more degree minus-n Pentarchy Prime Umbrellas, where "n" is a counting number, to have autonomy and active participation in the creation of prime directives for themselves.

Prime Governance Designation Displayed

Businesses and organizations will have prime identifiers clearly marked or displayed for prime governance. All businesses, commerce organizations, and service organizations will display and be easily accessible to all the degree prime designations whose set of business governing rules and guidelines are in effect.

Pentarchy Prime Organization Instruments

Specialized agencies charted by any designated prime will be empowered to make decisions on their own and to carry out these decisions. The designated prime has five days to decline any decision. After five days, the decision goes into effect. The prerequisite is for the agencies to forward a copy of the decision to the prime and the prime to acknowledge its receipt. Primes cannot refuse receipt of the copies. Primes can choose to invalidate the decision.

Environment and Commerce
Consortiums - Regulations and Guidelines

Continual Evolution

Viewed historically, business and commerce have gone through numerous "minute evolution moments". This will continue to be so in the future as well. However, the ebb and flow of prime directives will provide more timely responses.

Rules of Operation

Business will operate under the Rule of Five. Simply stated, the greatest degree Ascension Pentarchy Prime that makes decisions and directives is chosen when the business or commerce issue affects at least ninety-five of its Pentarchy Prime Umbrella members. No other degree Ascension Pentarchy Prime has oversight ownership when less that ninety-five percent are affected.

Equalizing Factor

For civil reviews and resolutions, an equalizing formula will be devised for allocation of resources between large business/commerce consortiums and prime members.

Business Rules of the Game

Business entities will be identified by their most ascension prime designation for the set of prime directives and companion business rules and guidelines based on the Rule of Five. All those who wish to do business in this Pentarchy Prime Umbrella must comply. No other set applies. This premise is established for simplicity and clear identification of the rules of the game being applied.

Non-Confinement Scope

Rules and regulations pertain to non-confined members of primes not in camps or secured fortresses. Auspices executive duty caretakers are charted to formulate them.

Confinement Scope

Confined prime members have confinement governance.

Environment and Commerce Consortiums - Positions and Roles

Contact is with Executive Duty Caretakers

Unlike pre-Pentarchy Prime systems, institution and corporation type organizations are not the "entities" informed about prime directives in Pentarchy Prime Framework. Executive duty caretakers are the primary entities for this information. Information includes what their roles and responsibilities are. Failure to comply can lead to their removal.

Environment and Commerce Consortiums - Fair Use Engagement Arena

Exclusion of Exclusion Clauses

Insurance will have no exclusion clauses that conflict with the purpose for the type of insurance that is being sold, for example life and wellness plans. The consumer pool will sustain any loss, or go out of business. The insurance may apply fair-use formulae to assess premiums.

Major Players

If a business consortium wants to be a big or major player in the marketplace, then a greater degree Pentarchy Prime Umbrella will be involved. The greater Pentarchy Prime Umbrella-related issues span this big or major business player consortium.

Rules of Engagement

The rules of engagement for business will be spelled out. More importantly, the code of conduct, which describes high qualities of conduct and aspirations, is supreme in this arena.

In the Kitchen Cooking Products

All naturally derived products from plants will have no restrictions on use and possession when cooking tools commonly found in food kitchens are used. The Rule of Five holds here in its commercial use.

"Seed Money"

For a major prime initiative, seed money in equal amounts will be given to the first twenty-five business entities that have been selected for research and development. After a pre-defined target date, a selection of five from the list will be given the go-ahead to move forward with the next phase of development and production for a period of five years. After that date, the marketplace influences will govern the outcomes. Examples of projects are new high-speed transport systems, like modern trains and tracks, for the Pentarchy Prime Umbrellas.

Pentarchy Prime Termination Points

Identification of commerce distribution and services termination points is essential for clear Pentarchy Prime Umbrellas business directives. It is advisable for ascension primes not to be too intrusive into more foundation prime domains. Have faith that these domains will on the whole do the right thing. Only in cases of weapons of mass destruction to include any man-made construction or mass biological contagion will ascension primes have oversight responsibilities.

Executive Duty Caretakers

Executive Duty Caretakers

This is a duty caretaker classification of caretakers that effectively oversee the vision and operation of an organization or association instrument.

Job Performance

It is not unreasonable to measure an executive duty caretaker job performance. After all, we require competent executive duty caretakers to engage in an active way.

Candidate Questionnaires

Candidates will answer questionnaires for positions as executive officer caretakers and their senior staff to learn of conflict-of-interest issues. Some examples are members of historical nation-state agencies or its official capacities. Depending on the position, the member can be disqualified and cannot serve. Reason: One cannot serve a belief system that is exclusionary in practice. Affidavits will be signed as to the truthfulness and accuracy of the responses with the knowledge that misleading and false replies may lean toward forfeitures of issue resolutions and possible exile from prime participation. The duration will start when the offending entity is effectively a part of primes by choice or when total prime sphere of influence and reach has taken hold. It must be made clear that this is a very serious offense with long period of prime directives' compliance consequence.

Term Limits for Executive Duty Caretakers

There are no term limits for non-Auspices executive duty caretakers. Removal is possible when there exists a pattern of failing to comply with one or more prime directives.

Auspices Executive Duty Caretaker

Auspices Executive Duty Caretakers

This is a duty caretaker classification of caretakers that effectively oversee the Auspices of an Ascension Pentarchy Prime instrument. She serves at the pleasure of the Ascension Pentarchy Prime and her skills and abilities are key factors in the prime's selection.

Auspices Executive Duty Caretakers Charter

The Auspices executive duty caretakers are empowered to implement prime directives assigned to them. The prime directives may be general or quite specific. When general, they are chartered with the responsibility for producing the detailed specifications and then implementing them. The Pentarchy Prime Umbrella that these caretakers serve will be provided with adequate resources to accomplish their directives.

Auspices Prime Secretary

An Auspices prime secretary -- a unique classification distinction among Auspices executive duty caretakers -- has the honor and duty of recording prime directives. Her duties include the safekeeping of the prime directives for posterity and the submission of copies of them to pent-degree archival recording centers. The requirements and procedures for these centers are described elsewhere.

Term Limits for Auspices Executive Duty Caretakers

There is no pre-set term limits for Auspices executive duty caretakers. To be removed from this position on the opinion of the respective Pentarchy Prime is not to be considered an offense. To violate one's own body of rules set forth for all in the domain under her care is considered to be a more serious offense. In this case, the highest penalties and/or exclusions will be imposed for such offenses. After all, an executive duty caretaker knows what is or is not an offense and will be held to the highest standards.

Removal of Auspices Executive Duty Caretakers

Removal of an Auspices executive duty caretaker holding a particular position requires three leader caretaker opinions for normal ending duration. This duration allows for a transitional period before another selected Auspices executive duty caretaker to assume this position. For immediate removal requires four or more leader caretaker opinions. The latter action would normally occur for serious position violations or the failure to comply with prime directives. The Pentarchy Prime Umbrella that these caretakers serve will be provided with adequate resources to accomplish their directives.

Vocation Caretakers

Duty Caretakers (Pursuit View 1)

This is a general classification of caretakers that perform a set of duties promoting the safety and well being of other entities.

Duty Caretaker (Pursuit View 2)

The duty caretaker is a general classification for any role in a position whereby a skill is learned and performed in a job environment. Her duties, in whole or in part, provide a service or product for another member of a Pentarchy Prime umbrella domain.

Specialist Caretaker Professionals

The specialist caretaker professional is a general classification that includes specialists such as doctors, dentists, nurses, scientists, mathematicians, and a whole array of other classifications. Primarily, the distinction is the result of narrowing the pursuit of interest in an entity's sojourn.

Degree of Caretaking Duties

Minimum standards are required for caretaker duties.

Certification

Certification for non-leader caretaker positions must be met when defined by the Pentarchy Prime Umbrella.

Job Performances and Retention

Duty/executive caretakers will be measured on their performances and dynamic prime domain developmental needs. It will indicate whether or not to retain each distinction of classification for the purpose of certification or be de-classified.

Vocation Duty Caretaker Removals in General

Leader caretakers will make decisions in matters of removals due to serious violations by a vocation duty caretaker in any category. They will make the suggestion for the vocation duty caretaker to resign before a more drastic opinion is issued to remove the caretaker from her position with serious consequences. Serious consequences can include the added provision that no holding of the same or similar caretaker positions from five up to twenty-five years depending on severity of the offense or refusal to step down.

The objective is to get the duty caretaker to leave her position in the most expeditious manner when the duty caretakers in charge failed to follow prime directives.

Non-Compliant Caretaker

The objective regarding the general classification of caretakers who violate prime directives is to remove them from positions and related privileges. Fines can be fixed amounts or be a percentage of an assessment. Usage of a fixed percentage will be found to be more equitable for all those who are in serious violations. Fines are best for minor offenses.

Sabbatical Decree

The sabbatical decree duration from holding a position once a decision is made for an entity's removal will commence five days after stepping down. This decree is specified in a prime directive or an Auspices executive duty caretaker's directive.

Natural Environment-Based Caretakers

Natural environment-based caretakers will be registered with the Pentarchy Prime Umbrella based on the Rule of Five. Support packages are provided when their missions are for the greater good of the Pentarchy Prime Umbrella. It may be necessary to rotate all who desire to participate when resources are fixed in amount. Natural environment-based executive caretakers will be identified to hold these long-term positions. They will be selected based on their skills and abilities matching the positions' qualifications.

Officer Duty Caretakers Responsibilities

Leader caretakers selected by particular Pentarchy Primes do not normally establish the detail rules or the monitoring of daily activities. They appoint executive officer duty caretakers to carry out responsibilities for the care of the general public. Removal of an executive officer duty caretaker is done with four out of five leader caretaker opinions of the Pentarchy Prime umbrella. Otherwise, the same rules set forth by executive officer duty caretakers are to be followed by everyone under the umbrella. For demonstration of support, Pentarchy Prime Umbrella leader caretakers are included with the rule set compliance.

Access to Information

Duty caretakers will keep no information secret when the information serves a vital public interest or the well being of all. All information will be available to leader caretakers without restrictions. Failure by knowingly withholding essential information by duty caretakers is a serious offense that will normally lead to immediate removal of caretaker duties and restrictions on similar positions in the future.

Review and Remedy Duty Caretakers

This is a classification of caretakers, historically known as court judges, to preside in matters that require review and resolution activities for disputed issues brought to the Auspices Review and Remedy Instruments by members of the community. These issues are not to be of the most serious kind, which are specifically the responsibilities of the Sentient Nexus Pentarchy Prime and Auspices instruments.

Pre-Adult and Adult Sponsor Caretakers

Sponsor Caretakers

This is a general classification whereby as sponsor caretakers of an entity, they will collectively participate in the caretaking decisions involving the entity. There will be no tolerance for selection determination confrontations. When primary determination confrontations ensue, those sponsor caretakers involved will be temporarily removed from sponsor caretaker status. Those sponsors remaining will be allowed to continue their responsibilities. With temporary sponsor removal status, those who show sincere effort to be viable sponsor caretakers once again will be allowed back in the caretaking activities of an entity. Sponsor caretakers are to be viewed as providing the best form of caretaking.

Pre-Adult Sponsor Caretaker

Pre-adult members will have oversight sponsor caretakers to assist them in their adult-maturing development. The pre-adult sponsor caretakers are normally first assigned to parental entities unless relinquished by parents or when there is a high certainty that grave safety or developmental harm is imminent.

Those who are sponsor caretakers for a pre-adult will have the designation removed when harm is done or the potential for grave harm is imminent. No more than five primary or principal caretakers are assigned per child.

Until they reach or are declared adult-status entities, children who have serious issues pertaining to them are to be reviewed by the first pent-degree ascension prime. Prime of degree five is another name for the same designation. This is based on the parents/custodians who are their caretakers.

The guidelines above apply when sponsor caretakers are available. In cases when none are available, please be the one to step in when a void is there. If you step in during emergency situations when they occur, your sincere attempts will not be viewed as prejudicial. Thanks go to all ahead of time.

Default Ascension Prime Pre-Adult Oversight

Pent-degree ascension primes automatically oversee the care of pre-adult within the Pentarchy Prime Umbrella unless specific expanding degree ascension prime decisions override due to harmful environments that were not being addressed by the pent-degree ascension primes. This issue ought to be rare.

Five Year Term Minimum

Pre-adult caretakers will be specifically identified for five-year terms. Those who do participate in caretaker duties will normally be renewed.

Guardian Auspices

Pre-adult members (children) are automatically under the Auspices of the first pent-degree Pentarchy Prime for matters pertaining to guardian oversights. No child will be invisible to this degree Pentarchy Prime. It is one of their primary responsibilities in making this so. Reviews are made at this designation for identification and re-establishing of pre-adult sponsor caretaker designation. Recommendation for child-care events ought to be followed. Removal of designation when recent child endangerment events have been found to be true or imminent child endangerment is very probable and ever present.

Pre-Adult Support Payments

Dependent support when decreed will not be greater than what is given as universal dependent deduction purposes. The first pent-degree prime will make that determination. Even for entities of limited resources, amounts are the same and owed over time to ease the burden.

Custody is not the Issue

The aim as it pertains to a child is not to decide who has custody, which is a historical entity property term, but rather who will be members in a group of caretakers for the child in all growth developmental matters pertaining to the child.

Automatic Sponsor Caretaker Assignments

Children will automatically have pre-adult sponsor caretakers assigned when natural adult family members are not available. These sponsor caretakers may not be perfect ones but will be ones who have the passion to do the best job they can. Only when serious harm is possible or has been done will the position be taken away. It is important to keep in mind that we are all growing. Sincere caretaking efforts are to be recognized and applauded.

High Priority Assignment

A very high priority for identifying child development caretakers (Pre-adult sponsor caretakers) is ever present whenever a child is without one. The fist pent-degree Pentarchy Prime will be primarily responsible for its oversight. The assignment will always be for a child development caretaker.

Urgent caretaking organization instruments may be needed for very short stays. "Big sisters and brothers" are asked to apply. You are welcomed.

Adult Designation

Bequeathing of an adult designation of an entity is made by the Nexus Pentarchy Prime or the first pent-degree Pentarchy Prime, whichever is closest to premiere foundation prime degree. This can be declared by an automatic age attainment directive or due to a prime determination request by an entity in question and subsequent opinion concurrence.

The Nexus Pentarchy Prime will establish the maximum adult attainment age for all entities able to make effective sentient decisions of their own. The degree of effective sentient decision creation determination will be defined to encompass close to one hundred percent of members within the nexus prime.

Adult Sponsor Caretakers

When an adult entity is not able to respond because of medical or bodily impairment, those who have personal involvement will decide on the entity's behalf. When a dispute arises that challenges a right of sponsorship, then the earliest degree Pentarchy Prime Umbrella encompassing all parties will select the sponsor caretakers. If, however, a sponsor caretaker is determined to have a very minor involvement or none at all, the degree prime that initially review the matter can defer a decision to the degree minus-one Pentarchy Prime Foundation encompassing the smaller Pentarchy Prime Umbrella.

When no adult sponsor caretakers are present, the Premier Pentarchy Prime Foundation is initially given the responsibility for the decision. When no adult sponsor caretaker is available and viable, the next Ascension Pentarchy Prime will be responsible for the decision. This repeats until the pent-degree Pentarchy Prime is found. Load balancing spanning a greater degree than pent-degree Pentarchy Prime Umbrella may be needed on occasions when major catastrophic events do occur.

Only interested entities who were/are involved with the well being of another entity are to be the primary ones who have the particular entity's best interest in mind and spirit. An Auspices instrument will not have ultimate decision over the welfare of the entity unless no sponsor caretakers have come forward with their declarations. Every effort will be made to have the entity's stay short.

Pentarchy Prime Associations

Initial Prime Framework Construction Associations

Five years will be the minimum membership association declaration with their respective Pentarchy Prime Foundations before making another selection. It is important to choose carefully because of this long-term commitment during the early years of Pentarchy Prime Framework construction. The aim in the beginning is to learn from our experiences in the turnaround of wise decisions formed in a shorter time. After this birth and early growth period, a minimum of twenty-five days from declaration signing is given before making another selection. After this minimum period, the entity is viewed as being a permanent member.

The reader may view the above guidelines as promoting a volatile environment. In time, it will be learned that it is more important to an entity to participate with their encounters in arriving at their own prime directives. The above guidelines provide escape clauses when prime associations become unbearable.

Single Domain Association Identification

Any entity can declare and be admitted into our Pentarchy Prime environment from a non-Pentarchy Prime environment. When this happens, identification for any non-Pentarchy Prime association domain is not recognized. Should an entity make a request to retain her prior identification, no Pentarchy Prime association is allowed and restricted visitor routes and sites are permitted only. Violations result in banishment from Pentarchy Prime Umbrella domains.

Change in Foundation Prime

Entity move requests to another premiere foundation prime are normally granted. There is a twenty-five day limitation on issues from initial notification before a different Pentarchy Prime Umbrella can review any issue regarding the entity. A twenty-five day to five year sliding scale is used as entity issue is reviewed at each step-degree Pentarchy Prime Umbrella to the nexus prime.

Prime Association Identification

A nexus universal symbol will define each Pentarchy Prime degree jurisdiction. A second uniquely designed symbol can be adopted by each prime of their own choosing to represent their distinctive prime identity.

Prime Designation

What is your prime designation?

Choice of Foundation Prime

All entities that are not confined can choose the premiere foundation prime of choice. Matters involving two or more members within a Pentarchy Prime Umbrella can defer the final opinion (decision) to a degree minus-n foundation prime that also is the Pentarchy Prime Umbrella to all parties. The view is that the opinion (decision) that the matter can best be handled is at the more inclusive prime. An example may be due to the close proximity of the matter (issue) with the prime identified. Examples are commerce, vehicle traffic patterns, air flights, sporting events, local sanitation services, etc. A partial decision may be rendered by the greatest ascension prime with the complement portions of the final decision deferred to an umbrella degree prime closer to premiere foundation prime.

Default Foundation Prime Selection

Foundation prime selection guidelines are imposed and enforced when an entity cannot decide her foundation prime identity. In this case, the designation prime that is determined is based on the interactions of other entities of the pent-degree prime regarding the entity in question and by the Rule of Five. Should this scenario not be easily determined, then the pent-degree prime with members in close proximity of the entity based on the Rule of Five will select on her behalf. Additional guidelines regarding more specific scenarios will be described in greater details at a later date.

Consider Rapid Turnaround Selection

One can consider proximity of prime members when joining a foundation prime. Also for prime leader caretaker, the same is true for ascension prime. This suggestion is not an absolute. However, rapid turnaround can be achieved more readily in prime review and directive activities.

Prime Separation Events

When Pentarchy Primes are separated due to natural barriers that are beyond control of the primes, temporary inclusive domain systems are formed in order to continue caretaking responsibilities until cohesive links with the others are restored. This means the establishment of a new premiere to Nexus Pentarchy Prime Framework.

Registration Research

Entity requests for foundation prime registration can select a characteristic category type for prime selection. A list of the primes and their affinity types are compiled and provided for selection determination. Archival Auspices Libraries are entrusted with this responsibility.

Consider a Viable Selection

In considering affinity type premiere foundation prime versus geographic positional foundation prime selection, the former will demonstrate its superior viability over time.

Registration of Visitors

During transformation and beyond, those who wish to visit or immigrate must register and declare their intentions. Once the immigration intent is registered and it is to immigrate, then they are given the chance to select Premiere Pentarchy Prime Foundation or are automatically assigned to one. In the latter case and once readjustment is complete, selection of a particular prime is allowed.

Pentarchy Primes Supersedes

In joining a prime, affirmation is made that decisions made by the prime in matters involving two or more member entities will be followed. All other decision-making systems do not supersede systems of Pentarchy Primes.

Pentarchy Prime Environment

Terrorist Regimes Identified

The policy of non-entry of entities into a domain defines it as a terrorist one as viewed by those who are excluded. In fact, this view will be shown to be universal. It will be so that terrorist regime will be dismantled wherever they may occur.

Non-Citizen Criminal Intent

No law or tenet will exist that defines sentient beings as being criminal because of being non-citizen. All non-harming sentient entities will have safe passage throughout primes' public passage routes.

Safe Passage

No entity can be considered a criminal for wanting to be free by entering a geographic boundary. A primary purpose of Pentarchy Prime is to ensure safe passage for all entities that travel throughout it.

All primes will allow safe passage through their primes for any entity. Exception for passage is when entity is confined for grave harmful acts.

Favorable Conditions

There is not to be condemnation so that conditions can be favorable for minimal or non cover-up on the true nature of the problem. The aim is to rectify harmful conditions quickly so that favorable conditions are restored.

Active Participation

Review your primes at all degrees and offer recommendations for improvements. You will find that the vast majority of leader caretakers welcome this.

Entity Information Access

Freedom to access any information on one's self is normally granted, except when murder or grave harmful acts have occurred and the investigations are ongoing.

Privileges Restored

When an entity's probation period is complete due to the serious nature of the violation or offenses, all privileges are to be restored unless specifically noted in the review directive.

Parallel Family Household Preserved

Pentarchy Prime Framework recognizes a family unit consisting of parents or pre-adult sponsor caretakers and children. This framework will not treat members poorly. To aid every member's basic viability needs will be explored and implemented. To help another will lead to the same being reciprocated.

Children's care will be under the Auspices of the first pent-degree Pentarchy Prime Umbrella as the primary Pentarchy Prime for review checks in favorable developmental environments. This Pentarchy Prime Umbrella has the first responsibility to intercede when harmful environments exist.

Urgent Charitable Work

When urgent charitable work is being carried out, obstacles will be removed by temporarily lessening the codes and standards that exist until the urgency has passed, at which time the higher codes and standards are restored.

Modes of Movement

A key success factor for Pentarchy Primes is to have various modes of transportation and access routes. There must be viability for all modes and not be limited to one or two primary modes. Alternatives ought to be pursued so that they can be accessible to all by using one of many modes.

Venues of Entity Pursuits

Good faith attempts will be made for specifying conditions that satisfy entity or entity group requests to perform pursuit ideas. Exceptions that prohibit them are when there is a high certainty that grave harm would be experienced by other entities.

Pentarchy Prime Governance

Leader Caretakers Oversee All

Historically, a government based on a nation-state framework is nothing more than having the elite in positions as land-based lords. Wars are started to secure and maintain artificial boundaries or fences. Leader caretakers do not require borders to wisely lead the pool that selected them.

General Reach

Historically, the legal system defined and handled matters that pertain to properties and their holdings of them. Entities are not to be viewed as property but rather are to be viewed in the well being and protection of primes. It is up to wise leader caretakers when entities may pose a danger to other entities and their well being and protection.

Minimum of Two

Primes deals with matters involving two or more members in their respective primes. For matters involving a singular member, that singular member handles them. Respect this.

Nation-State Jurisdiction

Nation-states have no jurisdiction over other nation-states. Only Ascension Pentarchy Primes do.

Evenly Spread

In historical legislative, judicial, and executive (triad) societal framework, massive laws and regulations must be passed, administered, and judged by few officials who preside over their application. With Pentarchy Prime, the decisions are spread more evenly and are more effective because matters are resolved at the optimum degree prime that spans all members and no greater!

Premier Prime Directives

When no rules and regulations exist to address an issue by two or more members of a Pentarchy Prime Umbrella, then the responsibility for their creation is the domain of the leader caretakers of the Pentarchy Prime Umbrella. Initially, they may be general in scope and application. Time may be needed for wise refinements. The wise usage of "time" applies here.

Geographic and Environmental Domains

Geographic and environmental domains are preserved under the Auspices of Pentarchy Prime Umbrellas based on the "Rule of Five" described elsewhere. Exceptions for non-preservation and non-sustaining activities can only be considered when an ongoing plague is present or a real possibility. In this case, a greater degree prime may recognize the situation to be of grave concern and intercede for the well being of all.

F. Dot

Bequeathing Caretaking to the Next Degree

Jurisdiction occurs at the umbrella degree prime that effectively encompasses all parties in an issue. Bequeathing jurisdiction on a subject matter can be made to the next ascension degree for a period of five years.

Access to Information

There will be no restrictions on an entity's own information recorded anywhere. Access to public information, which is maintained by any particular Pentarchy Prime, will be made available to all within the Pentarchy Prime umbrella. Those who administered treatments, for example doctors, will be regulated that describes the information to be collected and stored.

Revenue Sharing

Any resources, historically referred to as "revenue", collected by ascension primes are to be shared by the umbrella foundation primes. The shared resources allocation is based on wise usage and need.

Environmental Stewardship

Leader caretakers will, after much consultation with advisory duty caretakers, identify land, sea, air, space zones, etc. that can be given temporary stewardship for business, foundation prime, and/or entity usage. All usage code standards for its use must be complied with for continuous privilege usage.

Professional Certification Boards

Establish monitoring and evaluation Auspices boards for the professional duty caretakers. The Auspices will provide performance qualification ratings to aid any entity's need for such information.

A Primary Mission Statement

A primary mission statement of Pentarchy Primes is the identification and promotion of caretakers in their wise caretaking of entities in their domains. Historically, systems of laws in micromanaging behaviors maintained the premise that no uniqueness exists. Everyone and everything is identical in its application. This is a false premise. Diversity exists and is universal. Embrace it; promote it; allow for variances to exist! Wise decisions are welcomed. However, it would be wise to be uniform when common elements or application threads exist.

Final Decree

Leader caretakers are the final arbiters in all matters involving their Pentarchy Prime Umbrellas, inclusive. As described elsewhere in this guidebook, rely on the Rule of Five for matters pertaining to usage of natural resources, businesses, and commerce regarding efficiencies and to prevent review and resolution matters from going to a halt. Do establish auspice agencies to be instruments of Pentarchy Primes, where appropriate, to handle routine or common matters not pertaining to unique urgent consequence issues to the general Pentarchy Prime Umbrellas. Our respective Pentarchy Prime leader caretakers will etch well-formed principles and guidelines to assist us in our pursuits.

Ownership of Information

Information produced or collected in a Pentarchy Prime is to be shared by all entities within its umbrella. The referenced Pentarchy Prime may be required to share it with other Pentarchy Primes at the same prime degree. Here is how it works. A Pentarchy Prime Foundation can produce or collect information to be shared within its Pentarchy Prime umbrella. However, the next Ascension Pentarchy Prime must decide to collect the same type of information before it can be shared with its Pentarchy Prime Umbrellas. This constitutes the right to privacy and related matters.

Bequeathing Decision Review and Resolution Domain Review

Decisions are to be made at the earliest foundation degree prime whenever possible. Jurisdiction is to be respected and resolutions honored with no exception except as explicitly expressed elsewhere, because of the serious nature of the issue review item. Decisions can be delegated to the next Ascension Pentarchy Prime when review and determination requests are made by the foundation prime. The resulting decision by the ascension prime with sufficient opinions by leader caretakers is then binding. A request for insight can also be requested. The opinion may be used in arriving at a decision for the Pentarchy Prime Foundation decision. In both situations, a fee may be permissible. The criterion for a particular Pentarchy Prime to have responsibility for a decision is when an issue impacts two to five of the Pentarchy Prime Foundations within the prime.

Collection Set of Information

Information collected within a Pentarchy Prime umbrella remains within it unless a prime directive by the Pentarchy Prime Umbrella is made releasing the information to the ascension prime. This rule does not apply when the ascension prime is also collecting similar information by all degree minus-one member primes.

Ascension Prime Serious Issue Review

It will be one of the primary missions for primes to uncover the truth in matters that are of the serious nature initiated by more foundation primes when matters are not brought to ascension primes for a variety of reasons. The final onerous is on applying wise usage of prime activity avenues.

Pentarchy Prime Umbrella Re-sizing

When there are entities from other primes who have affected non-environment and commerce consortium actions by a more foundation degree Pentarchy Prime Umbrella and its members, then the Pentarchy Prime Umbrella encompassing the tighter degree will be involved.

Pentarchy Prime Governance Instruments

A Lease Arrangement

With Pentarchy Prime Framework, there is no propensity for war over land. The need to guard boundaries is non-existent. Besides, what would you defend? Land is a caretaker lease arrangement with the Pentarchy Prime Umbrellas affected. The wise usage of land is promoted by primes. Hoarding is not allowed. Feudal lords need not apply.

The Service of Institutions

Pentarchy Prime Framework requires leader caretakers take charge and make wise decisions. Leader caretakers do not serve institutions. Institutions, hereafter known as Pentarchy Prime Instruments, exist when prime directives warrant them.

Composition of Juries

Returning to the notion of an integrated system of justice, a more involved community participation in a just system will be found to be superior. For matters not pertaining to the highest degree of urgency, a panel of five jurors, two selected from one party's pool of peers, two selected from the other party's pool of peers, and one from the professional jurist pool, will preside in deciding the outcome of a non-harmful matter. This framework instrument is being proposed as an interim one or a long term one should leader caretakers choose it to be so to handle issues and matters not pertaining to present or future grave harmful acts. The earliest degree foundation prime that encompasses all the parties in an issue or matter defines the jurist selection pool. All parties may make any comment of their choosing, which has a bearing on the issue or matter, without censorship. A time limit may be imposed on each member who testifies so that it speeds up the process when needed. The goal of the proceedings is to be just and fair without the tone of condemning or victimizing. The aim should always be to deny privileges when a violation has been done, to recover loss of possessions by the violator, or to assist in the healing process when it is recognized that the assistant approach will have a long term lasting benefit to the whole. Confinement camps are cruel and are used as a last resort for blatant or habitual violations. An entity should be held when the entity flees from the scene of a harmful event like, for example, a serious accident, without first being released by a recorder-of-events officer duty caretaker on the scene.

Auspices of Pentarchy Primes

Instruments responsible for rules and guidelines based on prime directives exist under the Auspices of Pentarchy Primes.

Long Standing Instrument Organizations

The instrument organizations established by primes will certify professional ranks that are especially involved with the health, welfare, and security of its members. It is the responsibility of these same prime instrument organizations to review each certification on a periodic basis and when grave harm has been done or have a high degree of certainty of happening. The respective Pentarchy Prime Umbrella is liable for offenses when early warning signs were ignored.

No Second Guessing

Leader caretakers will not second-guess business decisions. However, rules and regulations on conduct and fairness will be established. Those particular rules and regulations that have high prime importance designation will be monitored by instrument Auspices of the primes. Removals of business executives are based on these high prime designations.

Pentarchy Prime Instrument Review Period

The leader caretakers of a particular Pentarchy Prime have five days to void proposed standards and guidelines produced by Auspices executive caretakers of the prime Auspices instruments. Opinion review feedback by leader caretakers can assist in rapid refinements when proposals are voided. In general emergency and when decrees are not related, the time for rejection is twenty-five days. These Auspices prime instruments are chartered with implementing guiding principles created by leader caretakers' prime directives.

Identification Access Speed Instrument

There is no need for bar codes on entities, since every entity is a member of at most one premier foundation prime. All ascension primes are derived from foundation primes that every entity can eventually be identified. However, an identification access speed instrument can be used to greatly speed up admission or perform transactions to primes' societal activities.

Pentarchy Prime Issue Formation

Prime Directive

A prime directive is the outcome of issue review and discussion activities by a particular Pentarchy Prime. This is due to an issue involving matters that pertain to two or more of its members. The prime directive reflects on the issue and specifies the resolution regarding it.

Candidate Issues

Candidate issues for prime decisions are based on the high probability that interactions of entities exist.

Size the Issue

The "size" of an issue is reviewed first. Then the review and resultant opinion of the issue is made at the correct "degree-size" Pentarchy Prime based on the issue's reach.

No Issue Delays

A prime has five days to validate an issue involving two or more members are in fact within their respective Pentarchy Prime Umbrella jurisdiction. Otherwise, the next ascension prime is involved in the issue unless the ascension prime cannot validate within five days. This process continues until an Pentarchy Prime Umbrella is found. This rule illustrates the importance of prime members' record keeping caretaking and preservation.

Types of Issues

Primarily, leader caretakers will be involved with types of issues that have not been addressed before. Established prime directives that are in existence at the present will govern normal or routine issues.

Matters brought to the Fore

Pentarchy Primes deals with matters not specified anywhere else as rules and guidelines that were implemented or previously defined prime directives.

New Issues

All existing prime directives must be in compliance before new issues raised by a prime member can be considered and handled by the prime's leader caretakers. To be in compliance can mean a scheduled action as set forth by prime directive(s). Exceptions are when matters pertain to grave harm that has been committed or there is a high degree of certainty that grave harm will be committed by the member.

Towards Ascension Prime

By registering your prime directives, future resolution petitions will more effectively review available information in rendering a newly created wise prime directive. These early directives set the stage for future directives at all degrees. All opinions do count.

Pentarchy Prime Issue Discourse

Review Delays

When an entity or leader caretaker requests review of an issue, the review will happen when all prime directives are complete or are making satisfactory progress towards their completion. Any delays are then due to the entity making the request. Exceptions are when grave emergencies exist.

Filibuster

A filibuster in prime terms means to withhold one's decision. Other leader caretakers within a prime can move forward with a final directive when sufficient opinion votes are present. Two filibusters can delay a permanent prime directive. Should the non-filibuster members provide the three sufficient opinion votes for a resultant prime directive, the prime directive is temporary for twenty-five days. The prime directive creation impasse will need to secure sufficient opinion votes to continue the same prime directive another twenty-five days. This is repeated whenever two leader caretakers in a prime choose to filibuster. Otherwise, the prime directive is permanent. When this filibuster situation event does occur, this type of event ought to alert members within a Pentarchy Prime Umbrella to take notice and get involved in assisting the resolution of this impasse. The assistance may lead to the selection of a replacement of one or more leader caretakers.

Pentarchy Prime Issue Resolution

Initial Pentarchy Prime Issue Requester

When a prime decision has been made and passed on to members within the prime who had the issue initially presented to the prime, the members must abide by it. Failure to comply by any member will cause suspension of further consideration for any current and future issue review requests brought by the non-compliant member.

NOTE: Consider using arbiters in Pentarchy Primes doctrines everywhere.

Interim Consuls

We will have interim consuls and arbiters to handle the transitional judicial reviews. Prime tenets are supreme and the consuls and arbiters will ensure that these tenets are not violated when reviewing historical references.

Leader Caretaker Opinions

For any prime, three yes opinions are needed for a decision to have creditable prime directive status recognition. In time of emergencies, one leader caretaker of the five in a prime is needed for a temporary decision to be carried out. Within 25 hours, the complement of the three minimum decisions is needed to remove a temporary decision to be longer term. Contingencies may need to be considered, which is why these temporary measures are needed. These events ought to be rare.

Text Available to All

The text to all prime decisions will be made available to all entities within the Pentarchy Prime Umbrella. The exceptions will be when there is a high probability that should a decision be made readily available, there is a high degree of certainty that grave harm may be committed by those who are viewed as violent entities and are not presently in containment.

A Procedure for Issue Review Escalation

For review escalation for non-harmful originating prime directive, the complainant must leave the Pentarchy Prime Foundation for another. This will encompasses a greater Ascension Pentarchy Prime before the initial complaint request can be considered by the greater Ascension Pentarchy Prime. An example of this is the following. A traditionally married couple in the same Pentarchy Prime Umbrella must "de-couple" before escalation reviews can be considered in regards to complaints between the marriage-bound entities. The respecting of Pentarchy Primes is normally given except for those provisions already spelled out elsewhere regarding grave offenses.

Record Keeping

An information system will be developed and maintained to keep track of all associations. Access to it is to be easily acquired by any member within the Pentarchy Prime Umbrella. Any matter involving two or more Pentarchy Primes at the same prime degree will be resolved by the immediate Ascension Pentarchy Prime encompassing all. A Pentarchy Prime session will convene as needed.

Source of Resolution Insights

Reviewing member foundation primes' prime directives by Pentarchy Prime Umbrella members does provide good insights regarding the health and wise decision making activities of the more foundation primes. Pentarchy Prime Umbrella can determine when assistance is urgently needed. Look there first.

The Rule of Five Review and Resolution Ceiling

On occasions, there may be appeals to the next ascension prime to determine if a particular prime directive is viewed as harsh. If so, a review is stated with comment and passed to foundation prime or petitioner requesting this review. A modified prime directive may be produced. This process repeats until five degrees of ascensions have been contacted. Review and resolution can yield a neutral outcome. It this case, the original prime directive is left as-is.

Interim Directives

Some issues can be deferred when the subject matter requires more thought and discovery. In those cases, an interim directive will be issued and have a preface stating that this directive is interim in scope and that the issue may be re-visited at a later time after additional thought and discovery activities.

Pentarchy Prime Issue
Resolution Implementation

Clarification Prime Directive Expansion

Prime directive refinements are needed only to clarify decision-making directives when the executive duty caretakers are unsure how to resolve an issue or when leader caretakers think the issue is of a greater importance to require a wise refinement.

Language of Choice

Dissemination of information and prime directives will be made using the language of choice selected by each Pentarchy Prime that issued them. One or more languages may be chosen.

Prime Directives Courier System

A separate Auspices courier system will exist to communicate prime directives to all foundation primes within Pentarchy Prime Umbrellas.

Archival Prime Directives

Permanent archival backups of prime directives are required. The activities and specifications are described elsewhere.

Further Classifications

Primes define the terms and conditions. Auspices executive duty caretakers will identify the items, properties, entities that are impacted by those terms and conditions.

Leader Caretaker Executor Refusal Requests

If a leader caretaker is selected to be the champion for the implementation of prime directives finds it difficult to execute a decision by the prime's group of leader caretakers because of strong beliefs, she may request that it be re-assigned to another, one who has decided with the majority. This request will normally be honored.

Auspices of Arbiter Caretakers

Actions and decisions by caretakers are based on prime directives where applicable. When excerpts become the norm through implementation, they become codified and under the Auspices of arbiter caretakers. The arbiter caretakers will preside over issue review and resolution outcome within their Auspices.

Member Restriction Database

Primes will maintain databases pertaining to privileges of entities that have been granted or restricted based on prime directives. A list of generalized categories will be used to identify privileges. An example is vehicle usage, public transportation (air, bus, train, shuttle, etc.), retail shopping, etc. Failure to comply with restricted privileges will result in being restricted to containment camps.

Umbrella Foundation Prime Allocations

Allocations of monetary instruments will normally be equally distributed to the umbrella foundation primes. To have unequal distribution of money allocations is when all five prime leader caretakers choose otherwise. An example is when a natural catastrophe has occurred and the passion to help out exists in this situation.

Most Favorable Displacement Options Status

There will be events when decisions require the closure to a way of life for an entity or a group of entities due to serious safety and health issues or due to a major shift in direction for the vibrant development of the greater Pentarchy Prime Umbrella. When this happens, then the entity or group will be given Most Favorable Displacement Assistant Options (MFDAO). These MFDAO are the same ones that are granted to anyone within the Pentarchy Prime Umbrella decreed by Pentarchy Prime Umbrella directives.

It is Imperative!

It is imperative that all prime directives be satisfied and carried out.

Pentarchy Prime Remedies for Failure of Implementation

Credit Worthiness

Transformation to the nexus is by way of decisions and the recording thereof. Failure of an entity to follow through on decisions from the primes will lead to suspensions of "credit worthiness status" of the entity in all future decisions involving entity. A specified duration after the entity complies is used to return the entity to "credit worthiness status" once again. This duration depends on the severity of non-compliance issue.

High Contractual Risk Entities

Those entities that fail to comply with prime directives after a reasonable period of specified time will be identified as "high contractual risk entities" in the respective Pentarchy Prime Umbrella issuing the alert. This may have the affect of rendering all future contractual agreements with other entities within the prime as having no value and will not be recognized by the prime.

Violation Review Consideration

No violations of prime directives are acceptable, lest they are in conflict with ascension prime directives or basic tenets. When there is a conflict, then the ascension primes may review foundation prime directives and render decisions when called into questioned as they pertain to ascension prime directives.

Longevity of Non-Compliance

An entity habitual failure to comply with prime directives will lead to the suspension of future issue review and resolution regarding that entity until all current directives has been complied. This identification will be made public so as to alert other entities that review and resolution for issues involving this particular entity will normally be at risk.

Warning: Serious Violation

Failure to comply with prime directives is a very serious violation. The warning will be disseminated throughout the prime.

Statute of Limitations

Statute of time limitations will exist so that performances of executive and duty caretakers can be measured. Pass the time statue limits and all information is available to anyone in the prime who requests it. Examples are murders, child endangerment, and child disadvantage action results.

Suspension of Review

The failure of one of five leader caretakers in a Pentarchy Prime and her Pentarchy Prime Umbrellas to comply with a decision made by the other four will be to suspend all further items that may be reviewed regarding issues originating from her Pentarchy Prime Umbrellas for consideration. This will result in the halt to decisions rendered pertaining to matters of the Pentarchy Prime Foundation represented by the one leader caretaker who refused to complied with one or more prime directives.

F. Dot

The failure of two of five leader caretakers in a Pentarchy Prime and their foundation primes to comply with a decision made by the other three will be to suspend all further items being reviewed from any foundation prime to the Pentarchy Prime Umbrella. A way to resolve this impasse is of the highest priority and ought to be found with the greatest earnestness.

An exception to the above can be made as it pertains to natural disasters or grave emergencies.

Non-Threatening versus Threatening Issues

An Offensive Event Defined

An offensive event has occurred when harm is done through the eyes of the victim and not those of the observers. All parties involved must work out fair resolution of the event. Exceptions are pre-adults and those who cannot articulate their perspectives. Compassion and understanding are the guiding forces in such matters. Recognition that every entity is developing at her level and pace will be recognized and adequate assistance provided when possible. A measured response is to be taken for the offense. No excessive response is allowed. It may be just as routine as issuing an order for the entity that is viewed as harmful to keep away from the entity that feels threatened.

Universal Violation

The ultimate act considered a violation of all is that which is of grave importance to all. It is the extinguishing of corporeal life of another member. The reason is that this act prevents the free association to any sect in the entire nexus prime.

Temporary Separations

There are times that some entities cannot function well due to not having sufficient preparations to make it so. In these cases, it may require separations from the general population so as not to bring grave harm to others. These separations, which are confined to camps with others of similar challenges, are to be as short as possible. All possible adequate preparation caretaking ought to be explored.

Far Less Than Grave Offenses

When less than grave offense discoveries have been made and identified by Auspices overseers, the leader caretakers representing the Pentarchy Prime umbrella have up to 125 days to charge the offenders and up to another 125 days to render a decision. This time duration is codified for performance evaluation activities and the pool members' early access to all information. The proceedings and decisions can be delegated to a decision-making body with appointees. This decision-making body can be a standing one with appointees appointed for fixed time duration.

Privilege Removal and Duration

As it pertains to violation resolution, the time limit ban for specific areas of activities or privileges must be spelled out in decisions. Total activities will not be banned unless maximum-security containment orders resulting in confinement were issued as part of the resolution order. Minimum basic needs are not to be denied.

Less Than Extreme

For more serious offenses other than extreme violent offenses, the next ascension prime will intercede to handle evaluation and remedy an opinion.

Suspension of privileges

For offenses not involving harmful acts to others, entities violating Pentarchy Prime decisions will have privileges suspended for a period of time. Repeated suspensions will yield longer privileges suspension time periods. Exile from the Pentarchy Prime may be a final resolution for habitual violations. Admission to another Pentarchy Prime is permitted after 125 days or multiples of 125 days, depending on the severity of the violation in the current umbrella Pentarchy Prime. The next Ascension Pentarchy Prime will decide in these matters unless it is the Nexus Pentarchy Prime already.

Time Limits on Charges

Only entities that commit murder (the deliberate extinguishing of life) can have up to twenty-five years from the date of the event to be declared guilty of the offense by the Sentient Nexus Pentarchy Prime. Serious physical or spiritual harm has a statute of limitation of five years after the offense for a declaration of grave opinion determination for the offense. The exception is when a child is involved. The child has five years after being declared an adult by age or by pent-degree leader caretaker opinion when another has committed a serious physical or spiritual harm while the entity was a child.

Case Example: Uncontrolled Vehicle Use

Case Example:

The uncontrolled usage of a vehicle by an entity resulting in grave harm or in extinguishing of another member in society:

Resolution:

The healing steps are:

1. Hold vehicle from entity.
2. Contain entity in camps.
3. Educate entity in the proper use of vehicle.
4. Impose a probation period for vehicle use.
5. Return the vehicle to the entity.

There ought to be a high degree of certainty that the harmful acts will not be repeated. Repeat violations by the entity will result in a five-fold duration increase in privilege removal for the entity. When it pertains to harmful acts, be clear regarding the seriousness of the events and the importance that serious containment actions are needed. Accidents are rarely "accidents" but due to the lack of preparations or blatant recklessness. Hence, prevention is the key to successful operation. Reckless operators will have their privileges suspended or revoked.

Case Consideration: Sizing Rape

The category of rape is historically considered to be one of grave endangerment to an adult entity. There is a tendency to overrate this violation especially when there are no convincing discoveries clearly identifying the event as such. Condemning provides no healing process to take place. Should there be misunderstanding of an entity's intent, then a decree will be issued that will state the clear perspectives of the entity who felt violated and that the entity who was perceived to be committing the harmful act to avoid proximity of the entity who felt violated. The proximity terms will be clearly specific in details. Any violation of these terms will result in declaring the original event as a serious violation. The actions to be taken for serious violations are described elsewhere.

Case Consideration: Sizing Statutory Rape

A variance of five years separating the ages of two entities will be used to determine statutory rape as historically defined when an age is used for specifying automatic adulthood and the child did not consent to romantic encounters or was coerced. The category of statutory rape is historically considered to be one of grave endangerment to a minor. There is a tendency to overrate this violation especially when consenting entities are involved. Condemning provides no healing process to take place. The changes described above will aid in the healing process of all.

Statute of Limitations

Statutes of time limitation are needed in a variety of areas to include grave harmful events in order to measure performances of our executive and duty caretakers. No delays beyond the time limits will be accepted for general prime pool participation by any entity showing interest in discovery activities.

The Way to Uncover the Truth

The need to get out of the condemning business is great. By not condemning, a greater chance for uncovering the truth is very possible. Make it so and be surprise when it happens when you least expect it.

317

Nexus Pentarchy Prime Rapid Response Auspices Team

Nexus Pentarchy Prime Rapid Response Auspices Charter

The Nexus Pentarchy Prime Rapid Response Auspices is chartered with peacekeeping duties to include apprehending and detaining entities that commit grave harmful acts. These duties will continue even in times of Nexus Pentarchy Prime impasses when there is a suspension of further prime directive creation events. Sufficient resources will not be withheld.

Nexus Pentarchy Prime Rapid Response Auspices teams comprised of five rapid deployment team members are formed to respond when one entity is committing grave harmful acts or are imminent. More teams are involved when there is more than one offending entity present.

Grave Harmful Truth Investigation Discoveries

Information discoveries learn as a result of truth investigator caretaking duties will only be revealed to the public or agencies when there are persuasive discovery findings in grave harmful acts. In certain situation, the dissemination of information may have to be withheld in protecting all entities involved. This is of prime importance! For example in the area of murder, which is the extinguishing of an entity, has been committed and there is a high degree of certainty that grave harmful acts will be committed but can be wisely prevented.

When discoveries do not pertain to grave harmful acts, the discoveries are confidential and the information cannot be disseminated beyond rapid response teams and the Auspices of nexus prime. Findings will require to be re-discovered in matters involving non-harmful issue resolving requests, which may result in prime directives or opinions.

Nexus Officer Duty Caretakers

This is a classification of caretakers selected by the Auspices of the Sentient Nexus Pentarchy Prime in performing duties as members of the Rapid Deployment Teams in ensuring that the set of Universal Tenets and Axioms are not being violated by members anywhere.

Nexus Officer Duty Caretakers Removal

Rapid-response nexus executive duty caretakers can be removed with three of the five Nexus Pentarchy Prime leader caretakers. The same as applies to all other degree prime designation of Officer Duty Caretakers.

Rapid Response Teams

A handful, five or fewer, of securing-the-peace personnel will intervene when one entity is killed. In this case, an automatic response team is made without approval of one or more of Sentient Nexus Pentarchy Prime leader caretakers. Escalation is warranted when killings of more than one entity exist. The response will be more paramilitary-like force sufficient enough to reduce the killings to zero. This situation ought to be rare. Also, periodic review of members of the response team is needed to ensure the best and wisest members are recruited and retained.

The most that a rapid response team officer caretaker can hold an entity is five days. Only a rapid response executive officer caretaker or Auspices securing-the-peace caretaker of the Sentient Nexus Pentarchy Prime can

F. Dot

hold one longer. A rapid response team caretaker (non-executive officer) can hold an entity for one day.

Alert Provisions

Alert provisions for missing members will be defined after twenty-five days since last contacted by the concerning party or when foul play is determined to happen by rapid response teams.

Producing and Implementing Containment Decrees

A decision made by executive officer caretakers delegated by leader caretakers can have up to twenty-five containment days given to members who fail to comply with issue review resolutions. Only the Auspices of the Sentient Nexus leader caretakers will have the final determination pertaining to matters regarding entities that extinguish other entities. They may request a standing review board be formed to gather information and recommendations. Immediate containment orders are issued to those considered highly probable suspects, based on reliable eyewitnesses, and evidence produced by rapid response teams. Without formal investigation findings, orders up to five containment days can be made by rapid response team executive duty caretakers for the safety of all. Suspect officer duty caretakers will automatically be assigned to suspects, with liaison duties to handle all reasonable suspects' personal matters. They are different from suspect advocate officer caretakers, who review and challenge the charges made on the suspect's behalf. When a containment sentencing outcome is made, the only reason for discharge is when new information overwhelmingly clears a suspect or after a minimum of twenty-five years and there is a very high degree of certainty that no further harm will be done by the entity once released into society. The twenty-five-year limit is given to entities when the gravity of the harmful events was of the highest of grievous acts. In the event that a second sentencing is made for capital offenses, life containment is automatic without release. A high degree of certainty from suspects committing further harm would then have been shown.

Confinement and Release

A Nexus Pentarchy Prime rapid response team executive caretaker can hold a dangerous entity until final investigation findings or set free due to convincing evidence to the contrary.

Duty Peace Caretakers

Honorable and inspiring are the duty peace caretakers.

Containment Environments

Historical Containment Views

Historically, court-ordered jail terms are nothing more than "time outs" for members of society. Jails ought to be for the security of communities and not to house members because of social issues that are not being adequately addressed. Think about this for a moment.

Dungeons Obsolete

The game of dungeons will no longer be played.

Non-Growth Industry

Prisons will no longer be promoted as an industry. Historical trends will not be used to build more prisons. A service will be provided by nexus prime to confine entities that are shown to exhibit grave harm to other non-threatening entities of the prime. When the numbers become large, urgent discovery activities are performed to determine hidden causes that can be rectified and return prime to favorable conditions. Action plans based on these findings will be implemented.

Minimal Containment Numbers

The incarcerating of large numbers of entities is not acceptable. Only the Auspices of the nexus prime will make that decision in times of grave emergencies. We are choosing to promote the health and vitality of all members of the nexus prime.

Containment Duration

Five years minimum confinement is required due to an accidental negligence that resulted in a death. An accidental negligence is when the accident has a high degree of certainty that the accident could have been avoided by entities in a pool of similar vocation using the Rule of Five to make that test.

Twenty-five years minimum confinement required due to purposeful acts leading to death. A purposeful act is when there is a certain degree of time and planning in committing the grave harmful acts.

In all confinement cases when an entity is extinguish by the entity in confinement and after serving a minimal duration, a very high degree of certainty must still exist that the entity will not repeat the harmful act again before the entity can be released from confinement.

Non-Capital Offense Duration

Containment for non-life extinguishing offenses will never be greater than the average duration in murder containment opinions. The primary concern must remain to separate violent entities from the more peaceful ones.

Violators Housed

Violators who are confined for offenses will be housed or camped with others of similar offenses. No mixing of violent and non-violent offenders is permitted.

Degrees of Confinement

More secure confinements are for those members who have performed acts of grave violence. There will be degrees of confinement based on the severity of the events and ongoing interactions with other members within confinement facilities.

Minimum Containment Facilities

Non-violent violators will not be housed in such maximum containment facilities. They will be housed in minimum containment facilities or camps. Duty caretakers carrying no firearms or weapons of any kind will guard non-violent facilities. These facilities will be self-directing containment camps whereby the tenants will learn by managing their own care.

Detainment Camps

Detainment camps are defined as limited access to confined entities whereby focused education and training avenues are provided to enable the return of entities to Pentarchy Prime Umbrellas. While in these camps, entities must also cooperate with others in the camp for basic needs. Abusers of privileges will result in more restricting confinement with other similar abusers. Self-directing training is needed to gradually return to general detainment pools.

Privilege Scale

Those entities in confinement will have reduced privileges. The degree of reduced privileges depends on the degree of severity in the entities' behaviors and actions.

Protected Separations

High security confinement facilities are to be used for very violent offenders. Confinement camps of varying degrees of security will be used for other offenders. No mixing of non-violent offenders with violent ones is allowed.

It's a Certainty

Containment of entities who commit grave harmful acts at other entities is generally viewed to be a certainty. A very high degree of certainty is needed and required to permit the offending entities to return to free primes once again. Much time is needed for such a consideration. Be patient.

Victims Have Input Rights to Remedy Resolution

When an entity is contained for offenses, there will be no caged lock-up unless violent offenses have been made and the victim who experienced the offense has agreed. Exception is when the victim is dead and the one closest to the victim will take her place in making that determination and when determination that violent tendencies have greatly subsided. Entities will manage their own care while in containment with sufficient resources for survival needs. No torture or execution of anyone in captivity will be allowed, ever!

When Confinement Term Limits Are Not Given

There will never be an order specifying duration for grave harmful committing entities. No violent person is allowed to be set free because no "timed" orders will be given, even if it means for life! The person will be set free when there is a high degree of trust and certainty that that person will not do similar acts of violence again and after spending a pre-defined universally applied minimum confinement duration.

Maximum Containment Facilities

When it comes to violent or grave violations to another entity or entities, containment is immediate with no end date. A minimum duration must be met which will equal the longest duration for non-serious or the least violent violations, whichever is greater. Any release after the minimum time will be granted when an extremely high certainty is realized whereby no serious and violent violations will ever occur again. The containment will be in maximum security and restricted facilities that confine only tenants that have committed similar grave violations. Duty caretakers of these facilities are permitted to protect themselves.

The Caretaking of Containment Facilities

There are those duty caretakers who will say that they were not involved with criminal acts that may occur in containment facilities. For Auspices executive officer duty caretakers however, if many such acts did in fact occur on their watch, then their title of Auspices executive officer duty caretaker will to be stripped from them. The aim is to have the best Auspices executive officer duty caretakers in charge.

No Executions on My Watch

No executions will occur on my watch. If you permit that to occur on your watch, your sentient awareness has been greatly diminished.

Escape Remedy

The mere fact that a violent entity is placed in containment ought to make the Pentarchy Prime Umbrellas secure. The containment is to be in a maximum-security facility. Auspices executive officer duty caretakers whose watches permit escape of those in maximum containment will be scrutinized and a determination made whether to have them replaced immediately. The duty caretakers being closest to the elements ought to be aware of such situations in advance. No violence will be done to those in containment is the primary rule when non-violent behavior is present by any entity. Forcible apprehension is permitted for those who continue violence to any entity around them.

Violent Issues Scope

Decisive Actions

Historically, there was a notion that the law will punish those who commit unspeakable crimes like murder. In fact, laws must first be passed that define harmful acts as crimes before these same acts can even be considered crimes. In the mean time, the killings continue because of delays in ensuring supposedly a person's rights. What is better is to have leader caretakers take decisive actions to contain those who have the highest probability of committing a serious offense based on available evidence. After a full inquiry and deliberation, the entity in confinement will be released or kept in confinement for the safety of all when that is the conclusion or opinion.

Grave Harm

It is important to contain entities whose purpose is to cause grave harm to others.

Response for Member Killers

Historically, the notion that someone who kills another is set free after a not-guilty verdict is simply not valid. The Sentient Nexus Pentarchy Prime leader caretakers are the only ones who have the ultimate responsibility to review containment of dangerous persons after new evidence is forthcoming.

The need to isolate threatening entities is great.

Condemning is going Out of Business

We will be out of the condemning business soon if not already. The business of condemning leads to our own destruction. Rapid deployment teams will have been required to process through rigorous selection process and training to become our supreme peace protection restoring caretakers. Characteristic traits are honesty, integrity, ethics, and wisdom in determining sufficient force solutions. Weapons of greater than required mass destruction will not be used. Executive peace caretaker of the rapid peace restoring team can determine low yield firepower defensive weapons usage. Non firepower and non-lethal weapons usage can be left to a member of rapid deployment team. In all cases where grave harmful events do occur, leader caretaker reviews are required. Valid use of non-lethal force is reviewed with the assistance of the pent-degree ascension prime.

Accountability for All Killings and Suspicious Deaths

All killings or suspicious deaths must be looked into. This is the ultimate responsibility of the Sentient Nexus Pentarchy Prime leader caretakers and their instruments. They may appoint investigators to look into the matter. However, the final determination responsibility still rests with them. Of course, it is natural to assume that these five nexus leader caretakers would be wise in selecting necessary Auspices consultancies to assist with timely opinions. Consider stepping forward when asked to.

Murder Investigations

Investigations of murders are open-ended. However, twenty-five years will be given as active status by the Sentient Nexus Pentarchy Prime. After twenty-five years, private concerns may take up the investigation and have access to all information collected to date and that will be collected by truth investigation duty caretakers and Auspices consultancies in the future.

Truth Discoveries

For serious harmful events, every entity must tell the truth during prime directing inquiry sessions. Those that were discovered to not have given true testimonies with more than a reasonable certainty will be confined in multiples of five days up to a maximum of 125 days based on severity of the false statements and resulting outcomes.

On the Side of Caution

Nexus leader caretakers can determine that an entity or entities can be confined as part of suspicious entity death investigation exhaustive findings to date, even when there is not persuasive evidence at the time. However, without very convincing evidence, the confinement is for a maximum of five years. Should more convincing evidence be forthcoming and are within its guidelines, then the conclusive confinement rules prevail. Should more persuasive evidence indicate that a member is innocent, release is immediate after discovery.

Official Endangerment

Officials whose orders result in grave harm to an entity or entities when an entity or entities are themselves not committing grave harm to others or is imminent, are to be considered dangerous for purposes of containment. Containment will continue until a high degree of certainty is achieved that a repeat of grave decisions and actions that could follow will not be made.

Assassination Response

When a leader caretaker is assassinated, everything within the prime stops that does not involve vital prime services while the prime is scoured for information and remedies! No further decisions are made until the investigation is complete.

Prime Privileged Information

A "hold" status on an entity is made when the entity has done a gravest act requiring containment. Information regarding the entity is privileged during this time to investigative discovery activity caretakers until significant conclusive findings are forthcoming.

Defender Duty Caretakers Assignments

Defender duty caretakers will aid in the investigation and advocacy of a defendant who has been sent to high security confinement.

On the Side of Safety

Consider being on the side of safety when an entity is determine to have a very high probability of being the one who committed a grave offense. Have the entity in confinement for the safety of all parties involved to include the entity in confinement.

Extinguish Issues Scope

Extinguish

The deliberate extinguishing of entities in corporeal form is the premier focus of resources and time by the Sentient Nexus Pentarchy Prime. The nexus prime can rely on all degree primes assistance in their investigations and remedies.

Measured Responses

Measured responses may be needed to contain or extinguish violent actions. No excessive actions are permitted.

Sufficient Force Application

Those who knowingly or purposefully participate in the decision and/ or execution of grave harmful acts in the guise of dealing with other entities' grave harmful acts will be viewed as committing similar acts. The exception is when performed while protecting oneself or selves. Only rapid response teams are given the latitude to provide measured responses when needed.

Percolate to the Top

Unless an entity departs by natural means, the gravity of the departure will percolate up to the top of the ascension primes and be detected by the nexus prime for investigation and remedy.

Non-Natural Departure

Only when extinguishing of corporeal existence is by non-natural causes will the nexus prime be involved. Questionable causes that may or may not be by natural causes will be investigated first by the pent-degree ascension prime. Acceleration to nexus prime is made immediately when a reasonable assertion is made regarding non-natural causes. Nexus prime have unlimited access to review information regarding all such happenings and conclusions. Periodically, nexus prime will choose selected cases for review.

Progress Reports

Provision for Confinement in Error

Since there is always a chance that an entity may be confined in error, once a new review followed by a new hearing has been conducted because significant new information and validations are uncovered, release is immediate, in less than twenty-five hours.

Dangerous Environments and Remedies

Robe of Violence Advocacy

Our historical criminal justice system will be dismantled due to its premise that members of society must be condemned so that its framework can exist. Do not be fooled in its view that justice is served when entities are condemned. This framework cannot hide behind its "robe of violence advocacy".

Stop Property Holdings Form of Terrorism

Stop terrorism in all its forms. In nation-state frameworks, citizens are properties and owned by the nation-state that declares them. When sentient entities are hunted down like criminals because of artificial legal status of being a non-citizen and that is the only reason for the hunt, then that act of apprehension is terrorism. Where is the humanity in this, this property-holdings premise by antiquated feudal lords?

Retiring Non-Issue Incarcerations

It is abominable to incarcerate entities whose only crime is the passion to be free to associate with any group and to go anywhere in the pool's reach. When no harm is being done to other entities or to environments, these behaviors are to be unrestricted when the impact is minimal. Let's retire these non-issue incarcerations.

In the Same Environment

Historically, benefits for soldiers in campaigns were provided regardless if severe harm was experienced or not. This was not so for members with medical problems. During those times, benefits must be determined first based on health diagnosis before a graduated degree of assistance is provided. In Pentarchy Prime Framework when entities are in the same environment, generally, benefits will be covered as well.

Sufficient Force Doctrine

Significantly more force than what can be done with sufficient minimal force that is sanctioned by historical nation-state is never acceptable. Gradual reduction in the use of force will be one of many purposes of primes. This is possible because those who are closest to the serious issues are more effective in resolving the issue. Choose not to turn back the historical clock in the harsh and overkill application in the use of excessive force.

Reduced to Rounding up Violent Entities

Historically, the reason for nation-state wars is because citizens are not allowed to leave! When entities are allowed to leave hostile environments, the actions are reduced to rounding up violent entities using rapid response teams. It will then be learned that far fewer entities are in fact violent by nature.

Die-Hard Spies

Spies that infiltrate primes with the objective of disrupting and dismantling the foundation will be exposed and identified within the prime framework to all prime members. A severe banishment is declared with the added directive that no further issue-resolution requests can be reviewed involving spies that violate applicable prime directives. The time period of banishment will be in multiples of five years up to twenty-five years, depending on severity. This information will be provided to all ascension primes to include the nexus prime. These degree primes will make appropriate prime directives for themselves.

Ecological Impact Activities

The harmful ecological impact activities produced by historical military framework do jeopardize national security. If allowed to continue, eventually, there will be no one else to argue on its use. Is this wise? These activities may have won the wars but loose the peace and nature's subsistence ways for the viable environment. Nature will make corrections based on usage. Nature reacts in time when it is raped.

Urgent Pursuits

An urgent pursuit of Pentarchy Primes, when it arises, is the dismantling of terrorist activities.

Hostilities Relocation

During the Transitional Period Towards a Nexus Pentarchy Prime Framework, entities joining the primes from hostile nation-states will be relocated far from the boundaries of these hostile nation-states. This safety measure is provided so long as the entities did not commit grave harmful acts anywhere that were not in self-defense. A vast barrier will have to be traveled for nation-states to impose forced repatriations. Any actions by these feudal nation-states will demonstrate their true terrorist persona.

Rapid Shut Down

If any agency is found to conduct terrorist activities, it will be shut down. It does not matter that a small part of the agency is conducting these activities or not. When discovered that these activities did in fact take place, the opinion will be that there is an element that is a fabric of the agency that is fundamentally amiss. If the agency is still needed as an instrument of Pentarchy Prime then it will be rebuilt from foundation zero. Executive officer caretakers will have to reapply. Once selected, then the general duty caretakers will be reassigned when it is warranted.

A Call to all Sentients

We will work towards breaking up all terrorist-producing organizations anywhere in the known world and beyond whose charters promote violent actions directed at other sentient entities as defined by prime tenets and directives.

Prime Member Impersonators

Offer no assistance and walk away from easy assistance and resources from convert prime member impersonators. Follow prime umbrella directives only. The built-in prime activities will expose these impersonators. With prime membership and related activities, the numbers are against impersonators from dismantling primes.

Contributing Participants

When accidents or grave events do take place, investigations are performed as to the cause. When it is found that caretakers, those holding positions that are chartered with preventive activities, were contributing participants in these events, then they are banned from their positions for specified periods of time. The duration is based on the severity of the neglect.

Urgent Happenings

When communications are cut off and information that is being spread cannot be confirmed, state it so to all who requests it and caution them not to take it as fact for the time being until further inquiry discoveries can be made. Use procedures regarding separation from Pentarchy Prime Umbrellas during emergencies. Prime directives that are produced but may be in conflict with the greater Pentarchy Prime Umbrella will not be admonished because of separation. However, all known prime directives and tenets will be recognized and carried out. Exception is in times of grave emergencies.

Natural Boundaries Instrument Charter

Identify and post natural boundaries subject to nature's laws. Interactions by prime members are at their own risks. Exclusions are when hazards produced by prime members within twenty-five years. Hazards produced by prime members are to be removed by the same members. Violators will be subject to stiff penalties and removal of related privileges when there is failure to comply.

Periodic Safe Passage Convoys

Frequent unannounced passage convoys will travel the domains in order to provide entities the opportunity to join the convoy. These convoys are opportunities to rescue oppressed entities or entities with self-directing pursuits. The awareness that we are all part of a greater pool is ever present.

Transitional Governance Reach

Nation-State Transformation

One by one, when the historical nation-state frameworks are replaced with Pentarchy Prime Umbrellas, all agreements made to other external nation-states will be terminated and outstanding issues referred to the corresponding Pentarchy Prime Umbrellas having span proximity to the frameworks. Rules and guidelines described elsewhere apply in these situations.

The Folding of Nation-States

One by one, nation-states will be declared obsolete and all prior contracts or treaties created when the nation-states were operational will be null and void. The complete suite of prime directives will be in effect everywhere.

Terrorist Officials Removal

Members holding ancient legislative official or representative positions who have passed laws of terror as defined by Pentarchy Primes will be expeditiously removed and replaced with others who are selected by primes to hold these transitional office-holding positions during the transitional period.

Pentarchy Prime "Elected Officials"

Primes are charter with issuing prime directives when needed. Other non-leader caretakers are required to take effective actions when asked to by leader caretakers that span their domains. Those who fail to perform their duties, as decree, will be subject to removal from their positions. This includes those who are "elected" by mass elections in historical governing systems. All prime directives covering "elected officials" are to be published for all to see within the Pentarchy Prime Umbrella.

Freedom of Movement

Terrorism exists when a nation-state prohibits free movements of sentients when the only "crimes" that were acted on were to cross artificial-borders (man-made ones). When there are no other detainment orders in effect, they must be allowed to freely pass without restrictions. The only restrictions are those established by Pentarchy Primes. The nation-state holds no ownership of sentients. Pentarchy Primes will pursue every effort possible in making this so.

Guilty by Association

The state that requires its citizens to do the police work based on its punitive laws regarding unlawful statutes in the area of providing humane behaviors and treatments toward "enemies (criminals) of the state" who commit "criminal" acts is shunning its responsibilities in these matters. No law ought to exist that make it a crime for any entity who helps in humane ways and not be aware of past, present, or future grave harmful acts. If we truly are to have a caring world, then no caring behavior will be prohibited.

Interim State Monopolies

Level the playing field by insisting on nation-state's monopolies for both prosecutions and defenses. Having one without the other reinforces the framework that lopsided abuses are ever present.

Restitution

Restitution, monetary or other forms, for events caused prior to Pentarchy Prime ascension will not be reviewed for remedies. After Pentarchy Prime arrival, restitution will have no meaning. It is very unlikely that any "awards" will be granted if basic needs are being supported. The focus is on uncovering root causes for failure to optimally provide caretaking activities that benefit all. In this way, corrective-action decrees can be taken and be ever present. In summary, there will be assistance and not compensation; there will be assistance and not restitution.

The Leashing of Politicians

Historical politicians have the propensity to be political. This is due to their training and limited view. That's all they know how to do. Our interest is to ensure that all our decisions are carried out and to remove anyone whom fails to comply. The politicians that are in violation will lose all privileges bestowed by the prime for significant periods of time up to twenty-five years.

Interim Courts

Historical courts can exist in the interim when no harmful acts are involved. Otherwise, leader caretakers have ownership and responsibility of decision/opinion outcome.

Declarations of Transfers

When primes supersedes the decision making of nation governing bodies, declarations made by these pre-prime governing agency bodies will be declared at the end of their life cycle. The historical agencies will be either shut down or transformed into prime agencies with new principles of conduct and objectives.

The End to War Machines

War machines will be dismantled. Rapid deployment teams will be created with its primary charter of diminishing and extinguishing entities' or groups of entities' violent activities no matter where these activities may be found. The Nexus Pentarchy Prime is supremely responsible for its charter and oversight with command centers located throughout all Pentarchy Prime Umbrellas.

Cartels

All historical non-violent entity-limiting government sponsored elite cartels are to be dismantled.

Time and Energy Well Spent

Do not expend much time and energy with historical governmental agencies in trying to persuade them to do the right thing. Instead, the focus ought to be on persuading and at times removing "official" non-prime caretakers whom no longer are capable of making wise decisions on behalf of all.

Heighten Terrorist State

During the transitional period, be mindful of renegade nation-states that violate prime directives. This may be an indication of a heightened terrorist state.

Warning/Advisory during Transition

When possible, it is unwise to make any agreements with a non-Pentarchy Prime member until such time that no other non-caretaker system exists or has collapsed. When that happens, agreements are based on Pentarchy Prime rules and guidelines.

We will perform no bartering with those Pentarchy Prime members caught in the containment snare of the non-caretaker system. The premise that no entity is a form of property prevails in this case. Activities and events over time will result in their release. However, we will provide timely escape assistance to all members in grave circumstances.

One Sided View of Prisoners of War

During the Transitional Period Towards a Nexus Pentarchy Prime Framework, if a nation-state uses the military to contain the populace of any other nation-state, then the opposing populous are soldiers of their campaign (issue). If captured by this nation-state's military, they are to be considered prisoners of war (POW). When "orders" are given for military action by this nation-state, their argument that only their soldiers can have POW distinction is a terrorist view. The reasoning is that the military is chartered for war. War results in prisoners of war in all cases.

In Pentarchy Primes, there will be no need to go to war. Release of "prisoners" will have no meaning. The whole concept of POW will become irrelevant everywhere. Containment for those who have the propensity to commit grave harmful acts is a prime directive.

Non-Pentarchy Prime Officeholder

One's measure of compliance by officeholder in non-Pentarchy Prime Frameworks is based on whether prime directives are being implemented. If not, no further decision or discussion with that officeholder will be made until prior decision is carried out. The officeholder will be removed from her position. Removal activities will commence at the earliest possible time for serious non-compliant activities.

Focus on Leaders

Focus on senior official actors who are self-appointed or forced imposed surrogates that interfere with our leader caretakers. Remove anyone from position of authority in historical belief systems when she fails to carry out our prime decisions. Do not be distracted with institutions with their methods and ways. They exist at the pleasure of our leader caretakers. Those who resist will have an entry made in their Pentarchy Prime public record stating that the entity or entities will be prohibited from holding compatible caretaker positions for twenty-five years commencing on the day that the member is removed from position. This is to be viewed as a very serious offense.

Interim Entry Points

Do not be concern initially with commercial and cultural exchanges with the known world. Work with your neighbors first. The affect will be like rainwater that eventually goes into creeks, then streams, then rivers, then lakes, and then oceans. Insist that nation-state laws be just and not violate basic prime tenets. There will be points into shared pools of primes. Eventually, only primes exist, which are something quite wonderful to strive for.

Implementation Plan for World Mobility

The implementation plan for gradual world mobility is first to have neighboring nation-states have freedom to cross their borders within five months of declaration with gradual entire world mobility completed in five years.

Transitional Commerce Center Embassies

Transitional Commerce Center Embassies (TCCE) will replace in the interim separate prime and non-prime centers for any issue involving both frameworks regarding commerce. The stewards will be comprised of five members from prime and five members from non-prime members. For the possible gradual implementation of resolution, three votes from the non-prime pools and three votes from prime pools are needed. For immediate implementation of resolution, four or more votes from each pool are needed.

Guests or Visitors

While non-prime members are within prime domains, prime directives regarding guests or visitors must be observed and vice versus. In order for TCCEs to exist, execution of detainees anywhere is strictly prohibited. When discoveries of executions are found, TCCEs' are temporarily closed until corrective actions are forthcoming and verifiable. Investigators will have unrestricted access to any confinement facilities for verification regarding any reported abuse discovered anywhere.

Society Member Sentencing Compliance

While in transition to prime framework, when a member of society fulfills conditions of sentencing, then no restrictions from having a job can be imposed. The only criteria for employment will be on job performances and other ancillary activities. This is reflective of Pentarchy Prime Directives.

No Persuasion Needed

Until Pentarchy Prime immersion, the elitists are a very small part of the world's population. Hence, there is no need to persuade them to join our foundation primes. By selecting officials who implement prime directives, their elitist ranks will dwindle and fall like an avalanche.

Reach of "Political" Review

To conserve time, resources, and the prevention of errors, focus on historical political spectrum domains whereby the Rule of Five prevails as it pertains to interactions with Pentarchy Prime and resulting outcomes.

Oath of Understanding

All who passes through primes must commit themselves to prime foundation governance or be treated as temporary guests with very limited access and privileges. Their oath of understanding must be clear to them or their pass-through must be speedy. In the latter case when pass-through is not speedy, then they will be escorted through the prime quickly.

Transitional Governance Instruments

To Whom the Courts Serve

During the Transitional Period Towards a Nexus Pentarchy Prime Framework, historical courts serve at the pleasure of the prime caretakers. This is strongly advised. When prime instruments are effectively in place, these courts will be given expiration dates. The time is near.

Interim Elected Officials

As part of the transition towards primes exclusively, officials selected to fill elected offices are on probation once elected. Failure to promote prime directives will lead to removal from office at the earliest possible time, e.g., the next election or preferably a recall. More than one recall or election may be needed as Pentarchy Prime Framework gains universal appeal.

Universal Care Support Amount

During the transition period, what the tax code states as the amount for dependent deduction, then that is the universal child-care support amount needed to raise a child based on these enacted "laws". In this way, no child will have a higher "value" than another. This amount will be used in all "child support payment" amount determinations. Eventually, children will no longer be property of anyone or man-made artifact.

Public Relations

No questions by non-member entities will be answered freely. Consultation with leader caretakers whose umbrella Pentarchy Prime encompasses the effective reach in non-prime domains will be made for the review and any subsequent response that may be needed.

Interim "Free" Elections

While there are "free" elections for elected duty officials, the selection of officials that carry out prime directives will be promoted. Failure to comply by any elected official will result in dismissal activities. The selection of the lesser of two evils will not be considered. When no viable candidate is available, write-ins of the chosen candidate will be promoted.

Obsolete N-Tier Courts

After transitions, there will be no n-tier justice systems as they pertain to quality and uniformity of the entire process. These systems based on nation-state land holdings to include sentients will have no meaning.

Interim Court Resolutions

During the Transitional Period Towards a Nexus Pentarchy Prime Framework, new court resolution must specify duration for prohibition on privileges. For prior resolutions, an automatic twenty-five year cap will be made in all cases not involving grave harmful acts.

Interim Official Review and Selection

During the transformational era towards Pentarchy Prime Foundation, Pentarchy Prime Umbrellas are chartered in producing directives regarding who in the current political spectrum must resign or face future long-term privilege limiting directives. In addition, identify all those in the current political spectrum who have consistently and dutifully carried out prime directives. Also a candidate rating system will be architect and implemented based on prime perspectives and acceptable scores. There can be multiple candidates selected and promoted by Pentarchy Prime Umbrellas for the same official position. The rating will aid prime members as to the proper voter selection.

Peaceful Strategy

By following a strategy of peaceful primes, we will expose the framework's violent "trigger-points" of nation-states. One by one, these points will be erased. In time, these artifact frameworks will collapse.

Interim Attorneys

During the Transitional Period Towards a Nexus Pentarchy Prime Framework, all "criminal" attorneys will be transferred to serving the public interest. Truth discovery pursuits will replace an adversarial system of posturing. No one is to be condemned. Wise courses of action will be promoted instead. Do not be fooled, effective remedies will be issued.

Multiparty Decline

Vying for territorial (land) use exclusivity by the two-party political system has no meaning in primes. Wise leader caretakers understand the needs and issues of Pentarchy Prime Umbrellas. Caretaking is taken seriously. Checks and balances are in place to ensure that this is so.

Test the Limits

We will test the limits of perceived "democratic systems" and then some until these elitist systems implode. Do not be fooled on the true nature of democratic systems. They are based on exclusion. Pentarchy Primes will then become universal.

One by One

One by one during the Transitional Period Towards a Nexus Pentarchy Prime Framework, laws that violate prime directives will be nullified. Courts then cannot pass rulings based on laws that no longer exist.

A Monopoly in Both Arenas

If the judicial system of an historical framework has a monopoly on prosecutions, then it will also be chartered to have a monopoly on the defense. In its historical existence, the system is not just. By having a dual system with prosecution and defense given monies in equal amounts by the artifact institution, both sides are served. Sharing of common services such as scientific analysis or access to any information permitted by either would be wise and cost-effective. Nation-state "legal institutions" will not have a monopoly in providing only prosecution services.

In addition, a historical "grand" jury will be comprised of skilled truth investigators when needed. Conscripts are not to be used. The premise is that it will be primarily chartered to uncover the truth so as to assist in a humane response to serious offenses. Therefore, those skilled in truth discoveries need apply. No condemning is permitted.

Bail Baggage

Bail concept baggage is a carryover of property rights and is no longer valid in a Pentarchy Prime Framework. Do not be fooled. No entity can hide for long. Therefore, bail is of little aid. Failure to appear will lead to more severe consequences. If entity actions pertain to grave harmful events towards other entities, then containment is immediate. No release is possible unless investigative discoveries proved otherwise. This is described elsewhere.

Realm of Business

The realm of business is adequately served in the interim by the judicial system as historically constructed. Note that this belief system is meant to include the judicial, legislative, and executive branches. This belief system is an interim one that will evolve into a more streamlined one.

Nation-State Defense Monopoly

Let it be emphasized that if a nation-state is going to have a monopoly in prosecuting a member of a society, then the state will also have a monopoly in providing the defense with access to all information collected by the prosecution team, and vice versa.

Fairness for State Monopolies

For balance to exist should we choose to continue in the interim with the historical judicial belief system, the same amount of resources shall be allocated to the defense of those that are being charged. It should not be considered unreasonable for a state institution to provide for such services, especially when it holds a monopoly in areas of prosecutions, since members of society cannot initiate prosecution proceedings themselves. We need truth investigation caretakers and not executioners.

Information Freely Recorded

There historically exists the legal notion that "evidential proofs" must be presented to reveal any truths. For the sake of argument, let us say yes. However, information should be freely recorded without censorship of opinions and ideas. They may be admissible. The information can be tagged accordingly. The passage of time and questioning of those who testify will validate the accuracy of their testimonies.

Time Limits on Business Laws

There will be an expiration date for all historical business laws passed even when other laws are built on top of them. If the validity of such laws still exists, the laws must be passed again.

The reasoning is that artificial (man-made) laws are to be viewed as not being cast in stone. The set of all laws do ebb and flow just like the history of sentients. It is only when rigidity for ancient laws exists that the framework snaps and implodes.

Re-passage of Laws

Historical laws over twenty-five years old are either re-passed as current laws or are made void by default on the twenty-fifth anniversary since the passage of the respective law. Within five years prior to the expiration of a particular law, a law can be re-passed. The initial enforcement of this rule will permit all laws falling outside the twenty-five-year limit an extra five years to have the laws reviewed for possible re-passage. They can be determined to be re-passed on a case by case basis or when it makes more sense to group related laws together and re-pass them as one package to preserve cohesion.

Non-Harmful Dispute Resolution

A proposal that each entity or group in a dispute be allowed to pick, say, two members from the community to form a review and resolution panel, with a tie-breaker coming from the Auspices of the jurist pool. It is the jurist pool that will be composed of experts or professionals trained to handle matters requiring resolution. Both sides will select this tie-breaker jurist. It is this system that will return power back to the members of society.

Interim Issue Resolution Instrument

The judicial system as it pertains to non-grave harmful acts can be maintained for some time until established Pentarchy Prime instruments are in place. Judges can only jail entities up to twenty-five days. Twenty-five days out of jail must pass before a repeat can be made when the offense is still the original one. Only leader caretakers can extend a stay longer when violent offenses occur or when imminent killings exist. The aim is to secure the peace using all resources available. No use of lethal force will be permitted unless serious life extinguishing acts or serious bodily harmful acts are in progress.

Withdrawal Prime Directive

When prime directives are made for the withdrawal from selected non-prime organizations and operations in the most expeditious manner, do so without causing grave harm to yourself.

Universal Passports

An interim transformation directive is to have what historically is known as the World Body provide universally recognized passports to be used to gain unobstructed passage anywhere in the known universe. Denial can only be made for entities that have been found to commit grave harmful acts or the imminent findings that potential grave harmful acts could have been committed had the acts not been kept in check.

Indicators for Interim Corrections

During the Transitional Period Towards a Nexus Pentarchy Prime Framework, officials must comply with prime directives even when other current institutions file suit against them in the courts. The ruling will indicate where changes will need to be made in either the laws or the constitutional framework. The offending parts will be dismantled.

Pentarchy Prime Umbrellas will provide assistance to personal matters when prime-selected officials are in confinement.

Prime Directives Shall Prevail

When there is a conflict of interest between official directives while an entity is an office holder in an historical framework and prime directives, then prime directives shall prevail. Officeholders will need to resign when "orders" are given that require them to violate prime directives.

Transformational Plan

One by one, nation-states that transform into primes will quietly withdraw members, resources, and money exchanges before announcing exits from treaties not recognizing primes as the supreme issue-resolution-decision-making instruments. When the historical "great" land (war) lords threaten in the use of force to return primes back to nation-states (war lords), they will have demonstrated how "feudal" and unjust they truly are. Do not respond with military responses. These "just war lords" will find that their own feudal members will dismantle their own systems when they learn that violence is being done on non-violent members. Ruling over the masses will be shown to be unwieldy. We have safety in numbers.

Transitional Identification Documents

Historical nation-states issued "passport" identification documents to members of their respective limited-access "societies" and must be shown to any other nation-state that is visited. Should there be a need for identification tags used for speedy processing, then the universal "world body" will issue universal entity speed instruments instead. No denial of entry is permitted unless containment of an entity is necessary because of grave harmful acts committed to others.

Time-Delayed Prime Directives

Prime decisions are to be made even when they cannot be carried out in the early phase of prime creation. Prime decisions will be recorded and archived for future implementation. Time is on our side. In time, all prime directives will be carried out. It is folly to think otherwise. The apparent delay will quite likely be due to the recognition that grave harmful acts can be avoided or minimized. During the Transitional Period Towards a Nexus Pentarchy Prime Framework, the only reason when prime directives cannot be carried out is when they violate basic tenets or conflict with more ascension prime directives that are discovered later.

The Framework of Caretaking

No Provisions for a Waiting Period

History shows that there was a notion that laws protect members of nation-states from grave harmful acts. However, if laws do not exist for specific categories of grave harmful acts, no laws have been violated and hence, it is viewed as if no grave harmful acts have been committed due to not having a legal standing in determining the merits of cases of this type. In this situation, how can society be really protected and secure? This void in securing legal protection from grave harm is the Achilles' heel for all law-based frameworks. The time lags for corrective responses cause more harmful acts to be experienced. *Prime framework waits for no provisions* when leader caretakers are chartered with unobstructed responsibility for wise resolution. Adjustments are immediate when determined to be on the side of caution when harmful acts are present or imminent.

At-Large Checks and Balances

The elite are just that. There are not many of them. For vast majority of members in society to grant vast powers to a few is alarming! Do select your leader caretakers wisely and allow them to make wise decisions. Our numbers are very large. With primes, there are checks and balances with the method of de-selecting leader caretakers when there is a history of unwise decision-making. Why minimize your importance and involvement? Be counted!

Uncovering the Truths Framework

The criminal courts as historically defined will transform from a defense plea of "guilty/not guilty" to one of uncovering the truths. Except for grave offenses when insufficient evidences exist, the charges, if declared, will be dropped and entity or entities are to be released. Twenty-five day confinement is the limit in these situations of truth discoveries with a moderate certainty. Only supreme Auspices for the nexus leader caretakers and the leader caretakers themselves can detain entities for longer than twenty-five days for grave harmful acts.

Decision Balancing Assured

With the historical judicial system, the vast majority of decisions are reserved to a very small number of members in society. With primes, the vast majority of decisions are reserved to the vast number of members in society through its umbrellas' span-caretaking reach. Sizing the decisions promotes every member's participation.

Good Samaritans Welcomed

Historically, Good Samaritans were no longer welcomed because of restrictive criminal code against assisting labeled criminals in providing even basic survival needs. By having a purely humanitarian perspective ought not to be a crime. It will be viewed as committing a grave harmful act when others did the offending acts prior to being in their care. In this example, it would be as if the Good Samaritan has possession of illegal weapons by associations with those who have. In a Sentient Dominion, Good Samaritans are welcomed. Consider removing one's self when discoveries of this kind exist and work with Sentient Auspices truth investigators.

Caretakers Needed

Historical judges are not caretakers. They are instead, administrators. Sentient well being is too important to be left solely to administrators. Caretakers are needed instead. Caretakers that are involved with the health and welfare of entities are best able to handle them. Caretakers are asked to apply.

Protected Shield

The protected shield factor goes up when primes freely produce their own prime directives. Autocratic land lords will have a most difficult time forcing their will on primes. Their castles and security motes will decay and return to Earth's domain. Their frameworks are short-lived.

Natural Environments Usage and Oversight

Hunting and fishing privileges will be allowed to interested entities. However, Auspices for nature's promotion executive officer caretakers' rules and guidelines will be adhered to. Violations can lead to privileges being revoked for a specified period of time.

Sanctuaries

Refuge of various kinds is like an oasis for species that are protected. These refuges will include those identified for sentients as well. Survival for all forms of expressions is assured provided these expressions do not violate basic tenets.

Harvest Yields

When "fishing the oceans of the world" for food, the fine tuning methods for yielding the greatest catch to the extreme will not be promoted. The methods that promote sustainable and/or return to historical ocean life populations and gains will be used and refined instead. The framework of caretaking applies here as well.

Inclusive Perspectives

It is important not to exclude anyone. All who are no longer in confinement are to be included. All perspectives are needed to make very wise decisions for domain vitality.

Charter of Care!

Very valid reasonable attempts will be made by environmental resource extraction duty caretakers. The "Charter of Care" will be created that defines directives that will promote the environment to renew itself. Design and construction of sentient habitats and work sites will be such as to minimize adverse impacts on the environment.

A Noble Trait

It is a noble trait to save others from harm even when harm is possible for one's self. The spirit grows when a way is found.

Hoarding

Hoarding of resources and claims on them are not in the best interest of primes. Resources are for the benefit of all. No ownership is allowed. Leasing to resource extracting caretakers for the benefit of all is allowed.

Returned to Prime Pool

Failure to comply with prime directives can lead to the return of land and property stewardships back to prime pool.

Hope for the Innocent

With the prime directive of no execution of an entity in confinement, this provides unending hope to save innocent ones.

Nature Bounty

Provide some resources to those few passionate entities that are protecting or making inquiries on the environment that indicate preservation and nature bounty promotions. The return will be bountiful.

Equalizing Support

There will be no existence of property and/or values attributed to entities in any issue review and resolution proceedings. Only equalizing support assistance can be considered. For example, suppose that there is a monetary support value given for every child. Those caretakers who can afford will be required to provide this value. Those caretakers who cannot effectively support this value will provide a level of support based on their financial portfolio and are not forgiven for the difference in monetary support. The payment in full is required over time.

Unrestricted Access

All Pentarchy Prime leader caretakers in the immediate degree minus-one foundation primes within a particular Pentarchy Prime Umbrella are to be given unrestricted access as spectators to Pentarchy Prime Umbrella activities. The only restriction is when a leader caretaker has committed a violent action without it being in self-defense. In that case, the particular leader caretaker is restricted from access. Checks and balances will ensure offending leader caretakers are de-selected and replacements made.

Choose Your Primes

An elitist belief system keeps all others in chains. Adherence to injustice promotes terrorism. The ones in power hide behind this belief system. Choose a different belief system. Choose adherence to sentient and wise leader caretakers. Choose your primes wisely. They are unique and so are we.

Nature's Sanctuary Domains

There will be defined vast sanctuary domains for life generating organisms to thrive on Earth so that no species are extinguished due to sentient catastrophic behaviors. These domains will also be used as a benchmark for sentient interactions on non-sanctuary domains. Sentients will not extinguish life so that they will be allowed to inhabit all of Earth. The only interactions by sentients are very limited non-intrusive visitations that are monitored by sanctuary caretakers who are given the Auspices caretaker keys to the sanctuaries. Choose them wisely.

Atonement Activities

By participating in prime directive creation activities, it will aid one in one's atonement since one will participate in wise and more effective issue resolutions. Is this important to you?

Entity Awareness Path

By establishing and promoting primes, an entity will evolve towards a higher level of awareness. This evolution may not be apparent in this moment in time. However, time will prove the evolution to be dramatic and profound!

Thoughts and Affirmations

Know your Primes

Work with your primes. Have your opinions known to them.

Condemn Not!

You don't actually condemn me. It is reflective. You condemn yourself.

The End to Condemnations

A nation-state that condemns will be extinguished. It will condemn no more!

The Life of Primes

A prime has a life of its own. You can be a part of this life.

No One is Alone

When we come together as primes, no one is left alone.

Being Sentient

No law will exist that negates an entity for being sentient.

"What-Ifs"

Speculations on "what-ifs" regarding the shaping of historical belief systems are not promoted during transition to Pentarchy Primes. Pentarchy Prime disclosure of prime directives to its members is the source of our strength.

Metamorphose Into Something Greater!

With a Pentarchy Prime sentient promoting environment, one will find one's self. From this awareness, go further and metamorphose into something greater!

It is only a Matter of Time

A system that condemns cannot long endure. It is only a matter of time

It Starts With One

I am one entity. I need four more to make a prime. This is the start to the propagation of primes. For this to happen, it starts with one.

Start by Building Primes

We don't need institutions. We need caretakers. When primes reach a pentacle, it is of prime celebration!

Tipping the Scale

Your one vote, one action, could make the difference in tipping the scale in Pentarchy Prime installment.

Prime Rules!

Leader caretakers are supreme to all other systems.

Prime Foundation and Beyond

The Fallacies of Triage

By adopting the framework of Pentarchy Prime, your activities will expose the fallacies of the historical triage belief systems, which have the premise of advancing feudal lord rules and the distinction of the elite with their exclusive privileges over the masses.

Break the Cycle of Land Wars

One may consider the notion that the need for transformation can be put off indefinitely. To hold onto the framework of land lords will promote land wars indefinitely. Understand the true nature of entities to be set free is the same as fighting for land, even though it was not apparent at the time. With the framework of Pentarchy Primes, no land boundaries are defined. Hence, no need to fight for land and hence, for freedom. To fight for land is more than the exclusion of entities. History has shown that in every single case, slavery, terrorism, and genocide are the resultant events. Choose to give governance power to the many and not to the few elite.

Micro-View Governments

History is clear. Governments can only deal with other governments. Translation, the elite can only deal with other elite groups. Another way of looking at this is that "micro-view" governments can only interact with other "micro-view" governments. Responsibility for decisions is the actions that are the result of these decisions, which can be defused and hidden throughout governmental institutions. With Pentarchy Primes, there is no diffusion. The selection of leader caretakers is made by all. Choose your leader caretakers wisely.

Prime Construction

Do not be concern about convincing entities that are not interested in the framework of Pentarchy Primes. They will not be aware that a healing wave of prime construction is taking place in full view. The triumph is when prime directives will require them to comply or be removed from their positions and privileges withheld. Complying will be swift.

By nourishing and promoting primes, we will have the most effective conflict-resolution-solving framework ever achieved.

There is a Choice

Pentarchy Primes are only for those who wish to elevate themselves from slavery and servitude that have been enforced by feudal lords. What choice will you make?

Sentient Responsible Organization

We are a sentient responsible organization, not a political action one. This distinction will be readily refreshing in time.

Controlling Interest

Do not be discouraged that the framework of Pentarchy Primes will take years to bring to collective consciousness. Take comfort with the knowledge that with anything, when folks are free to choose a higher evolved prime framework, then it takes just fifty-one percent of the votes in historically voting establishments to gain a more unobstructed controlling interest. This will provide us with the critical awareness to take universal hold. This Sentient Framework will be implemented everywhere from that moment on. This will truly be The Nexus Moment.

Nexus Prime at any Degree

Nexus prime can occur at any degree. With premiere founders, we will use the pent-degree Pentarchy Prime to be the Nexus Birth of Universal Directives. Each degree ascension prime thereafter will be to re-affirm or refine these directives. Failure by any member of society to comply will be noted and prime decisions recorded. It may appear that an entity is getting away with non-compliance. However in time, all debts will be cleared with compliance.

Nexus Fundamental Changes

Fundamental nexus tenets and principles can only be modified by the unanimous decision of the nexus prime leader caretakers and the plurality opinions of the degree minus-five of foundation primes within the nexus prime. With the event of having the unanimous opinion of the nexus prime leader caretakers, a significant tenet change request is made known to all. With the participation of the degree minus-five of foundation prime members within the nexus prime, the checks and balances are preserved.

Truth Discoveries

The truth is what will always be pursued and expounded. It will not be done in a manner of convenience and cost effectiveness when very harmful acts are being investigated. Determining the true causes for the acts will bring to the fore opportunities to remove harmful generating environments. This refinement will truly promote peace and tranquility.

Sentient Life-Forms Recognized

Human form will be one of many sentient life forms or species in a greater society. It did take society a very long time to acknowledge that other races of man are part of a greater society. To advance to the next level of an even greater society is to apply the same characteristics and attributes applied to human form evaluations so as to admit other candidate species with the same degree of protection from execution or annihilation. The spawning for this greater society is to eliminate ALL references to members of society being subjects or property of a feudal state. Decisions are made by wise caretakers and not by institutions as they are currently defined, which exist in form and not substance. Institutions are to be instruments and extensions of caretakers. They are to carry out the opinions of our wisest caretakers.

Prime Foundation Specifications

This book provides specifications for any prime to operate in, even when developing primes are not aware of each other. Should two or more developing primes make contact, this book handles the ascension prime as well. This is a great feature of primes because the nexus is the limit.

Closing Remarks

Once there were Guerrilla "Freedom Fighters"

Historically, the once most powerful nation on earth was a guerrilla terrorist regime fighting the Great Feudal Empires of its time. Later in history, the "Geneva Convention" dictated the terms regarding prisoners of war (POW) during wartime. This is the result of a collective nation-states decree. The decree applies primarily to opposing nation-state solders. Conclusion, non-solders that take up arms are considered guerrillas and are not protected. This is hypocrisy since all countries were founded by guerrilla activities. Therefore, guerrillas cannot be considered terrorists or the same claim must be universally applied regarding "established" nation-states. Choose to terrorize no more.

When the military is used for defensive or offensive purposes, then those entities that are captured because of their participation in the conflict are to be considered as prisoners of war (POW). Only when civilian police forces are involved is the term POW not used. However, this definition will be a moot point once nation-states expire. The solution is to dismantle all land-based nation-states. The need for guerrilla or terrorist activity, depending on your point-of-view, will no longer be needed. Later in history, there will be no land claims to fight over. Land will be Auspices of all sentients.

Living and Breathing Foundation Prime

Over time, this book will be a living and breathing one due to revisions that will be incorporated as a more complete set of nexus tenets and foundation principles is defined or established ones refined based on discovery and learning activities.

Timely Responses

Historical trilateral systems; legislative, executive, and judicial; waits for tragedies to occur first before acting on them. Wise decisions are not done by this reactionary mechanism (machine). Using their historical ways of adversarial processes, uncovering truths were drowned out. There is, in general, no rapid response team on the scene of grave harmful events. In a Pentarchy Prime Framework, the nexus prime has ultimate responsibility to ensure that effective truth discovery activities do take place and the outcomes published.

Law is Reflective

For those who do not think that the laws maim, torture, oppress, etc., guess again. Do your own research and discover for yourself that the methods that are being used to accomplish them have been kept hidden from the non-elite. The law is criminal when it condemns. The law is reflective. See for yourself.

Exclusion Implosion

Historically, power was derived through exclusion and through the labors of others. This kind of forced attainment will expire, if not already. The propagation of primes will ensure that exclusions do not exist.

Terrorism no more!

This original author is working to eliminate government-sanctioned terrorism in all its form. Forms of terrorism will be exposed no matter how deeply hidden they may appear to be. In time, there will be terrorism no more. Will you be there with the rest of us?

Primes Engulf the Landscape

Create Primes and then watch as primes engulf the unsuspecting "old guards" and "landscapes" as more and more of the "nation-states" get absorbed. One by one, the treaty organizations will expire and be replaced with prime directives. The need to maintain military hardware and personnel will dwindle and then be disbanded because there will be no more "land boundaries" to protect.

Society of Self-determination

Pentarchy Prime Framework is not a political party. It is a vast societal pool of sentient entities resuming their right of self-determination.

Impending Implosion

A society based on condemnation will implode. It will not long endure.

Rogue Nation-States

The belief in nation-states permits rogue states to hold the majority at bay. Primes encompass and embrace the entire umbrella pool so that no entity is overlooked.

It is "Within Reason"

It is not unreasonable to expect decision-making bodies to make decisions that would benefit all of society. If any confess that little can be done to make this so, then they are not that great after all. Maintenance and propping up of feudal systems are their primary objectives. We can choose to promote the preferred path. This guidebook will assist.

It Starts With One

This book describes the establishment of foundation primes. This birth begins with the sentient awareness of entities. Will you be one of them?

Nation-State Fall Back

The framework of land-based nation-states cannot long endure and evolve into a higher framework. The "evolution" can only lead to the return to more barbarous feudal states whereby ethnic cleansing is the law for instant wealth and "new land" ownership.

Prevention of Total Annihilation

Retaining the framework of nation-state as ever-greater technological advances are made will lead to total annihilation by these "technological advances". How great can it be when its use returns all to rubble?

Individual Recognition

By promoting individualism by the nation-state makes it possible to extinguish an entity. With Pentarchy Primes, a pool will have to be extinguished. This is a very great feat unless mass destruction is promoted. If the nation-state does in fact do it, the result is its implosion. Hence, there is safety in numbers.

What took so long?

Time will pass and entities born in the not so distant future will look at this contemporary period of time, as of the writing of this guidebook version of primes, and ask what took society so long to adopt the Charter of Primes? They will view the detractors and force resisters not in a favorable light. In fact, they may even be scorned for their actions and in-actions.

Out in the Cold

Pentarchy Primes will not initially be well received. However over time, the repeated demonstrations of decision making by all entities will be realized and be well received in greater numbers. The naysayers will discover that they are "out in the cold" by their own activities.

See the Future Today

When all is said and done regarding the planting and nurturing of primes, future sojourners will find it difficult to understand why society took so long to embrace a universal member growth-developing framework as Pentarchy Primes. Can you see the future today? It is all around us.

Premier Founders

The first five to the fifth power members will be given the designation of "Premier Founders". This is a great honor because their resolve and stamina have changed the course of societal existence forever! Development towards a higher level of awareness is assured.

Guidebook Ready!

This book is written to be available when the time comes to evolve, as a society, to something greater. It may appear that much time has passed and nothing is happening requiring this guidebook. However, the time will be ripe for the seeds described in this book and others in the series by this scribe to germinate. It will then catch on like wildfire as artifact feudal systems implode. A system based on shifting landmasses is shaky indeed and may ultimately return to the sea.

Book Fund

A fund will be established to help pay for copies of this book in those cases when the interested person meets a hardship need level, which is defined as subsistence or below.

Disclaimer

For those who need a disclaimer in order to continue to exist in their framework, any usage of Pentarchy Prime Framework specified in manual scripts and books are based on the interpretation of the readers and users of them. This fact must be publicly stated for the reader and user. The author does not attest to any accurate interpretation made by any reader or user. Her actions are self-determined.

Spectacular Results

Allow primes to flourish. You will be pleasantly surprised with its spectacular results.

Primes Endure!

Primes endure!

Bulletins

Revisions

Within a short period of time after the initial publishing of this book, the changes (refinements) will be found to be minimal. Over a longer period of time and after much discoveries and experiences, the refinements may be somewhat more significant. However, do not be surprised if the Pentarchy Prime Framework and related tenets and principles remain largely intact.

Living Foundation Guide

Minor revisions for this book are scheduled in five years of published date. Input from prime members is welcomed and appreciated.

Comprehensive embellishments pertaining to this book is scheduled in twenty-five years of the original published date. I recommend that Pentarchy Prime Umbrellas at pent-degree and greater reach be the primary authors for the twenty-fifth year revision, which will most likely be expansions on the basic premise.

Your Feedback and Suggestions Welcomed Here

I welcome your feedback and suggestions from any prime member. Your suggestions will be reviewed and may be incorporated in an updated version of this book five years from the original published date.

When feedback indicates certain passages of this book requires a greater degree of clarity, the addition of tenets, or the addition of prime guiding principles then a bulletin will be forthcoming so that there are not delays in disseminating this information. Should there be many bulletins then an updated book will be published. It will be another twenty-five years whereby much will have been learned and articulated, at which time the author relinquishes authorship to the nexus prime umbrella.

Printed in the United States
By Bookmasters